REMAINS

Historical and Literary

CONNECTED WITH THE PALATINE COUNTIES OF

Lancaster and Chester

VOLUME XXXIV —
THIRD SERIES

MANCHESTER
Printed for the Chetham Society
1987

FOR WENDY, TOM AND FRANCIS

WAR AND SOCIETY IN MEDIEVAL CHESHIRE

1277 – 1403

Philip Morgan

MANCHESTER

Printed for the Chetham Society

1987

Published for the Society by
Manchester University Press
Oxford Road, Manchester M13 9PL, UK

British Library cataloguing in publication data
Morgan, Philip, *1953-*
War and society in late medieval Cheshire, 1277–1403.—(Remains historical and literary
connected with the palatine counties of Lancaster and Cheshire. 3rd series; v. 24)
1. Militarism—England—Cheshire—History   2. Cheshire—History—Military
I. Title   II. Chetham Society   III. Series
355'.0213'094271   UA647

Library of Congress cataloging in publication data
Morgan, Philip.
War and society in medieval Cheshire, 1277–1403.
(Remains, historical and literary, connected with the
palatine counties of Lancaster and Chester; 3rd ser.,
v. 34)
Based on the author's thesis.
Bibliography: p. 228.
Includes index.
1. Cheshire—History.   2. Cheshire—History, Military.
3. Great Britain—History, Military—Medieval period,
1066–1485. I. Title. II. Series.
DA670.L19C5 3rd ser., vol. 34   942.7'14s   87-11044
[942.7'103]

ISBN 0–7190–1342–9 *hardback*

Printed in Great Britain
at the University Printing House, Oxford
by David Stanford
Printer to the University

CONTENTS

MAPS AND TABLES

ABBREVIATIONS

BIHR	*Bulletin of the Institute of Historical Research*
BJRL	*Bulletin of the John Rylands Library*
BL	British Library
BPR	*Register of Edward the Black Prince*, 4 vols. (1930–33)
CCR	*Calendar of Close Rolls*
CFR	*Calendar of Fine Rolls*
Chet. Soc.	Chetham Society
CPR	*Calendar of Patent Rolls*
CRO	Cheshire Record Office
Econ. H.R.	*Economic History Review*
EHR	*English Historical Review*
JRL	John Rylands University Library of Manchester
KUL	Keele University Library
LCRS	*Record Society of Lancashire and Cheshire*
LRO	Lancashire Record Office
PCC	Prerogative Court of Canterbury
SHC	Staffordshire Record Society (formerly William Salt Archaeological Society), *Collections for a History of Staffordshire* (also called *Staffordshire Historical Collections*)
THLC	*Transactions of the Historic Society of Lancashire and Cheshire*
TRHS	*Transactions of the Royal Historical Society*
VCH (Cheshire)	*The Victoria History of Cheshire*

ACKNOWLEDGEMENTS

Like all historical work this monograph owes much to the encouragement and advice of others. In particular I am indebted to Paul Booth, whose seminars on medieval Cheshire at the University of Liverpool did much to shape my own research. Dr Christopher Allmand and Professor F. R. H. Du Boulay, who examined the thesis on which this study is based, offered much valuable advice. Dr Michael Bennett read the whole book in draft and made several suggestions towards its improvement. Professor J. S. Roskell of the Chetham Society was more than kind in the help which he gave in preparing the text for publication. Above all, however, I would like to thank Professor Rees Davies whose teaching and supervision of my research have been a perpetual source of 'good lordship' during the years in which I have been concerned with the history of medieval Cheshire.

Much of the necessary research was carried out in a variety of record offices. To the staff of these I can only offer the customary acknowledgement. Their encouragement and conversation often lightened the dull routine of record searching. I am grateful to the chancellor of the duchy of Cornwall for permission to quote from the *journal* of John Henxteworth. Miss G. Matheson was particularly helpful in assisting my search of uncalendared records at the John Rylands Library. Miss A. Kennett arranged for me to consult the Eaton charters at the Chester Record Office.

The maps in this volume were drawn by Wendy Morgan. To her and to the rest of my family this book can be but poor reward for their help and support. My thanks are nonetheless heartfelt.

P.M.
Keele, June 1986

PREFACE

This study has three broad aims. It seeks to establish an account of the military service of Cheshiremen in the century between the Welsh wars of Edward I and the risings of Owain Glyn Dŵr and Sir Henry Percy (Hotspur); to identify those who served in war, whether on a single occasion or as part of a military career; and to study the nature of the relationship between military service and the fabric of local society within the county of Cheshire.

Consideration of the lordship of royal earls, notably Edward I and the Black Prince, reveals that the county played an important role in the emergence of the indentured retinue and in other changes in the organisation of war during the fourteenth century. Much of the county's militarism may have developed from a traditional role in the March of Wales, although the military experience of the Cheshire gentry is seen to have been more firmly developed during the lordship of the Black Prince and the campaigns of the Hundred Years War. The heaviest demands for manpower, however, are seen to have arisen in the factional conflicts of Richard II's reign.

Detailed study of the structures of lordship and society is used to explain the extent of militarism in the county and to illuminate what is known of the dynamic of the retinue. Membership of what is termed the 'military community' had various derivations, but especially lordship and locality, kinship and careerism. Each is explored in a number of well-documented examples. Military service is seen as a career which attracted those without an important role in local society, and as an incident in the lives of men who fell under the weight of lordly rule, but also as an avenue along which prominent courtiers and other careerists travelled.

The intimacy of the relationship between war and local society is also explored in an examination of the crisis of faction which developed in Cheshire, as in the rest of England, during the reigns of Richard II and Henry IV.

INTRODUCTION

War and its impact on society have figured prominently in the historiography of later medieval Europe. In England detailed study grew out of the work of J. E. Morris on the Welsh wars of Edward I, and concentrated initially on the organisation and history of retinues as an aspect of social relationships, conveniently, if rather misleadingly, characterised by the term 'bastard feudalism'.[1] The social and economic impacts of war, upon the nobility and civilian population, have been the subjects of historical controversy.[2] More recently research has examined the formation and character of the late medieval attitudes to war, the development of theories of the 'just war' among canonists, and the regulation of the laws of war among the participants.[3] The general direction of these works, however, has fallen well short of what the French historian, Philippe Contamine, has described as '*une sociologie de la guerre*'. In an important work he argues that medieval warfare was overwhelmingly fought in the name of established authorities and that, as a consequence, the structures of military society reflected more or less faithfully the structures of society as a whole.[4] Research on the social composition of armies should, he postulates, identify any dissonance between this model and the reality in any particular historical context.

This monograph is concerned with the character and development of military society within a particular regional community, the county of Cheshire, over a period of little more than a century from 1277 to 1403. The general aim has been the formulation of '*une sociologie de la guerre*' for Cheshire during the Hundred Years War; to that end it has been necessary to identify those in local society with military experience, and to study the changing form of this military community between the end of the Welsh wars of Edward I and the defeat of Sir Henry Percy (Hotspur) at the battle of Shrewsbury (1403). The organisation, equipping and payment of retinues, together with a study of the social and political impact of the military community within county society as a whole, provide the thematic framework.

In several respects Cheshire promised to be the ideal choice. The county enjoys a reputation for having been a highly militarist society for much of the medieval period; a judgement reflected in several contemporary sources. Lucian, a monk at Chester before 1195, observed that 'seldom have they respite from columns and troops'.[5] In common with the counties of the northern border and to a lesser extent of the maritime lands of the south-east, Cheshire had a military responsibility woven into the fabric of tenurial relationships to a greater degree than in the rest of England.[6] This responsibility was exemplified in the coincidence of the county and the earldom in Chester, granted to Hugh of Avranches in or shortly after 1070 as a compact lordship designed to provide an offensive base for the conquest of Wales. After 1254 the earldom was customarily part of the endowment of the king's eldest son, who as the earl remained the largest single landowner in Cheshire for much of the medieval period. Concessions to a military responsibility in Wales fostered the development of an institutional independence from the rest of England, while the sheer weight of the earldom's lands and institutions within the county tended to impose a degree of political and social uniformity.

Lucian noted of the men of Cheshire that they were 'like the rest of mortals throughout the world, partly unlike the rest of the English, partly better (and) partly equal'.[7] Michael Bennett has convincingly observed the existence of a 'county community', which, with other lesser 'solidarities', reinforced the insular character of regional society in the north-west of England in the late fourteenth and early fifteenth centuries.[8] The independence of Cheshire in ecclesiastical terms had no legal basis, but the inability of the Bishop of Lichfield to cite Cheshire men in his courts was rationalised in a series of agreements with the archdeacon of Chester, who paid the bishop a pension to hear cases in the ecclesiastical courts within the county.[9] The military and administrative distinctiveness of Cheshire was matched by the existence of a regional community and by a measure of ecclesiastical separation.

The impressive and largely intact collections of palatine records and an insular and militarist society appeared to offer an ideal community within which the organisation and effects of military service might be discerned. However, the form of the surviving evidence has imposed certain constraints on the shape of the work. Not least, the place of the secondary sources within the historiographical tradition of Cheshire's military identity needs to be discussed.

I. THE HISTORIOGRAPHICAL TRADITION

The traditional view of the character of late medieval military service in Cheshire was formed during the period from 1540 to 1620, paradoxically at a time when preparation for the profession of arms was not regarded so highly in the social repertoire of the nobility and gentry. The education of a gentleman now had a predominantly literary core, in opposition to the traditional skills of warfare and the hunt. If the Tudor gentry thus differed from their predecessors, they nonetheless held them in high esteem. At a time of rapid social change a claim to ancient blood, displayed in heraldic devices and coats of arms, provided an outward sign of social status. Antiquarians assisted in the assimilation of new families into the ranks of the gentry through painstaking, if occasionally spurious, genealogical research. John Lumley, a Durham lay magnate and member of the Elizabethan Society of Antiquaries, embellished the exterior of his castle with armorial shields and filled the parish church of Chester-le-Street with lines of medievalised, and mostly sham, effigies of his ancestors.[10] Elsewhere heralds fabricated arms for their clients, often, at their visitations, unscrupulously providing pedigrees which usurped the arms of medieval families and simplified quarterings to suggest antiquity.[11]

Central to the already mythologised view of the late medieval period in the general histories of Polydore Vergil and others was the Tudor conception of military skills as the preserve of nobles and gentry. While employment in military service decayed, gentry wills still recalled the martial glories of the family past; and the armour they bequeathed became less an item of war equipment than a uniform of ancient status, lavishly decorated and embellished. More important incidents of military service were amplified into feats of martial glory, or else simply fabricated, as in the case of John Phillipot's claim that the Pelham family had taken part in the capture of King John II of France at Poitiers.[12]

In Cheshire the ruling *élite* of gentry families appears to have been unusually stable during the early modern period, few families emerging as newcomers to the county through purchases of monastic land.[13] The Cheshire gentry, however, shared the great interest of their class in past history. At Doddington, south-east of Nantwich, for example, the hall built for Sir Thomas Broughton during the last quarter of the eighteenth century by Samuel Wyatt vies for attention with the castle constructed by Sir John Delves after 1365.[14] The castle incorporates a carved porch, a fragment of the earlier Jacobean hall, with statues of the Black Prince, and Sir James Audley and his four esquires, who appear in Froissart's chronicle in receipt of a 500-mark reward from the prince.

The identification of the Doddington porch can be traced no further back than the seventeenth century, and the porch may well be contemporary with the fabrication, if not its source.[15] The role of Sir John Delves in the service of the prince, clear enough in the pages of the Prince's *Register*, needs no modern amplification. However, during the sixteenth and seventeenth centuries the competition in fabrication induced several families to embellish their pedigrees with details of military careers. The military careers of the four Cheshire esquires were real enough, but evidently had lacked the lustre that participation in a specific and notable event could give.

This attempt to emphasise, even to fabricate, a military reputation for Cheshire families is to be seen elsewhere in the county, as at the parish church of Macclesfield, a few miles to the east of Doddington. In 1620 Sir Peter Legh of Lyme restored the Legh chapel and its monuments to the Legh family, adding a brass to Peter Legh (d. 1399) which incorporated 'some ould verses written upon a stone in this chappell'. Some evidently accurate lines commemorating Peter Legh's service to Richard II and his subsequent execution by Henry IV are bolstered by a fictional military pedigree of service at Crécy and in the campaigns of the Black Prince. Clearly, however, not all such accounts deserve to be dismissed as mere fabrications. The account of Laurance Maisterson in 1612 of his own family history appears to be firmly rooted in original documents, now lost, but which can be verified from other sources. Even Maisterson's account, however, set out his claim to 'nobility' through the military service of his ancestors. He wrote of Thomas Maisterson (fl. late fourteenth century), 'of all the Maistersons before, I find him to be of the greatest note and account and the best servitor. Moreover he is called esquire by those great princes ...'[16]

During the late middle ages such was the conception of war that mere soldiering was held to be a noble calling in itself, one which fostered a social equality among combatants on the battle field. Ennobling and hereditary status were the rewards of gallantry, and a soldier's descendants might reasonably base a claim to nobility on the grounds of military distinction alone.[17] As a result, in Maisterson's narrative, an indenture between Thomas Maisterson and John of Gaunt is embellished with portions of Froissart's narrative of the Black Prince's victory at the battle of Nájera (Navarre) in 1367.[18] An emphasis on military fame has persisted until recent times. Although the county histories of the eighteenth and nineteenth centuries were unashamedly compiled on the basis of land ownership (the history of the land and the noble and gentry families who owned it), George Ormerod, writing his history of the county in

1819, excused the inclusion of the Maistersons of Nantwich on the grounds that 'although they never appear to have possessed manorial property in Cheshire ... [they] were a family of high antiquity and importance, distinguished for military prowess'.[19] The commonplace nature of Maisterson's indenture had become the particular event of valour at Nájera; a transfiguration that can be matched in numerous Tudor genealogies. In the manner of the multiplication of fragments of the true cross, the antiquarians of the early modern period were to populate the already mythologised events of the Hundred Years War with the ancestors of leading county families. None with a claim to ancient status was to be without its own illustrious warrior.

A cursory comparison of the evidence of the early modern copyists, notably the Randle Holme family and Sir Peter Leycester, with extant collections of deeds reveals that most of the evidence concerning military service within private collections remains much as it was during the sixteenth century. The dispersal and disappearance of what may have been the commonplace evidences of such service, in the form of indentures, receipts and writs, was quite possibly contemporary; the survival of such documents into the modern period results, not from accidental inclusion within packets of land deeds, but because such documents were later regarded as evidence of gentry status in the same way as ancient charters relating to land title. Just as the military reputation of late medieval Cheshire and of its families was established and elaborated in the Tudor period, so it was then also that the longbow and the longbowman were extolled in historical retrospect.

The popular weapon of the later medieval period had, by the time of the publication of Roger Ascham's *Toxophilus* in 1544, become a weapon of sport. Ascham's polemics were directed, not in favour of the weapon's military worth, which he found self-evident, but in support of the pastime of archery as a fit sport for scholars and in the education of gentlemen.[20] The emerging class of small landowners, among the lesser gentry and the yeomanry, found their pedigrees and claims to ancient status in the role, as they perceived it, of the longbowmen in the Hundred Years War. In part the judgement as to social class implicit in the anonymity of the late medieval archer had already been breached before the decline of the longbow as a weapon of war. Sir Richard Assheton, who rebuilt the parish church of Middleton near Manchester, incorporated a window, now in the south wall of the chancel, to celebrate his part in the battle of Flodden Field in 1513. The sixteen archers of his company are depicted in the lowest portions of the window, below the portraiture of the Asshetons; not, however, in anonymity, for each archer carries his bow across one shoulder, his name written along the bow-string. By the mid-seventeenth century the quickly mythologised view of the role of the longbowmen in the later medieval period had accorded them a place in the social hierarchy, as in this recommendation from Thomas D'Urfey in 1653:

> Let nobles shoot, cause tis a pastime fit.
> Let Yeoman shoot for th' king's and nation's good.

What historians might describe as 'archers raised in Cheshire' have in like vein become that more heroic figure, the 'Cheshire archer'.[21]

These social assumptions form an indispensable part of the received tradition of military service in the localities, which it is important to recognise. The jingoism of early accounts of the Hundred Years War has been dispelled from academic studies of the character of late medieval warfare, but remain in the works of local antiquarians. In Cheshire, Ormerod's *History*, and the revision by Helsby in the late nineteenth century, though achievements of the first order, are in scope little more than copyist's work, firmly anchored in the antiquarian traditions of the sixteenth and seventeenth centuries. The qualitative picture of the nature of local military service had already been established in the Tudor and Stuart period; new sources of evidence available to later researchers have been used largely to reinforce assumptions made in the early modern period, rather than as a basis for a critical analysis of the position of military service within the county.

The accepted view of the origins and development of military society in Cheshire is based ultimately on the work of H. J. Hewitt, first published in 1929.[22] The conclusions advanced there have been modified little, and find their most recent presentation in an account of the rising of 1393.[23] The confused events of that year are interpreted as a revolt against the prospects of a peace with France; the rising stands, therefore, at the apex of a developing tradition which finds its origins in the Welsh wars of Edward I. Insistent and heavy demands for manpower during the late thirteenth century, it is argued, fostered an experience and an expectation of military service within county society which continued during the campaigns of the Hundred Years War. Edward I's choice of manpower, based on the proximity of Cheshire to Wales and a traditional and localised responsibility of service, hardened into custom, encouraged by administrative separateness and the military commitments of successive earls, notably the Black Prince.

In socio-economic terms this hypothesis follows Malthus in the view that 'the ambition of princes would want instruments of destruction if the distress of the lower classes did not drive them under their standards'. In a predominantly pastoral economy, so it is argued, warfare absorbed large supplies of surplus manpower and encouraged a growth of population beyond the ability of local agricultural production to sustain it. In that respect the peace proposals of John of Gaunt and Thomas of Woodstock in 1393 constituted a real threat to living standards and employment for a significant section of the population of Cheshire. Military service also provided an outlet for the violent and aggressive tendencies of local society which are recorded in the increasingly strident accounts of chroniclers during the reign of Richard II. The endemic violence characteristic of the whole of the Welsh March was further aggravated by the existence within the county of criminal sanctuaries or avowries which attracted criminal elements into Cheshire and into the retinues of the Hundred Years War.

For a number of reasons Hewitt's theories now stand in need of some modification. Any estimate of the level or quality of the recruitment in the county before the close of the fourteenth century is still largely conjectural, but the manpower demands of Edward I do not seem to have weighed more heavily on Cheshire than on many other English counties. Almost certainly Hewitt also overestimated the extent and importance of pastoralism within Cheshire's economy, and recent work suggests that in Cheshire, as in the rest of England, the bounds of arable cultivation had expanded in response to population pressure. Accounts from the earl's demesne manors, Sir James Audley's manor at Newhall, and evidence from the inquisitions *post mortem* all suggest the widespread importance of arable cultivation within the manorial economy.[24] Furthermore, any theory of underemployment within a pastoral economy does not account for the maintenance of manpower demands and the expansion of military service which followed the loss of population during the Black Death and subsequent plagues. Equally, no connection can be demonstrated between the organisation of avowries in Cheshire and recruitment by the earl of Chester for campaigns in France, and an assessment of the degree of militarisation within Cheshire society is preferred to an arid discussion of relative levels of violence and lawlessness within medieval society in general.

Whilst accepting Hewitt's general hypothesis, Michael Bennett has recently argued that soldiering, and the profit associated with warfare in the fourteenth and fifteenth centuries, may be part of the explanation for the region's 'widespread reputation as a seed-plot of gentility'.[25] Nevertheless, it will be argued that the importance of military service as a formative element in Cheshire society has been greatly overstressed.

The county was far from unique in the extent or delineation of its military obligations, and at no point did the degree of stratification in local society exhibit the rapid change often associated with the dominance of military service in the framework of social and economic relationships.[26] Indeed, many successful soldiers appear to have found it difficult to enter polite society in Cheshire with the profits of their service.[27] The military community in the county was never more than a significant, if complementary, minority within the ranks of landed and office-holding gentry.

The county does, however, exhibit significant local variations from the overall pattern of military service in the rest of England. The proximity of Wales and the relative militarisation of the March from an early date may well have engendered a society that was amenable to the demands of warfare in the Hundred Years War. More significantly the role of the Earl of Chester as a consistent and often large-scale employer of troops maintained the continuity of military service and ensured an expansion in the levels of manpower demands during the 1340s. Any view of the county as a monolithic royal enclave is, however, simplistic. The antiquarian tradition of the county historians, in which a catalogue of occasions of service served virtually to establish a regional claim to ancient status, fails to illuminate crucial areas in the formation and development of the military community, or strictly to define the profits and attractiveness of military service.

II. THE DOCUMENTARY SOURCES

In any historical study the direction of the enquiry may be at variance with the character of the surviving evidence, assembled by contemporaries for different purposes; at other times, however, the character or completeness of the evidence may itself favour a particular approach or conclusion. In terms of the development of military service in late medieval Cheshire, the essential features of the primary sources are the constantly changing pattern of the documentation, and the fact that all too often the surviving evidence falls short of enabling us to answer basic questions entirely satisfactorily. It is important to recognise, therefore, that the shape of this work will in part be a reflection of the uneven pattern of the documentation, as also of the conclusions of the writer.

Cheshire occupies a somewhat unusual position in relation to the evidence available in the rest of England. The county does not appear in the national records to any great extent, and until the mid-nineteenth century the records of medieval Cheshire remained where they were generated, in Chester Castle. The collections of palatine records are impressively large and only now being fully explored by medieval historians. Selections from some classes of documents have been published by the local historical societies, and others were indifferently calendared by the Public Record Office during the last century, but in the main the historian must use sources that are still in manuscript.[28]

There were two major institutions in the county administration during the medieval period: the exchequer and the county court. The chamberlain of Chester was in effect both treasurer and chancellor of the county, responsible for the revenues of the earl in the county and for writs issued under the Cheshire seal. The accounts of the chamberlain survive intact for much of the fourteenth century, with the exception of the years of the Principality of Aquitaine (1362 – 70), and contain details of the earl's income from lands, wardships and minorities, courts, and fees of the seal; as well as expenditure on fees, wages, annuities, and building works. These are the final accounts submitted to the earl's council and generally survive in two copies. In addition, the subsidiary accounts of comital officials, on which the final accounts are based, survive in large numbers in the accounts of the escheator and sheriff of the county, bailiffs, foresters, and farmers and receivers of lands in the earl's hands.

These accounts provide information on the financial administration of the earldom, and also cast some light on the wealth and status of landholders in the county. All the land in the county was held from the earl who exercised rights over wardship of lands and minorities, and the inquisitions *post mortem* held by the escheator in the county form one of the more important groups of subsidiary accounts. They survive in significant quantity from 1349, although their value is lessened by the growth of enfeoffments to use during the latter half of the fourteenth century. Difficulties arise, not only in considering the value of these sources in forming a general view of the pattern of landholding and the economy of the county, but in relating them to the military community in particular. J. M. W. Bean could find little evidence to suggest that military service had played a significant role in the development of uses during the later medieval period, but such arrangements were clearly popular within the military community.[29] The possibility of death in battle encouraged a significant number of Cheshire men to convey their land to feoffees before leaving on expeditions for France, and as a result the declining value of inquisitions post mortem is particularly true of the military community. The arrangements of Sir Ralph Mobberley before the campaigns of 1355 – 7 and 1359 – 60 can be established from private evidences, but few members of the Cheshire soldiery are well served by such sources. Sir John Ward, Sir Hugh Calveley, Sir David Cradock and Sir Thomas Wettenhall, for example, are all poorly served by the palatinate records.[30]

The chamberlain's accounts do, however, reflect the extent of the earl's expenditure on warfare and military service, although an important rider has to be added. Throughout the fourteenth century the earl was rarely expected to live of his own, and liveries of money from the earl's other English lands or direct from the royal exchequer were often used to pay for the military service of Cheshire men. Three major categories of expenditure can, however, be derived from the accounts.

The expenditure of the earl in the maintenance of the castles of Cheshire and Flintshire was consistently and often exclusively organised by the chamberlain of Chester, whose accounts therefore reflect those aspects of military service. For almost the whole of the fourteenth century the crown acted as paymaster to military expeditions in France; liveries of cash for the payment of wages to men-at-arms and archers were organised through the earl's household and do not therefore appear in the Cheshire accounts. On three occasions, however, a variety of political circumstances encouraged the earl to use the revenues of the earldom of Chester for military purposes. During Edward I's Welsh wars the entire revenues of the county were devoted to the payment of military expenses for three years (1281 – 4), and during the years of the Principality of Aquitaine (1362 – 70) it seems likely that English lordship there was financed partly from the Cheshire revenues. In both cases the financial arrangements remain obscure, but during the last years of the reign of Richard II the accounts of the chamberlain yield vital information on the payment and movement of troops, often identifying the leadership of companies of men-at-arms and archers. The distribution of information over the period under examination is, therefore, very uneven.

A more consistent source of information is given in the details of annuities and rewards paid to those in the earl's service. The extent of comital patronage cannot, of course, be judged solely on the evidence of the annuities drawn on the Cheshire revenues. The assignment of the income of lands formed perhaps the smallest item in the provision of noble and royal patronage, and was often restricted to the more important retainers. The grants of the Black Prince to the members of his retinue, mostly drawn from men recruited outside the county, so burdened the Cheshire revenues during the reign of his son that few new annuities were granted at a time when the patronage of the king as Earl and later as Prince of Chester reached its peak. The assignment of income was a relatively small and inelastic source of patronage. Nevertheless, the information contained in the chamberlain's accounts makes an essential contribution to the composite picture of military service and its pattern of rewards.

The chamberlain was also responsible for the issue of writs under the Cheshire seal in his custody. The enrolments of these writs are contained in a group of records erroneously described as 'recognizance rolls'.[31] They contain a record of appointments of comital officials and grants in favour of individuals which clearly reflect *inter alia* the rewards of military service. Letters of protection, grants of office and land, exemptions and pardons as rewards for service in France, and the appointment of commissions of array for the raising of troops are enrolled for most of the fourteenth century, again with the exception of the years of the Principality of Aquitaine (1362–70).

The chief officer of the county was the justice of Chester who presided over the county court. The county court of Chester was unlike that in the normal English county in that its functions reflected the supreme competence of the earl; it could hear pleas of all kinds and encompassed cases which would elsewhere be within the jurisdiction of the King's Bench. In addition the courts of the justice were itinerant like the sheriff's tourn, the records of the latter surviving in an uneven and poor condition. We are, however, concerned less with the competence and operation of these courts than with the direct and indirect information on military service which their records contain.[32]

The information is of two kinds, personal and political. In the first instance there are cases involving soldiers who are so described: hearings which involve the production of letters of protection or the suspension of legal proceedings as a reward for service, cases which involve offences committed by soldiers going on expeditions and returning from campaigns, or offences against soldiers' lands and families during their absence. Cases of this nature do not, of course, amount to a significant proportion of the business before the courts, but each instance adds to the picture of the military community within local society and reflects the relative importance of military service. The second category involves the hearing of pleas in connection with the major political and military crises of the period – the trailbaston court of 1353, the risings of 1393 and 1400, and the battle of Shrewsbury in 1403 – in which the participants appeared before the courts. As well as providing information on the progress and organisation of these events, they supplement surviving retinue rolls in the identification of the military community.

As well as the rolls of the proceedings of the several courts, there are the groups of subsidiary documents available to the justice and his clerks. Foremost of these are the rolls of indictments before the county court which have already been explored for the 'rising' on the estates of St Werburgh's abbey in 1381 and the progress of 'the revolt of the earls' in 1400.[33] The information contained in these rolls is often fuller than the version given on the corresponding plea roll of the county court and sometimes reports events which did not subsequently appear in those rolls. They are, for instance, especially useful in measuring the success of Sir Henry Percy (Hotspur) in raising the county in 1403.[34] Of occasional value are other classes of subsidiary documents: the *gaol files, writs etc.*, in reality the documentation available to the clerks of the county court for each session during the fourteenth century and containing the indictments, writs, jury lists and coroners' inquisitions. For a short time before the Crécy campaign the *Essoin* rolls note the excuse *'quia in servicio domini regis'* against the names of those indicted for non-appearance at the county court, although such entries did not continue. Each of these records contains information on the nature of military service which is often not to be found elsewhere.

The records of local courts may also be used to illustrate the operation of local society in a way that has already been attempted with the trailbaston roll of 1353. An analysis of pledges for the payment of fines among the lesser gentry in Wirral, for instance, can be used to illustrate the existence of an interest group centred on Sir William Stanley and the social structure which lay behind much of the criminal activity revealed by the general eyre of 1353.[35] This kind of information is the inevitable by-product of many of the palatinate records; the enrolments of recognizances for debt and other private evidences, or disputes relating to lands, fees and the execution of wills, all reveal in part aspects of local society. It is, however, important to recognise that the palatinate records reflect a particular view of medieval society, a view in which the ownership of land formed the basis and core of essential social relationships. The ownership and transmission of lands and offences against land or property which dominate the public records of Cheshire can only be used to illustrate a partial view of local society and, by implication, are less revealing of its military aspects.

The evidence of the official records is in the first instance secondhand, the interpretation of events and relationships undertaken by the courts and comital officials or presented for official scrutiny by the participants themselves. Such records inevitably concentrate on the higher levels of local society and on horizontal social relationships between near social equals; they provide an inadequate view of the social hierarchy, being based on conflict rather than co-operation. Well-documented figures in the military community, such as Sir Hugh Calveley, Sir David Hulgreve or Sir David Cradock, fail to make any impression on the records of the palatinate, and their omission suggests the danger of relying exclusively on such sources.

Cheshire is disappointingly served by the survival of manorial accounts, with the exception of those demense lands consistently in the earl's hands or of lands held in wardship, and there are fewer manorial court records. The impact of ecclesiastical lordship on the county was slight, and little survives to illuminate the management of gentry and noble estates. An exception is the documentation preserved by the duchy of Lancaster and relating to the lordship of Halton in north and east Cheshire. Here the court rolls of Halton, Congleton, Whitley and Runcorn, with the bailiff's accounts of the lordship, reflect the impact of noble recruitment in local society.[36]

The weight of documentation in the public records generated by the ownership and exploitation of land is matched in importance by that generated by the family. The extended kinship group, expanded within the locality, shaped the character of many of the retinues in the county during the later medieval period. Cheshire is unusually well served by the survival of impressively large collections of family deeds which compete for interest with many of the public records.

Primarily, a deed is a reflection of personal life, rather than a record of government. A commission which appoints men as keepers of the peace says something about their status, but we can only presume any relationship between members of such a group. A deed, on the other hand, touches upon a whole system of social relationships – land tenure, kinship, a passing need or simple friendship. The evidence for these relationships seldom found its way into the legal record and does not, therefore, survive, if indeed it ever existed, but can be reconstructed in some degree from witness lists and charter appearances. Gentry archives further illustrate the distribution of patronage and the rewards of military service at the lowest levels of the military community and, as has been suggested, they preserve much of the commonplace documentation relating directly to the performance of military service, namely indentures, pardons, and receipts.[37] Collections of deeds containing marriage agreements, wills, details of the transmission and exchange of lands, and the interest groups revealed in witness lists allow access to a much broader spectrum of medieval life. Such collections are, however, statements of social success over an extended period and, although they successfully reflect the careers and affinities of soldiers like Sir William Mainwaring, John Leycester or Sir Ralph Mobberley, and even Sir Hugh Calveley, they serve little to lift the veil of anonymity from men like Knolles, Hulgreve and Cradock.

The palatinate records, those of the lordship of Halton, and collections of deeds may be used to illustrate the growth and impact of military service in the county; they do not in themselves describe or identify the military community. The evidence listed above has been used in the later stages of the enquiry. An immediate objective was to identify, as far as possible, the military community, i.e. those who served, and especially those who served fairly regularly.

Two relationships dominate the military life of the county: that with the king, and that with the Earl of Chester, who were the most significant employers of Cheshire troops. With one or two exceptions the crown was the ultimate paymaster for military expeditions during the fourteenth century, and the English commitment to warfare during the late middle ages can be measured in the records of the wardrobe, exchequer and chancery. These sources are well known and have been much used by historians, although their value in relation to the development of military service in Cheshire needs to be examined.

There are perhaps two major objectives to be considered in any evaluation of these records. In attempting to provide a comprehensive picture of the effect of military service in Cheshire society we are interested in what H. J. Hewitt has described as the 'organisation of war' – the methods employed in the locality in mounting an expedition. In this respect we may seek to establish the nature of military service in the county, the methods of recruitment and reward, the level of manpower demands and the changes in military organisation. In the final analysis, however, we are perhaps more interested in the social pattern revealed within the military community as far as that community can be identified from the sources so far mentioned.

Fluctuations in the overall financial responsibility for the conduct of war within the royal administration as between the exchequer and the wardrobe are well established. Until 1340, and for a brief period during the later years of Richard II, the wardrobe accounts are perhaps the most useful for the military historian; during the intervening years the records of the exchequer usurp that position. It is important to note, however, that neither department exercised an exclusive responsibility. Both sources have been used extensively by historians and their character requires little notice here.[38] Within the tradition of such research one may establish a chronological framework for the development of military service in Cheshire between 1277 and 1403.

The documentation does, however, present problems in any attempt to identify the membership of the military community. Much of the research on the social and economic effects of war relies on a discussion of occasionally well-documented careers. Among the nobility the effects of war may be judged with reasonable accuracy, for that class is on the whole well documented.[39] Below the nobility, however, there is a real difficulty in deciding whether the examples of men such as Fastolf, Molyneux and Winter, Knolles and Chandos are in fact representative of military society as a whole.[40] Within a smaller area, a single English county, it may be possible to assemble a representative sample of those involved in warfare, although in comparison with Fastolf the evidence relating to individuals may be very incomplete.

The organisation of war during the fourteenth century generated an extensive documentation, reflecting the complexity of relationships between the crown and its troops. Perhaps the most valuable sources are those which are in some way comprehensive, or identify the total demand on the county at a particular time. The nomenclature of the retinue roll of a noble captain may bear close resemblance to the area of his greatest landed influence or personal presence, and the military contribution of some of the boroughs can often be identified; but such sources are seldom valid for an area as large as a county. In Cheshire, however, the rapid expansion of military service during the 1340s coincided with the personal rule of the Black Prince, whose position as Earl of Chester gave him a virtual monopoly of the raising of troops in the county. The militarisation of society with which we associate Edward III's campaigns in France had, in Cheshire at least, a focus of personal service.

The existence of a major focus of recruitment within Cheshire society during the period between 1343 and 1376 does not, however, solve all the problems of personal identification, and a study of the retinues of the Black Prince presents its own difficulties.[41] Nevertheless, the picture of military service in Cheshire society which emerges during this period occupies a central position within this study. The patronage of the Black Prince introduced Cheshire men into the retinues of other noble captains and to positions of influence within the English administration of lands in France, and it conditioned the framework of local politics and military recruitment into the fifteenth century. There are three important sources, each associated with the prince's household, for the study of this vital period in the military history of Cheshire.

The *Register* of the Black Prince contains copies of letters issued under the prince's seal and is perhaps the most impressive single surviving register from a noble household of the fourteenth century.[42] Although its contents have been described as a 'depository of miscellaneous memoranda', the information of value to this study is of two kinds. First are copies of letters addressed to the justice of Chester which deal with the recruitment, equipping and payment of troops and the appointment of leaders for the retinues. Second are details of rewards, pardons and grants to members of the prince's retinue both before, during, and after particular campaigns. The direct information on military service is, however, more than matched by the importance of the overall character of the document. Within the *Register* the recruitment of retinues is found alongside the ordinary business of a magnate controlling his estate; the register not only identifies many of the lesser soldiery in the prince's service, but often relates them to the local society from which they were drawn. The extant sections of the *Register* cover the prince's three major campaigns before the peace of Bretigny; Crécy (1346), Poitiers (1357) and Edward III's final expedition (1359).

The campaign in Gascony between 1355 and 1357 is further illuminated in the *journal* of John Henxteworth, a day book of payments made by the controller of the prince's household at Bordeaux during the winter of 1355 – 6.[43] The miscellaneous character of daily expenses and payments to leaders of retinues, archers and individual men-at-arms in this journal supplements the information on the Cheshire retinues contained in the *Register*. It was used extensively by H. J. Hewitt, in his study of the campaign, to identify the membership of the prince's retinue.[44] In a Cheshire context it has been possible to identify the membership of several knightly retinues, and a discussion of the 'affinity' of Sir Ralph Mobberley has, as a result, been used to illustrate the social context of military service in the county at this date.[45]

The years of the Principality of Aquitaine (1362 – 70) form an obvious lacuna in the pattern of documentation, only partly filled by the survival of evidence relating to the defence of the Principality in 1369. The campaign is well known from the testimony of witnesses in the later Scrope-Grosvenor heraldic dispute in 1385, many of whom claimed to have served on it.[46] An unnoticed retinue roll of the Black Prince does, however, relate to this campaign and has been used both to supplement and verify the testimony of the Scrope-Grosvenor witnesses.[47]

Each of these sources may, of course, be supplemented both by the palatinate records and private evidences already described, and by other less comprehensive documents which add to the information available

for individual campaigns. The *Register* does not include copies of letters
from the prince requesting letters of protection for members of the
retinue; these may be recovered from the French and Gascon rolls of
the chancery. A few original replies dealing with the progress of recruitment in Cheshire during 1345 survive among the ancient correspondence of the exchequer, and some documents relating to the organisation
of the retinue in Gascony in 1355 were transcribed by the Cheshire
antiquary, Randle Holme III.[48]

III. MILITARY SERVICE IN LATE MEDIEVAL CHESHIRE

Military service during the fourteenth century implied a variety of inter-
personal relationships – with the king, through royal provision of an
adequate system of defence and as revealed in the records of royal
government, and with other lords, often noble, with whom men entered
into relationships which included the provision of military service.
The action of the crown, however, dominates the surviving evidence
relating to military service, and even where a significant body of
evidence survives for a noble lord, as in the case of John of Gaunt or
the Black Prince, survival is often due to the fact that the documentation had passed within the administrative competence of the crown.
Historians have generally concentrated their attention upon the permanent retinues of the magnates and the crown, those men closely
associated with the household of the king or a noble lord at the centre
of political life.[49] The relationship of the crown and the magnates was,
however, at the apex of the system of military recruitment. We remain
much less well informed of the ways in which individual retinues were
assembled in the localities, although a number of recent articles suggest that documentation may well survive in local record offices.[50] The
organisation and social context of the extended retinue, perhaps
assembled for a single campaign, is nonetheless of crucial importance.
The disposal of royal and noble patronage was successful only as far as
it was cognisant of the realities of local society, and important episodes
in the development of military recruitment in Cheshire are only intelligible in such terms. The relationships which governed the participation
of an individual archer as the smallest component of a noble retinue may
never be readily understood, partly because the widespread survival
of documentation chronicling the arrangements between the noble
captains and the crown far outweighs the evidence relating to men
lower in the administrative hierarchy of military recruitment. A purely
narrative approach to the problems of military service in the county

based on the supposed pre-eminence of the crown and the Earl of Chester will, therefore, fall well short of establishing any 'sociologie de la guerre' for the county of Cheshire. The rewards and attractions of military service also remain poorly documented. The extensive rebuilding at Bunbury and Nantwich, and the construction of an east end and chevet, unique in England, at Vale Royal abbey may well be examples of the investment of profits of war, Leland's 'ex spoliis nobilium bello Gallico captorum', but until we can attempt some long-term judgement on the profit accumulated or loss incurred by individual soldiers, assessments based on isolated examples of booty or lucrative ransoms must be unrepresentative.

It may indeed be possible to establish the development and fluctuations of royal and comital demands on manpower within the county from the evidence of royal or comital government, although any discussion of the organisation of war which ignores the hierarchial bias of such documentation will yield only an imperfect understanding of the social and political context of military service. These two themes, therefore, overlie and expand the narrative approach which dominates consideration of the period between 1277 and 1340.

The association of war and politics needs little justification in a society where the continuance of royal government so often depended on the ability to marshall effective military support. In practice there might be little discernible difference between the force raised for an expedition to France and that mustered in support of a noble faction. Purely mercenary contracts between a noble captain and a small retinue of men-at-arms and archers were common, but often the raising of troops corresponded in essentials to the raising of political support. In 1387, to quote a well-documented example, the force under Richard, Earl of Arundel, at the factional battle of Radcot Bridge showed little variation from that which had recently returned from the earl's naval victory at Sluis.[51]

At this level the functioning of local society depended on the downward percolation of the largesse and patronage necessary for the maintenance of 'good lordship'. The feudal obligation of landlord and tenant was augmented by the rewards of service in the household or the retinue, and by access to the monopoly of office-holding exercised by the crown or the earl. Military service, therefore, implied a relationship which was often deeper than that expressed in the precise contractual obligations of the indenture. Philip Hardeshull, who undertook to serve Edmund Stafford in 1297 'for as long as the war lasts between the king of England and the king of France', did so because Stafford was lord of Madeley in north Staffordshire where Hardeshull was his tenant.[52] The relationship between tenurial ties and the formation of retinues was perhaps the most vital element in the development of military recruitment during the fourteenth century, and some attempt is made therefore to determine the pattern of landholding in the county.[53] Military recruitment did, however, extend beyond the bounds of direct tenurial relationships and served to broaden and strengthen lordship and political influence in the localities. Grants of fees, offices and the incidents of feudal tenure formed part of the system of patronage whereby a lord maintained his status and dignity in the locality and attracted the support of its gentry affiliations. For the most part, as Anthony Tuck has suggested, it was 'an ordinary, uncontentious, and regularly functioning part of the administrative and financial system'.[54] Although most expeditionary forces were raised through a system of sub-contracting in which the permanent retinue formed only the nucleus, nevertheless the pattern of military recruitment might often reflect the character and extent of gentry support dependent on the patronage of the captain. The potential incidents of military service were clearly a notable aid to recruitment; and the prospect, though not necessarily the realisation, of ambitions for booty, ransoms, land and office exercised a measure of control over the choice of sub-contractors in the mounting of an expedition.

In Cheshire the development of military service, over a period of more than a century between 1277 and 1403, had a magnitude and rhythm which was directly related to the political circumstances of its system of patronage. Even the most cursory examination of the evidence reveals the existence of a single faction society in which the earl (whether king or prince) was the centre and focus of gentry affiliations aspiring to hold a leading role in the politics of the county. This fact is borne out by the recruitment of troops by the three Edwards and the Black Prince during the period between 1277 and 1376; and the right to exclusive recruitment within the county exercised a formative role in the development of military service there that was only parallelled in the Welsh March and the palatinate of Durham.[55]

It is suggested that the declining role of the Black Prince after 1370 and the minority of Richard II broadened the basis of military recruitment and represented a successful challenge to the operation of a single faction in Cheshire. This is reflected in a study of the patterns of recruitment by Richard, earl of Arundel, and John of Gaunt, who appear as large-scale employers of Cheshire troops during the late fourteenth century. Both were lords of land in the county – Gaunt, as baron of

Halton, was the largest individual landowner – but other magnates make an appearance as retainers of troops often by virtue of holding office as justice of Chester.[56]

The multiplicity of noble captains can be related to the political turmoils of the reign of Richard II which were shaping the overall pattern of recruitment. Following the factional battle at Radcot Bridge in 1387, in which Cheshire troops were prominent on both sides, Richard II attempted to re-establish the single faction in local society and between 1397 and 1399 recruited a Cheshire retinue and distributed fees and grants on an unprecedented scale.[57] The social and political tensions generated by the fragmentation of comital authority re-emerge, however, in the factional conflicts early in the reign of Henry IV when Sir Henry Percy, who was justice of Chester, was able to recruit extensively in Cheshire. Only at the battle of Shrewsbury in 1403 was the complete authority of the earl's affinity finally restored.

The political conflicts of the final quarter of the fourteenth century are apparent in the competition for offices, custody of lands, wardships and marriages where the higher nobility often wielded political power on behalf of local lords. The pattern of gentry support can be identified from appearances in retinues, recognizances and from the direct evidence of noble support and patronage enrolled among the palatinate records. Such support was often vacillating or suspect but clearly illustrates the relevance of politics and faction in the development of military recruitment.

Developments in the pattern of military recruitment by the lords of Halton – Thomas of Lancaster, Henry of Grosmont and John of Gaunt – are followed over the whole period from 1311 to 1403 and related to changes in political circumstance and the continuity of lordship. Any consideration of retaining by Thomas of Lancaster is, however, hampered by the lack of evidence to establish the pattern of gentry affiliations. What does emerge from consideration both of the crisis of Edward II's reign and that under Richard II is that competition among the lower ranks of the gentry often emerged in the guise of political acts.[58] The pattern of gentry affiliations which supported the noble factions of the later medieval period, and through which the distribution of patronage was organised, was itself shaped by tenurial and inter-personal relationships in the locality.

It is perhaps a truism that the conduct of war was merely a reflection of the domestic social organisation; a continuation of social intercourse and command by other means. However, it is apparent from the study of a well-documented knightly retinue, that of Sir Ralph Mobberley between 1355 and 1360, that the factors which governed the formation of a gentry affiliation and its reflection in a military retinue were complex rather than simple. In this case it is possible to identify a significant proportion of the retinue from the evidence of John Henxteworth's *Journal* and the Black Prince's *Register*, and to compare it with an isolated rental and the witness lists of charters and deeds. Although Mobberley's lands exercised a clear geographical constraint on the formation of his retinue, its form was far removed from a muster of tenurial support.

Sir Ralph Mobberley's estates and influence in local society established him as a focus for the aspirations of small landowners and tenants, and his retinue drew its membership from the younger sons of neighbouring gentry families and from relationships of kinship and political support in the locality. The character of the retinue was formed over a period of some thirty years and can at several points be satisfactorily related to a response to the conflict between Thomas of Lancaster and Edward II and the fragmentation of political authority between 1322 and 1330 which encouraged an increasingly violent approach to the tensions in local society. The conclusions advanced for the formation and character of Mobberley's retinue in Gascony are supported by examination of other retinues during the fourteenth century, notably those of John Leycester and Sir William Mainwaring. Such studies are, however, dependent upon the conjunction of an adequate retinue roll with the survival of significant numbers of deeds or charters which will allow consideration of the substantive relationships within a retinue.

The direction of the study is, however, still inescapably hierarchial in character and firmly based on the assumption of corporate military service in the retinues of the earl and other noble captains. Although in a study of the retinues of Mobberley, Leycester and Mainwaring we approach closer to a wider spectrum within the military community, conclusions as to the social context of military service are drawn mainly from the evidence of deeds and charters. The survival of such evidence is firmly rooted in a kinship society where the family makes regular and adequate provision for relatives. Where kinship links are weak, or the extent of the family lands insufficient to meet the demands of an extended kinship group – unless the younger son or cadet branch succeeds ultimately in establishing its own claim to gentry status through the ownership of land in the same county – there is a marked paucity of evidence of a private nature. This was particularly true for a recognisable class of soldier most obviously represented in the career of Sir Hugh Calveley, whose role in Cheshire society is barely visible in the sources so far described.

Some attempt is made, therefore, to broaden the scope of the surviving evidence through a number of individual studies through which
it may be possible to test the assumptions based upon a consideration
of the recruitment of the earl and established gentry families in the
county. The period between 1360 and 1370 has been taken as a base,
largely because a weaker operation of royal authority, both in England
and France, allowed the widest expansion of independent and individual
military enterprise.

A number of individuals, Sir Hugh Calveley, Sir David Hulgreve
and John Norbury, first emerge as the leaders of freelance companies in
the Breton March; others such as John Jodrell, Sir Thomas Wettenhall,
Sir David and Sir Richard Cradock as members of the English administration and garrisons in Aquitaine under the Black Prince. The
evidence for their careers is far from comprehensive; few are well served
by the survival of deed collections or private evidences, and fewer still
would feature in a survey of the development of military service in the
county based on the evidence of comital recruitment. The military
arrangements which survive in the *Register* or among the palatinate
records are, on the whole, those between the prince and the leaders of
landed society. They deal with the raising of troops within the prince's
lordship and the grants and rewards of service distributed within those
lordships following campaigns. Henxteworth's *Journal*, which deals with
the ordinary daily business of the retinue during the campaign of 1355
in the way that the *Register* records the ordinary business of a magnate
controlling his estates, is in that respect a unique record.

The garrisoning of Aquitaine and the speculative adventures in Spain
and Brittany enable us to identify that section of the military community
which served regularly and for long periods rather than for the mere
duration of single campaigns at regular intervals. The distinction, as
we might expect, is to be made largely on the basis of landed status;
military service over an extended period was more attractive to the
landless younger son or member of a cadet branch than to the lord of
important estates in Cheshire. The evidence is both fragmentary and
uneven: an appearance in the records of the English administration of
the Rouergue, a petition from captivity in Saintonge, payments from
the treasury of Duke John IV of Brittany or a minor role in Froissart's
narrative. Retinue rolls survive for Hulgreve and Calveley, together
with a small number of deeds, but on the whole we are in a position to
form judgements about the rewards and attractions of military service
in such individual cases rather than to relate these persons to the fabric
of local society. Here there are knights and esquires whose military

service is less well reported, but whose experiences add to a study of the social context of military service in the county of Cheshire.

The treatment of the central issues posed by the subject of this monograph has of necessity to be episodic. Such an approach is dictated both by the unevenness of the documentation and by the fact that military service was an episodic experience for most of the men of Cheshire in the period under discussion. By approaching the subject from a variety of angles and over a protracted period (1277 – 1403), however, a cumulative impression of the nature of military obligations and service and of the changing character of the military community in one county may emerge. Such an impression can be used to test the generalisations – often based on a single campaign or the careers of individual soldiers or the haphazard survival of certain kinds of documentation – which have often been made about the impact of military service on late medieval English society.

NOTES

[1] The following provide a guide to the principal work in the subject: J. E. Morris, *The Welsh Wars of Edward I*, 1901; A. E. Prince, 'The Strength of English Armies in the Reign of Edward III', *EHR*, xlvi, 1931, pp. 353 – 7; *idem*, 'The Army and Navy', in J. F. Willard & W. A. Morris (eds), *The English Government at Work, 1327 – 1336*, 1940, I, pp. 332 – 93; N. B. Lewis, 'The Organization of Indentured Retinues in Fourteenth-Century England', *TRHS*, 4th Series, xxvii, 1945, pp. 29 – 39; J. W. Sherborne, 'Indentured Retinues and the English Expeditions to France', *EHR*, lxxix, 1964, pp. 718 – 46.

[2] K. B. McFarlane, 'Bastard Feudalism', *BIHR*, xx, 1943 – 5, pp. 161 – 80; *idem, The Nobility of Later Medieval England*, 1973, pp. 19 – 40; *idem*, 'War, Economy and Social Change: England and the Hundred Years War', *Past and Present*, xxii, 1962, pp. 3 – 13; M. M. Postan, 'The Costs of the Hundred Years War', *ibid*, xxvii, 1964, pp. 34 – 53; *idem*, 'Some Social Consequences of the Hundred Years War', *Econ. H.R.*, xii, 1942, pp. 1 – 12; A. R. Bridbury, 'The Hundred Years War: Costs and Profits', in D. C. Coleman & A. H. John (eds), *Trade, Government and Economy in Pre-Industrial England*, 1977, pp. 80 – 95; H. J. Hewitt, *The Organization of War under Edward III*, 1966.

[3] M. H. Keen, *The Laws of War in the Later Middle Ages*, 1965; F. H. Russell, *The Just War in the Middle Ages*, 1975; J. Barnie, *War in Medieval Society*, 1974.

[4] Philippe Contamine, *War in the Middle Ages*, 1984, pp. 238 – 9.

[5] *Liber Luciani de Laude Cestrie*, ed. M. V. Taylor, LCRS, lxiv, 1912, p. 66.

[6] See below pp. 18 – 20.

[7] *Liber Luciani*, p. 65.

[8] Michael J. Bennett, *Community, Class and Careerism. Cheshire and Lancashire Society in the Age of Sir Gawain and the Green Knight*, 1984, pp. 21 – 52; J. S. Morrill, *Cheshire, 1630 – 1660: County Government and Society during the English Revolution*, 1974, pp. 1 – 5.

[9] P. Heath, 'The Medieval Archdeaconry and Tudor Bishopric of Chester', *Journal of Ecclesiastical History*, xx, 1969, pp. 243–52.

[10] M. James, *Family, Lineage and Civil Society: A Study of Politics, Society and Mentality in the Durham Region, 1500–1640*, 1974, pp. 109–10.

[11] *Ibid.*, p. 108; M. Maclagan, 'Genealogy and Heraldry in the 16th and 17th Centuries', in L. Fox (ed.), *English Historical Scholarship in the 16th and 17th Centuries*, 1956, pp. 38–42.

[12] *Ibid.*, p. 41.

[13] J. S. Morrill, *op. cit.*, p. 3.

[14] N. Pevsner & E. Hubbard, *The Buildings of England: Cheshire*, 1971, pp. 198–200.

[15] H. J. Hewitt, *The Black Prince's Expedition 1355–1357*, 1958, appendix A, pp. 192–3.

[16] B. L. Harley MS 2119, f. 87–8.

[17] M. H. Keen, *The Laws of War in the Late Middle Ages*, 1965, appendix II 'The Peerage of Soldiers', pp. 254–7.

[18] B. L. Harley MS 2119, f. 87d.

[19] G. Ormerod, *The History of the County Palatine and City of Chester*, 3 vols., ed. T. Helsby, 2nd edition, 1882, III, p. 438.

[20] L. V. Ryan, *Roger Ascham*, 1964, pp. 51–4.

[21] Cited in R. Hardy, *Longbow: A Social and Military History*, 1976, p. 143; Charles E. Kelsey, *Cheshire*, Oxford County Histories, 1911, p. 110.

[22] H. J. Hewitt, *Medieval Cheshire: An Economic and Social History of Cheshire in the Reign of the Three Edwards*, 1929. The Cheshire evidence is also discussed in *idem, The Black Prince's Expedition, 1355–1357*, 1958, and *idem, The Organization of War under Edward III*, 1966. A descriptive account of military service in the county is to be found in *idem, Cheshire under the Three Edwards*, 1967, and for the period 1387–1513 in J. T. Driver, *Cheshire in the Later Middle Ages*, 1971.

[23] J. A. Tuck, *Richard II and the English Nobility*, 1973, pp. 165–6.

[24] P. H. W. Booth, '"Farming for Profit" in the Fourteenth Century: The Cheshire Estates of the Earldom of Chester', *Journal of the Chester Archaeological Society*, 62, 1980 for 1979, pp. 73–90.

[25] Michael J. Bennett, *Community, Class and Careerism*, p. 189.

[26] In a society with a high military participation ratio, where military service could compete successfully with the ownership of land or birth and lineage, a rapid movement between social classes or the enhancing of warrior status might be expected. See for instance M. C. Gerbet, 'Les Guerres et l'Accès à la Noblesse en Espagne de 1465 à 1592', *Mélanges de la Casa de Velasquez*, viii, 1972, pp. 295–326.

[27] Michael J. Bennett, loc. cit. See below chapter 3, especially pp. 118–20, 129–30, 136–8; chapter 4, especially pp. 150–2, 154–6, 162–8.

[28] Most of the Cheshire records are listed in the *List of Records of the Palatinates of Chester, Durham and Lancaster, the Honour of Peveril, and the Principality of Wales*, Public Record Office, *List and Indexes xl*, 1914. The records of local courts and ministers' accounts are listed in *List and Indexes*, iv and v. Published records are listed below in the list of sources.

[29] J. M. W. Bean, *The Decline of English Feudalism 1215–1540*, 1968, pp. 144–8.

[30] See below pp. 52–4, 134–8, 170–1.

[31] Public Record Office, Chester 2. (All references to unpublished records refer to collections at the Public Record Office, unless otherwise stated.) They were known as 'recognizance rolls' because the first membrane of each roll was generally taken up with such entries. They are calendared, in a form which does not reproduce the character of the original, in the *36th Report of the Deputy Keeper of the Public Records*, appendix II, 1875.

[32] An account of these records is given below in the list of sources.

[33] E. Powell & G. M. Trevelyan, *The Peasants' Rising and the Lollards*, 1899, pp. 14–16; Michael J. Bennett, *Community, Class and Careerism*, pp. 93–5; P. McNiven, 'The Cheshire Rising of 1400', *BJRL*, lii, 1969–70, pp. 375–96.

[34] See below p. 213.

[35] P. H. W. Booth, 'Taxation and Public Order: Cheshire in 1353', *Northern History*, xii, 1976, pp. 30–1.

[36] DL30 (Court rolls), DL29 (Ministers' accounts). See below pp. 72–4.

[37] See above p. 5. The major deed collections are noted in the list of sources.

[38] Some of the principal work in this field is to be found in the following: A. E. Prince, 'The Strength of English Armies in the Reign of Edward III', *EHR*, xlvi, 1931, pp. 353–7; *idem*, 'The Army and Navy' in J. F. Willard & W. A. Morris (eds), *The English Government at Work 1327–1336*, 1940, I, pp. 332–93; N. B. Lewis, 'The Organization of Indentured Retinues in Fourteenth Century England', *TRHS*, 4th Series, xxvii, 1945, pp. 29–39; M. Prestwich, *War, Politics and Finance under Edward I*, 1972; R. Nicholson, *Edward III and the Scots*, 1965.

[39] K. B. McFarlane, *The Nobility of Later Medieval England*, 1973, pp. 19–40.

[40] M. M. Postan, 'Some Social Consequences of the Hundred Years War', *Econ. H.R.*, xii, 1942, pp. 1–12; *idem*, 'The Costs of the Hundred Years War', *Past and Present*, xxvii, 1964, pp. 34–53; K. B. McFarlane, 'War, the Economy and Social Change: England and the Hundred Years War', *Past and Present*, xxii, 1962, pp. 3–13.

[41] See below pp. 103–14.

[42] *Register of Edward the Black Prince*, ed. M. C. B. Dawes, 1930–33, vol. I, 'England, Wales, Cornwall and Chester 1346–8'; vol. II, 'The White Book of Cornwall 1351–65', vol. III, 'Palatinate of Chester and Flint 1351–65', vol. IV, 'England 1351–65'. It is described by M. Sharp, 'The Administrative Chancery of the Black Prince before 1362', in A. G. Little & F. M. Powicke (eds), *Essays in Medieval History Presented to Thomas Frederick Tout*, 1925, pp. 321–33.

[44] Duchy of Cornwall Office, *Journal* of John Henxteworth. I am grateful to the Chancellor of the Duchy of Cornwall for permission to quote from this document.

[44] H. J. Hewitt, *The Black Prince's Expedition, 1355–1357*, 1958, Appendix C, pp. 195–216.

[45] See below pp. 115–20.

[46] N. H. Nicolas, *The Scrope-Grosvenor Controversy*, 2 vols, 1832.

[47] E101/29/24; see below pp. 131–3.

[48] See below p. 112.

[49] J. R. Maddicott, *Thomas of Lancaster, 1307–22*, 1970, especially chapter II; A. J. Pollard, *John Talbot and the War in France, 1427–1453*, 1983, pp. 68–101; K. Fowler, *The King's Lieutenant*, 1969, appendix III.

[50] A. Goodman, 'The military Subcontracts of Sir Hugh Hastings, 1380', *EHR*, xcv, 1980, pp. 114–20; *idem*, 'Responses to Requests in Yorkshire for Military Service under Henry V', *Northern History*, xvii, 1981, pp. 240–52; Simon Walker, 'Profit and Loss in the Hundred Years War: the Subcontracts of Sir John Strother, 1374', *BIHR*, lviii, 1985, pp. 100–6.

[51] See below p. 190.

[52] CRO, Crewe of Crewe MS DCR/26/3D/6.

[53] See below pp. 66–78.

[54] J. A. Tuck, 'Richard II's System of Patronage' in F. R. H. Du Boulay & Caroline M. Barron (eds), *The Reign of Richard II*, 1971, p. 4.

[55] Michael Powicke, *Military Obligation in Medieval England*, 1962, p. 156.

[56] See below pp. 72–5.

[57] J. L. Gillespie, 'The Cheshire Archers of Richard II: A Royal Experiment in Bastard Feudalism', University of Princeton PhD, 1972. Some of its conclusions are, however, disputed. See below pp. 000–00.

[58] A similar thesis is advanced in S. L. Waugh, 'The Profits of Violence: The Minor Gentry in the Rebellion of 1321–22 in Gloucestershire and Herefordshire', *Speculum*, lii, 1977, pp. 843–69.

CHAPTER I

THE MILITARISM OF CHESHIRE SOCIETY AND THE ORIGINS OF THE RETINUE

The campaigns of Edward I in Wales and Scotland and the military disasters of Edward II are of crucial importance in the identification of the military obligations and performance of service in late medieval Cheshire. However, the sources for individual campaigns during this period are founded upon a particularly narrow base in the wardrobe and exchequer. In these records troops outside the royal household, and below the leadership of the noble retinue, maintain a virtual anonymity which cannot be adequately made good from other sources. Brief career details can be obtained only for a handful of Cheshire knights, and there is for these years a lack of evidence of the kind which later allows us to link the lesser soldiery with particular gentry and localities within the county. Nevertheless, a study of military recruitment during these years provides a valuable background and introduction to the characteristic features of retinues and campaigns later in the fourteenth century.

I. THE MILITARISM OF CHESHIRE SOCIETY

Edward I's campaigns stand at the end of a long period of containment and largely ineffectual responses by the crown to the independence of the Welsh princes in central and northern Wales, the results of which were keenly felt in Cheshire. During the two centuries after the Norman conquest a state of intermittent warfare had marked border society in the northern March, a condition reflected in the two major Chester chronicles. The writings of Lucian, perhaps sub-prior of St Werburgh's in 1195, contain little more than the brief comments already noted, but the chronicle commissioned by abbot Simon of Whitchurch before 1290 reports in detail the persistent campaigning in Wales and the effects of warfare.[1] Perhaps the most notable of these involved the loss of one of the county's religious foundations, with the removal of the monks at the Cistercian house at Poulton on the Dee to a new site at Dieulacres in Staffordshire in 1214 as a result of the continued incursions of the

Welsh.[2] The political conflicts of Henry III's reign served to exacerbate the county's military problems, and in 1264 the pro-Monfort author of the *Annales Cestrienses* recorded that a row of houses in Chester belonging to the abbey of St Werburgh was demolished to allow construction of a ditch around the city as a protection against 'the barons or the Welsh'.[3] In considering the Edwardian campaigns, therefore, one needs to emphasise the traditional impact of war on Cheshire society.

Many of these characteristics predate the Norman conquest by several centuries and have their origins in the Mercian occupation of this area (despite the battle of Chester in 615), although it is with the Norman conquest in 1066 that we encounter a new element in border society. The earldom of Chester, coincident with the county, had originally formed part of the chain of Marcher earldoms founded in the aftermath of the conquest as bases for the conquest of Wales. The earldom of Shrewsbury fell victim to the political aspirations of Robert of Bellême under Henry I, while the position of the earldom of Hereford was quickly undermined by the rapid penetration of South Wales and by the forfeiture of its earl in 1075. Their decline can be matched in the body of England by that of the earldoms of East Anglia and Kent before the end of the eleventh century.[4] In North Wales parts of Gwynedd had been granted to Robert of Rhuddlan in anticipation of a projected conquest to be mounted from the earldom of Chester. In the event the conquest failed after Robert's death, and during the twelfth century the Welsh recovered many of the lands in North Wales which had been surveyed in 1086.[5] Apart from a small group of manors south-west of Chester, a fragment of the 1086 hundred of Atiscross, the river Dee remained the border with Wales until Edward I's campaigns at the end of the thirteenth century. The product of a passing military expediency, Cheshire's independence hardened into custom as successive kings failed to apply themselves to the military problem in Wales.

The proximity of Wales provided one important stimulus to the survival of the earldom of Chester and to the maintenance of a military element in local society, but the rights and privileges of that earldom owed more to the political wisdom of successive earls and their landed position in the rest of England.[6] The hardening and elaboration of this 'framework of disconnected rights' into palatine status can be related to the continuity of comital lordship between 1071 and 1237. The reversion of the earldom to the crown in that year served to recognise and perpetuate the liberties and independence of the county of Chester which had been formed during the reign of Henry II and which, according to the late Geoffrey Barraclough, were not fully articulated until after 1237. During the later medieval period the earldom customarily formed part of the endowment of the king's eldest son, and was granted to the future Edward I in 1254. Immunity from royal taxation and the operation of the king's courts did not amount to complete autonomy, and the king did not hesitate to violate or define the liberties of Cheshire as and when reason demanded. This was particularly true when the earl was also king, and at such times the privileges of the county lacked definition. The county contributed to several subsidies under Edward I, although it was subsequently exempt from royal taxation. Judicial and military privileges were equally subject to the tests of royal expediency.[7] It is in the role of successive earls, however, that we must seek the formation and shaping of the political life of the county, and with it the establishment of the limits of military service.[8]

The position of military service within Cheshire society is noticed first in the charter issued by Earl Ranulph III in 1215 – 16, probably shortly after King John's death in October 1216.[9] Its most important provisions laid down the militia duty of the free sub-tenantry, that 'they shall have coats of mail or hauberks and defend their fees by their bodies, even if they are not knights'; and the territorial limits of service were defined as 'not beyond the Lyme unless by their grace and at my costs'.[10] The Lyme refers here to the traditional name for the boundary with the uplands of the Pennine massif; and the eastern boundaries of the county therefore set the limits of service, by implication defining that service as relating mainly to Wales. At this date the county shared a special but not unique military position with the Durham palatinate and the Marches. The early recognition of these rights and obligations did not in any case insulate the county against the military demands of the crown during the early fourteenth century. Numerous grievances in Cheshire as elsewhere in England centred on the payment of shire levies from the time they left the borders of the county, an obligation established by Edward I and challenged by both Edward II and Edward III.[11] Notwithstanding the provisions of the 1216 charter the county shared the imposition of royal demands, and in 1300 troops raised in Cheshire for Scotland were actually paid from the date of muster at Carlisle, and not from the county boundary.[12] The re-establishment of the concessions of Earl Ranulph III belongs to the rule of the Black Prince, at the same time as the crown itself was making belated concessions concerning the payment of shire levies.[13]

During the thirteenth century the surviving sources concentrate on the definition and performance of feudal obligations, and as a result research has concentrated on the provision of knight-service.[14] The earliest statement of the knights' fees in the county dates from 1253 with a return for an aid for the knighting of the king's eldest son, and revealed some seventy and one twentieth fees.[15] In 1277 the re-opening of campaigns in Wales by the crown was partly financed by demands for a scutage on knights' fees. Writs were directed to the justice of Chester, and the returns endorsed with a note that the men of the county had performed their service. As a result the jurors appear to have submitted a copy of the 1253 list without alteration or revision.[16] A more comprehensive list dates from 1288 with an inquest in the county as to the service due to the king in time of war with Wales. Here some seventy-nine fees and thirty-seven sixtieths are recorded – an increase on the 1253 list which prompted Tait to argue that the 1288 list was based on an earlier and fuller source approximating to the original Norman assessment of eighty fees, fixed between 1071 and 1086.[17]

The subinfeudation of these fees can in several instances be recovered from inquisitions *post mortem* and from occasional feodaries, but it is important to consider the relationship of these lists to the actual provision of men-at-arms by the county.[18] How far were the obligations recorded in the 1288 list and in the inquisitions *post mortem* fossilised survivals reintroduced, like the list of 1253, in the face of military commitments which in reality bore a different form?

Michael Prestwich has established that the distinction drawn between feudal and contractual troops in the armies of Edward I is largely unreal, and that the composition of armies in the field, however raised, remained essentially the same.[19] The experience of Cheshire provides examples of each form of service, both feudal and contractual. The endorsement on the 1277 scutage return noted that the men of Cheshire had performed their feudal service 'and more than that at the king's request', an instance of unpaid voluntary service. In the aftermath of the same campaign three of the men who figure in lists of knights' fees were serving for pay near Flint.[20]

Service outside the county boundary was not initially an issue under Edward I, as campaigns were restricted to North Wales. The possibility of opposition to service occurred, however, as expeditions were mounted in South Wales and Scotland. On two separate occasions in 1287 and 1297 – the former for a campaign against Rhys ap Maredudd in South Wales, the latter for a winter campaign in Scotland – the service of the men of Cheshire was to be considered gracious and not drawn into custom.[21] This caveat did not extend to subsequent campaigns in Scotland, and it is possible that the king's absence from the campaigns of 1287 and 1297, rather than concern over 'foreign' service, prompted the claim of the knightly class to gracious service. The county did join in the opposition to service in France and Gascony under Edward I, and indeed strengthened that opposition during the reign of Edward II. In general, however, Cheshire offers little variation on the themes of military service to be found elsewhere in England during these years.

Even in these terms, however, the county's pre-eminent role in the Welsh campaigns of Edward I separates its experience of war from that of the majority of the English counties. That role is well reported in the secondary sources. The city of Chester lay at the centre of the organisation of the king's campaigns in Wales, serving frequently as a port and site for musters and as the headquarters of the royal household during preparations for expeditions into North Wales.[22] The county also provided large numbers of both men-at-arms and infantry, quantities of supplies and equipment, and acted as host to retinues and levies en route from the rest of England. The general character of Edward's campaigns between 1277 and 1295 is well established and may be briefly summarised.

Following abortive attempts to arrange a meeting with Llywelyn near Chester in September 1275 preparations for war began in earnest, and in 1277 a three-month campaign mounted from Chester had captured the Welsh harvests in Anglesey and forced Llywelyn to come to terms. In 1282 Llywelyn's brother, Dafydd ap Gruffydd, dissatisfied with his reward from Edward, had sponsored a rising in Wales which quickly became a general revolt. As in the campaign of 1277 a royal army advanced from Chester along the coast of North Wales, finally capturing the castle at Bere in April 1283. Four years later Edmund, Earl of Cornwall, drew on troops from Cheshire to assist in the suppression of a rising in South Wales led by Rhys ap Maredudd, mounted during the king's absence in Gascony. A final popular rising, again aimed at exploiting the diversion of resources towards an expedition to Gascony, led Edward to North Wales in 1294. The king's army marched from Chester towards Anglesey as the earl of Warwick, moving from Montgomery, defeated the Welsh at Maes Moydog in March 1295.

Edward's campaigns in Wales were fought largely with Welsh infantry recruited in South Wales and the border lands of the northern March; but among the infantry forces raised in England the county of Cheshire maintained a dominant role which continued during Edward's campaigns in Scotland. The raising of troops was always unevenly distributed among the English local communities, and in the Welsh and Scottish campaigns the burden fell most heavily on the counties of the Welsh March and the north of England.[23] Proximity to Wales and

Scotland seems to have been the most important consideration, although in counties like Derbyshire military skill also appears to have played a significant role. Equally important is the fact that the armies in Wales between 1277 and 1295 maintained the Marcher coalition with which Edward had countered Simon de Montfort at the battle of Evesham in 1265 and reinforced Edward's own role as the foremost Marcher lord.

During the first campaign in Wales in 1277 the Cheshire foot accounted for roughly fifty per cent of the infantry forces during the earlier stages, falling to thirty-three per cent with the arrival of reinforcements during the late summer and autumn.[24] In all some 1,620 foot from Cheshire served during the first Welsh campaign; a level of demand which was extended during the campaign of 1282–3 when some 2,000 foot were to be found in the various armies.[25] In 1287 the rising in South Wales brought an army of 11,000 foot into the field under Edmund of Cornwall, of whom 700 were raised in Cheshire under the justice, Reginald Grey.[26] Finally, a body of 1,000 foot from Cheshire were with Edward as he entered South Wales in May 1295 during the last Welsh campaign.[27] The levels of demand indicated by these figures reflect both the traditional position of the county *vis-à-vis* Wales, and the role of the king as a Marcher lord.

This latter point is clearly made in the employment of a guard of archers within the royal household, both in 1277 and 1282. In 1277, 100 archers from Macclesfield led by Henry Davenport were paid 4*d* a day for the duration of the campaign.[28] Davenport later served a bailiff of the hundred of Macclesfield, and the connection with the demesne lands of the earldom of Chester is echoed by a note in the exchequer account explaining the inflated rate of pay, '*quia sunt de terra regis*'.[29] The guard reappears during the campaign of 1282, although its rate of pay had declined to the customary wage for foot soldiers of 2*d* a day.[30] There is little evidence to suggest that Macclesfield archers were especially renowned for their skills, or that the guard had been specifically selected for that reason. Certainly the employment of such a rigidly local guard was a precedent that was not followed by the crown at any time in the fourteenth century, even during the reign of Richard II.[31] The guard does not appear after the campaign of 1282, and the raising of troops from the demesne lands of the earldom is perhaps to be related to Edward's brief interest in Marcher lordship which declined with the broadening of royal concerns in Gascony and Scotland.

The size of infantry levies in Cheshire during the Welsh wars was initially maintained in Scotland, and in 1297 4,000 foot were requested from the county to join the Earl of Warenne at Newcastle-upon-Tyne for a winter campaign during the king's absence in Flanders.[32] In the event only 3,000 foot were raised in Cheshire and reached Newcastle too late to join Warenne; they were simply paid for the march from the county boundary.[33] The campaign was unusual in several ways, not least because it represented the heaviest demand for manpower on the county during the medieval period. The leadership of infantry levies had also previously rested with the lesser gentry and younger sons of the knightly class. In 1297, although later a common feature of military organisation in the county, the important landowners were for the first time associated with the leadership of infantry, perhaps as a result of the absence of both the Earl and the Justice of Chester from the campaign. In the following year the king's campaign which led to the battle of Falkirk attracted some 1,283 foot from the county; some 300 more than were summoned.[34] Thereafter demands for infantry fell away, and in 1300 only 330 archers from the county served in the Caerlaverock campaign.[35] Cheshire was far from unique in this respect and the size of royal armies showed a marked decline after the battle of Falkirk, as infantry armies of great size proved increasingly difficult to keep in the field.

We must fairly assume also that those men who figure in the lists of knights' fees were to be found serving in the armies of Edward I, and in fact where details of service can be recovered they mostly relate to men in this category. However, the service from eighty knights' fees in Cheshire, as from such sources in the rest of England, was clearly insufficient to meet the demands of the crown for mounted troops, and various expedients were adopted to extend the basis of the *servitium debitum*. Foremost of these were the various attempts to set wealth qualifications for service, and on several occasions between 1279 and 1300 writs distraining twenty, thirty and forty librate landholders were addressed to the justice of Chester.[36] These efforts aroused almost universal opposition, culminating in the crisis of 1297, although it seems unlikely that the crown had been able to make any significant gains in increasing the basis of recruitment. In Cheshire this is made all the more unlikely in the light of the single surviving return to such a writ. This dates from 1300 when the king had revived wealth qualifications for service, and despite renewed opposition had lists of forty librate landholders drawn up.[37] The writ addressed to Richard Mascy, justice of Chester, referred to the salvation of the kingdom and community as the pretext of action, entered the customary plea of necessity, and ordered the muster of forty librate landholders at Carlisle by June. The returns, compiled by Hugh Audley and Fulc Lestrange, merely repeated the details of the list of knights' fees in 1288.[38]

In the absence of detailed records of service we have no way of
knowing whether the holders of knights' fees always performed their
service in person, or of identifying the methods employed in putting their
retinues in the field. The only knight who emerges with any degree of
clarity is Hamo Mascy, Baron of Dunham Massey, whose tenure of the
Mascy estate neatly straddles the period under discussion: he received
livery of his lands in 1277 and died in 1325.[39] The brief details of his
military career which emerge in the surviving records amply illustrate
the difficulties to be overcome in compiling such military biographies
at this early date. The anonymity preserved by the records of the
exchequer has already been mentioned, while private evidences only
rarely contain military documents of this period. The contractual
system, already well established under Edward I, may well have been
largely verbal; and until the documentation recording the relationships
between knights and their retinues survives in greater quantity, the task
of identifying social and economic groupings in the smaller retinues can
only be putative.

The known instances of Mascy's own service probably form only a
selection from his actual military career. In 1297 he was commissioned,
along with Ralph Vernon, to lead the 4,000 archers chosen in Cheshire
to join the Earl of Warenne in Scotland.[40] In the following year he
appears on the Falkirk Roll of Arms, with at least six other holders of
knights' fees and thirty-four other Cheshire knights.[41] Finally in 1301
he was summoned to lead the levies of Welsh foot to Carlisle to join the
retinue of the Prince of Wales.[42] It seems inconceivable that these
examples are in any way comprehensive, and in any case one lacks
details of Mascy's involvement, and that of his peers, in Edward I's
earlier Welsh campaigns.

The militarism of Cheshire society is, however, not to be seen solely
in the context of those campaigns, nor indeed should the limits of
military service be seen to rest purely on the feudal service demanded
by the crown in these years. The earldom and county of Chester had
for much of the medieval period formed the military frontier of English
royal power. The impact of a permanent frontier on the character of
local societies has been closely followed, notably in the development of
early medieval Spain. There, the constant demands of warfare served
to create a noble class in which military prowess could compete successfully with the traditional elements of birth and lineage. Social stratification thus depended on the employment of the wealth and honour
consequent on military success; and following a chronic shortage of
manpower the attributes of nobility were allowed to percolate to the

lowest social levels, creating a class of 'commoner' knights.[43] It is perhaps unsafe to postulate that society in late medieval Cheshire might approximate to that of Spain in the thirteenth century, but it is suggested, by Hewitt and others, that the county, in common with the rest of the March and the northern border, was militarised to a greater extent than in the rest of England.

The archaeological evidence hardly confirms that thesis for although the hand of Edward I is still visible in the landscape of north Wales, in that series of castles which provide a climax to the military architecture of the medieval period, little survives in Cheshire to testify to the role of the county in the military events of the late thirteenth century. The line of motte and bailey castles built under the Norman earls along the Cheshire border at Shotwick, Dodleston, Aldford, Shoklach and Malpas lay far behind Edward I's front lines, and their scant physical remains appear to bear witness to an earlier phase in the history of the March. The pace and scale of building activity at Flint, Conwy, Caernarfon and other Welsh castle sites was matched only at the site of Vale Royal Abbey, founded by Edward I in 1277 and the scene of an intensive building programme until 1281.

Manorial records, however, offer more direct confirmation of the militarism of local society. A survey of the Earl of Arundel's lands in 1301, for example, allows a comparison of tenurial conditions in southern England and the March, and reveals in Shropshire and Cheshire the retention of military obligations long after their commutation to cash payments in Sussex.[44] The Fitzalans' pre-eminent role as Marcher lords was ultimately supported by the persistence of a military element in the framework of tenurial relationships. Thus in Cheshire William Helsby held the village of Helsby for the service of a horseman with armour for forty days in time of war, Richard Brown a disparate group of lands for the service of a man with a bow and a quiverful of arrows for forty days.[45] What might seem anachronistic in the feudal host in Scotland remained vital to military lordship in the March. A survey of the manor of Dunham Massey in 1401 even points to the updating of military obligations, perhaps during the early fourteenth century. There, the tenant of Bredbury owed the service of 'a man called a *hoblar* for fifteen days in time of war with Wales', suggesting that the service of a number of footmen had been rationalised in the face of changing military techniques.[46]

It is in this light that one must approach the remains of Cheshire's castles and the evidence of inquisitions *post mortem* at the end of the thirteenth century. Castle guard along the line of Norman motte and bailey castles lay at the heart of the obligations of military service as they are revealed in inquisitions *post mortem*, Richard Orreby owing service at Aldford, the tenants of William Boydel at Newhall and Geoffrey Griffin at Dodleston.[47] It is difficult to envisage the military importance of these sites in the context of Edward I's Welsh castles, particularly as at several sites the medieval parish church occupies the bailey, over-shadowing the motte. The reality of border warfare can, however, be gauged from several sources. In 1286 a case at the county court centred on the performance of castle guard at Dodleston, John Boydel claiming that William Lancelyn had failed to perform the service of a horseman with arms for fifteen days.[48] At Malpas, where the church-yard adjoins the motte, the lord of Cholmondeley petitioned to establish a chapel there on the grounds that 'the dead in time of war are buried in the fields because Malpas church is so near Wales that part of the parish belongs to the English, part to the Welsh wherefore the English dare not go in war time ...'[49] The campaigns of Edward I and the organisation of his war in Wales only temporarily superseded the traditional, local responses to border warfare which had shaped Cheshire society.

During the course of the thirteenth century manors along the western edge of the county had been particularly vulnerable to attack, and jurors claimed not to be able to approach either Malpas or Dodleston in time of war. The manor of Dodleston had formed part of the lands of the abbey at Poulton which were retained by the new foundation at Dieulacres. In 1299 the abbey leased the manor to William Doncaster, a citizen of Chester, and included the provision that the buildings were to be rebuilt in the event of their destruction by fire during time of war with Wales.[50] The threat of border raiding did not diminish with Edward I's political settlement, and as late as 1338 it still seemed expedient that a new bridge across the Dee at Holt should be fortified.[51] Six years later the abbot of St Werburgh's in Chester was still able to petition the pope success-fully for compensation for the loss of the manors of Broughton and Dyserth, and the church at Holywell, 'by reason of the wars between the kings of England and the princes of Wales'.[52] To the traditional burdens of a border society we must also add the temporary, but none-theless destructive, presence of Edward I's infantry armies in Chester and the equally disruptive Welsh levies under Edward II, who in 1319 rioted in the city for three days before their departure for Scotland.[53]

What then does this study of Edward I's campaigns reveal about the nature of military service in Cheshire at the end of the thirteenth century? There is little doubt that levels of demand for manpower were at their highest during this period, although it remains difficult to offer precise statistics. The county was included in the Domesday survey and on that evidence J. C. Russell estimated a population in the late eleventh century of some 8,000 people.[54] In the absence of poll tax returns for the lay population, estimates of the later medieval population have been based upon application of population densities in neighbouring counties, giving Cheshire, in Russell's estimation, a population of 15,503 in 1377. Later revisions of Russell's work have produced a figure closer to 20,000.[55] More recently, however, Michael Bennett has challenged both the basis of comparability between the adjacent counties of the north-west, and the degree of under-enumeration in the poll tax of 1377. His estimate of the Cheshire population at this date is 48,000.[56] The heaviest demand for manpower came in 1297 when 4,000 foot from Cheshire were requested for a winter campaign in Scotland, although the more usual levels of recruitment had been between 1,000 and 2,000 for other Welsh and Scottish campaigns. On this basis between 10 and 15 per cent of the adult male population in the county was likely to have found service in the armies of Edward I.

An implicit suggestion, however, is that although that recruitment remains important in the definition of military obligations, it must be seen in the light of a border problem of some two centuries' duration. Cheshire was already a highly militarised society in which the physical effects of warfare were more marked, and where military service persisted as a valid part of tenurial relationships after it had fallen into disuse elsewhere in England. Hitherto the response to the threat of Welsh incursions and raiding was essentially local and operated through a system of castle guard, or by the raising of forces under the justice of Chester.[57] The rule of Edward I, who after his creation as earl of Chester in 1254 had been established as a leading magnate on the Welsh border, not only extended these military commitments but placed them firmly within the national context.

II. MOUNTED ARCHERS AND THE DEVELOPMENT OF THE RETINUE

The level of manpower demands in real terms was to fall throughout England in the fourteenth century as large infantry armies proved increasingly difficult to keep in the field. As the population of England was also to fall as a result of famine and plague, the level of military recruitment by the crown was to remain proportionately as significant as it had been under Edward I. It is the contention of this monograph, however, that military service, tended no longer to include those elements lowest in the social scale, partly as a result of changes in the organisation of medieval armies. The virtual disappearance of the poorly-armed footsoldier and his replacement by the mounted archer was to cause a significant increase in the levels of military service amongst certain sections of the local population after the 1330s.

Developments in military practice which dramatically increased the efficiency of Edwardian armies grew from the lessons learnt on campaigns in Wales and Scotland. The payment of wages was first mooted in the Welsh war of 1282, although opposition amongst the nobility continued until the reign of Edward II. Efforts to broaden the basis of military obligations were not, on the whole, successful, but the introduction of contracts between the crown and the magnates, although not used to raise whole armies until 1337, had an immediate impact on military recruitment. At Boroughbridge, Dupplin Moor and Halidon Hill English armies also observed the effect of positioning dismounted men-at-arms in lines and schiltroms, with archers on the flanks.[58] A recurring problem had been the lack of mobility of large infantry armies, and attempts were made to simulate Scottish mounted raids in 1298 when 200 cavalry were to be supported by pack horses. Ultimately the introduction of the mounted archer was to solve the problems of the cumbersome infantry army, but the same precedent had been set in the employment of the hobelar or lightly-armed horseman.[59]

Social and military conditions had long favoured the use of lightly-armed horsemen in Ireland, and as early as 1188 Gerald of Wales had recommended the combination of archers and cavalry. Faced with difficult terrain, within which there were few opportunities for mounted shock combat, the Anglo-Norman lords developed native military techniques which stretched back centuries. Irish hobelars, used primarily as reconnaissance troops, were employed in increasing numbers between 1296 and 1322, with as many as 500 serving during the Scottish campaign of 1303.

The earliest English hobelars were raised from the northern border counties where the Cumberland knight, Andrew Harclay, employed them to great effect against the Scots and in 1322 against Thomas of Lancaster at Boroughbridge.[60] The wardrobe book for the Scottish campaign of 1322 reveals that Cheshire provided the larger of the two groups of hobelars raised by the English counties.[61] Cheshire hobelars were also summoned for service in Gascony in 1324 and 1325 and were clearly playing an important role in changes in military tactics.

Such developments were not for the most part either sudden or premeditated, and assessments of the state of change reached during particular campaigns serve only to disguise the nature of that change over a longer period. The availability of a novel weapon or technique does not necessitate its immediate employment, and the widespread introduction of the mounted archer after 1334, as of other innovations, is perhaps to be related as much to social changes in military recruitment as to the apparent tactical superiority of the lightly armed horseman.

In any society 'the military participation ratio' (the proportion of men taking part in war) is closely related to the relative cost of the armaments and to the length of training required for particular military skills.[62] In the medieval period the most obvious example is that connected with the introduction of the stirrup and the development of mounted shock combat, which restricted the role of warrior to a narrow privileged *élite* dependent on the income of estates for the maintenance of horse and armour. At the end of the eleventh century the mailed shirt had become so intricate that it equalled the price of a good farm.[63] At the end of the thirteenth century the cost of equipping a knight continued to restrict the membership of this social and military *élite*, although the military participation ratio had risen with the increasing use of large infantry forces. The equipment of the foot soldier was fixed by custom and statute; but the expense of providing an aketon or bascinet, or a particular type of offensive weapon, seldom affected the social character of the levy. In practice the cost of equipment fell upon the community, which assumed responsibility for the choice of men for service. The wages of the foot soldier at 2*d* a day compared favourably with those for unskilled labour, but military service with its attendant risks can have been an attractive prospect for only a few members of the local community. Customary obligations for possession of arms were often disregarded, and infantry levies in Scotland were frequently poorly armed and clothed, and prone to high levels of desertion.[64] During the late thirteenth century, therefore, the military participation ratio reached its highest levels; no class in society was exempt from service and in 1298 up to 5 per cent of the adult male population may have been summoned to serve.

The widespread introduction of the hobelar and the mounted archer increased the expense of equipment and the length of training associated with the skills of warfare, and therefore favoured a reduction in the military participation ratio and the retreat of military service into a narrower social spectrum below the nobility, or alternatively the development of a better-trained, and therefore more permanent, pool of military recruits. Both developments may be observed in Cheshire during the course of the fourteenth century. The retinue of Sir James

Audley in Gascony in 1345 was, for example, equipped with three horses for each man-at-arms and one horse for each archer: an investment beyond the means of much of the population and a potent sign of social status unlikely to be offered lightly by the community. Indeed it has been argued that investment in horses by knights could, at the start of the fifteenth century, represent between six months' and a year's wages.[65] The lowest common denominator in Edward I's armies was the poorly-armed foot soldier, often recruited at the lowest social level, and at whose speed the whole army moved; in the retinues of the Black Prince each man was equipped with a horse and was proficient with a weapon which required a long period of training and continuous practice, i.e. the longbow.

In 1175 the Council of Woodstock's decree on the carrying of bows and arrows east of the river Severn suggests that the weapon was novel in these areas, but that its use was spreading.[66] The gradual eastward spread of the Gwentian bow during the twelfth and thirteenth centuries is apparent in a variety of evidence, from its appearance in the design of floor tiles in use along the Welsh border to its rapidly increasing use as a weapon in assaults and homicides. In 1242, however, a writ enforcing the assize of arms required the use of the bow from those with lands worth between 40s and 100s a year, or goods to the value of 120s. The bow, it seems, was not yet regarded as the customary weapon of the peasantry, although a later clause advocated its wider use. This recommended that those outside the forest who were able should have bows, whilst those within the forest areas should have crossbows.[67] This official sponsorship of the crossbow, a weapon of great expense and restricted availability, suggests that within the forest areas offences against the vert and venisom committed by archers had already reached significant levels. At a time of rapidly increasing population the attractiveness of the longbow amongst the landless and smallholding population is clear enough, and the place of the forest areas in the spread of the weapon seems likely.

The introduction of the longbow as an infantry weapon is to be seen during Edward I's Welsh and Scottish campaigns when the greater part of the foot soldiers are described as archers.[68] The majority of foot soldiers at this date were Welsh friendlies from the March and South Wales where the longbow was already a customary weapon. When the English counties began to provide archers, they were drawn largely from the forested areas in Derbyshire, Nottinghamshire, the Forest of Dean and Cheshire. The 100 Macclesfield archers who served in the body-guard of Edward I from 1277 reflect both the king's position as a

Marcher lord and the early and widespread use of the longbow in Cheshire.

Cheshire too was to play a leading role in the introduction of the mounted archer in the 1330s, but it would be misleading to assume that men of the same class as had fought on foot in large numbers in the armies of Edward I were now mounted in smaller numbers in the armies of Edward III. Even the earliest mounted archers would appear to have been men of some standing in local society (as, for example, those raised by the city of Norwich), and at the end of the fourteenth century, sanctioned no doubt by the achievement of the mounted archer in the retinues of the Hundred Years War, the longbow makes appearances on gentry seals and in gentry wills.[69]

The progress of coincidental and seemingly accidental technical innovation now appears less important than other gradual changes during the 1330s and 1340s, a time of marked decline in the contribution of shire levies and infantry in general, and of the rising importance of retinues capable of assuming a variety of military roles. Increasingly, expeditionary forces would be composed of men-at-arms and mounted archers, the latter capable of affording infantry protection in a static engagement with larger forces, but serving within a mounted and consequently highly mobile force. In that respect the mounted archer may be seen as a solution to that persistent military problem which had perplexed both Edward I and his son. The early importance of such retinues, composed of men-at-arms and mounted archers, is, however, not easily recognised in armies which still maintained a substantial infantry element, and as long as the size of such armies in Scotland is seen as the sole index of serious military purpose on the part of the crown. The expedition of 1336, during which Edward III, accompanied by 400 men-at-arms and 400 hobelars and mounted archers, moved to devastate the highlands and Aberdeen and to relieve the siege of Lochindorb castle, is consequently generally dismissed as being of little significance. The interest of a contemporary account which emphasised the pace at which that force moved across Scotland is, however, clear enough and provides an important indication of the early employment of the typical retinue of the Hundred Years War.[70] In considering the development of military practice between 1327 and 1338, the significant change is not so much the tactic of dismounting men-at-arms and ranging archers in flanking wings, or the expedient of equipping hobelars with the longbow, as the way in which the retinue and the *chevauchée* came to dominate the organisation of war under Edward III. The importance of that brief ride through the highlands in 1336 is not lessened by the fact that it avoided, as the Black Prince in Gascony did not, an engagement with superior forces at its culmination.

The period of Edward III's Scottish campaigns has long been characterised as a form of military and political apprenticeship, a forcing ground for tactical innovation in which the crises and conflicts of the previous three decades were reconciled on the basis of consent and co-operation.[71] By 1341 the leadership in war rested firmly with the nobility at the head of a contractual army raised on the basis of the individual retinue. Experiments in compulsion and the hardening of military obligations which had moved temporarily to the advantage of the crown were rationalised by the emergence of a system of public finance which liberated Edward III from the problems which had confronted the crown after 1297. Purveyance and taxation, rather than personal military service, were henceforth the more insistent burdens of warfare in the local communities as the shire levies were increasingly devoted to local defence or minor supportive roles on continental expeditions.[72]

The distinction between communal and contractual obligations is perhaps unreal, for the two forms continued to overlap in the raising of armies. The muster of troops by the Black Prince in Cheshire would be firmly based on the communal obligations of the county, as expressed in the charter of 1216, although the prince nevertheless sealed indentures with individual knights and esquires for the raising of archers, and many of those same knights would often later be appointed as commissioners of array.[73] An apparent terminological confusion signifies little more than the matching of new and traditional forms in the raising of troops, and however summoned the composition of armies would remain roughly constant.[74] The crucial point is that the burden of recruitment had passed from the crown into the hands of the noble captains who now undertook to provide the number of soldiers specified in their indentures. A continuing, and in some respects increasing, concern with distraint of knighthood, with the provisions of the Statute of Winchester and with customary obligations in general, each a feature of Edward III's rule, ensured the survival of a reserve of troops and added to the sources on which the captain might draw in mustering his company.

Of the methods of recruitment adopted, perhaps the best documented is the use of retainers, men bound by indenture, either for life or for the duration of particular campaigns on payment of fees or annuities, and in return for the provision of military service.[75] Such men offered a lord the prospect of ostentatious display, gave counsel in peace and war, and staffed the administration of his estate. In time of war they

provided the core of the lord's military retinue.[76] The range of relationships which were encompassed within the retinue were not confined
to the nobility but reached down into the ranks of the gentry, whose
own forms of domestic organisation mirrored those of the nobility.
The organisation of war was therefore a reflection of relationships within
local society, and in Cheshire it was a relationship restricted to those
above the peasantry.

War in that sense had again become the province of an *élite* which
supported itself financially on the economy at large. In narrowly fiscal
terms it could only be profitable when the incidents and advantages
gained through ransoms, *appatis*, land and office exceeded the yield of
taxation raised to finance its conduct, or for as long as the main burden
of that taxation fell elsewhere. Warfare was, however, the greatest
consumer of public finance and often the mainspring of royal largesse;
its conduct clearly favoured the transfer of wealth into the hands of a
nobility which had maintained its hold on the leadership in war. Indeed
during a period of declining demesne profits the organisation of war was
to provide a new route by which the profits of agriculture and the trade
in wool and cloth, in the form of taxation, flowed into the hands of the
magnates and their retinues. Herein lies the interest of the retinue, not
simply as a means of providing military service, but as perhaps the most
dynamic social form of the later medieval period.

These separate questions are clearly not capable of a single or simple
solution, and in Cheshire the emergence of the mounted archer and the
concurrent development of the retinue is approached initially through
a study of the career of a minor knight, Sir John Ward of Sproston.

During the winter campaign in Scotland in 1334 perhaps as many
as 1,660 'mounted archers' had served in an army of little more than
6,000 men, principally within the retinues of the magnates.[77] Notwithstanding an isolated reference in the previous year, this remains the
earliest documentary evidence of their employment in the English
armies of the later medieval period. In view of their service on so large
a scale, however, it seems unlikely that their appearance was totally
without precedent, and it is perhaps more probable that the equipment
of the hobelar, from whom the mounted archer had perhaps evolved,
had been subject to some variation throughout the period since the early
1320s. The wardrobe clerk, in his account of the levies from the West
Riding of Yorkshire, had in fact described the arrival of 103 '*hobelarios
sagittarios ad equites*', revealing an administrative terminology in process
of change.[78] Nevertheless, troops described both as hobelars and
mounted archers continued to serve in armies for a further decade.

Not least of the body of mounted archers in 1334 were 100 under the leadership of John Ward, 'chosen for the body[guard] of the king in the county of Cheshire', whose strength was gradually augmented during the autumn months, reaching a level of some 214 men in late November when two standards bearing the royal arms were presented to Ward and Henry Pledour to carry before the king. The whole body served from then until the end of the campaign in February 1335.[79] Ward's service clearly recalled that of a similar group of archers raised in the lordship of Macclesfield during the first Welsh war of 1277, whose recruitment had been the product of Edward I's brief interest in Marcher lordship.[80] The employment of a guard of mounted archers raises the question of the relative importance of such troops within the royal household, and of the character of military service in Cheshire at a date when crucial changes in military usage were under way.

A guard of royal archers had indeed been a relatively common element in the household, developed by Edward II in the years after Gaveston's death. In 1315 a force of thirty Welsh and English archers drew $3d$ a day 'staying in the king's household as his bodyguard (*pro corpore suo*)' on his journeys, and the arrangement appears to have continued until after the fall of Thomas of Lancaster.[81] Beyond a certain preference for the Welsh, there appears to have been little discernible territorial bias in the recruitment of these archers, although the relative obscurity of those who served often makes a firm judgement difficult. Once within the household, those recruited both by Edward II and Edward III seem to have shared a variety of tasks, principally in the carrying of royal letters.[82] Under Edward II many were further employed in the garrisons of royal castles along the Scottish border, and several may earlier have been among the household troops at Scarborough prior to Gaveston's capture there.[83] Although the experience of Edward II's household did establish a number of precedents later taken up by that of his son, most notably in the employment of hobelars, it would perhaps be premature to identify any consistent and continuous development in the organisation of the king's household.[84] The guard which served Edward II was literally a personal bodyguard, and accompanied the king as a permanent part of the household receiving fees and robes; that which found service under Edward III, and indeed Edward I, was rather that part of the expanded household which made up a royal expeditionary force recruited for the duration of particular campaigns. The connection between the Macclesfield archers and those under John Ward must remain problematical.

The level of the crown's demands upon the county of Cheshire, as revealed in the wardrobe accounts of the 1330s, do, however, serve to establish the character and extent of military service during a vital decade. It has been suggested that the weight of the crown's demands upon the English local communities had reached a peak of oppressiveness during that same decade, and had fuelled a crisis in the country and in parliament.[85] That Cheshire would appear to have played little or no part in the popular movements of the period and indeed to have escaped the demands of royal taxation and purveyance is clearly a fact of some significance.[86] It remains to be seen, however, to what extent the county had escaped from what was perhaps the less onerous burden of military service.

Table 1   *Military service in Cheshire 1334–1342*

Date	Numbers	Leaders	Service
Oct 1334 – Dec 1334	214 king's archers	John Ward	Scotland
May 1335	40 hobelars & 200 archers		Scotland
June 1335 – Jan 1336	162 king's archers	John Ward	Scotland
June 1336 – Dec 1336	60 king's archers	John Stamford & Henry Pledour	Scotland
July 1336	100 hobelars & 300 archers	John Arden & John Legh	Scotland
May 1337 – June 1337	45 king's archers	Henry Pledour	Scotland
Aug 1337	200 mounted archers	Alex Wastenays & Ralph Morton	Flanders
Sept 1337	150 mounted archers	Alex Wastenays & Ralph Morton	Scotland
July 1338 – Nov 1339	202 king's archers 150 mounted archers	John Ward John Hide	Flanders Flanders
Nov 1341 – Jan 1342	50 king's archers 195 mounted archers	John Ward Alex Wastenays & John Grey	Scotland Scotland
Sept 1342 – Feb 1343	80 king's archers	John Ward	Brittany

(Sources: B. L. Cotton MS Nero C VIII; E101/388/5; E36/203; E36/204; *Parliamentary Writs and Writs of Military Summons.*)

Ward's archers had returned to serve during the summer campaign of 1335 when the 162 men under his leadership were joined by eighteen 'king's archers' raised in Radnor by Hugh Tyrell.[87] Thereafter, however, the decline in the king's ambitions in Scotland brought about a shrinkage of military activity on the border. Sixty king's archers under John Stamford and Henry Pledour were present on the Lochindorb campaign; and forty-five under Pledour's leadership appear in the summer of 1337, when they were joined by a further fifty archers raised in Knaresborough, and forty-two archers raised by Tyrell in the March.[88] Preparations for the king's expedition to France continued to dominate the details of military organisation, and 200 mounted archers raised in Cheshire were retained in London in August 1337 in anticipation of a summer crossing. In the event the campaign was postponed until the following year, although 150 of the Cheshire archers were apparently diverted to the Scottish border to serve under the earl of Warwick.[89]

In July 1338 Edward III at last embarked for Flanders where the earliest military campaign of the Hundred Years War reached an inconclusive end, notable only for the indiscriminate pillaging of Cambrai. By this date the shire levies were playing an increasingly minor role, for the burdens of war on the local communities had now moved firmly into the areas of taxation and purveyance. The army in Flanders was recruited mainly by contract, although the mounted archers were still entered separately in the accounts of the wardrobe and did not share in the inflated wage rates given to the men-at-arms in the retinues of the magnates.[90] John Ward again had led a force of some 202 king's archers, although the final Cheshire contribution to the campaign was a good deal higher as a result of the service of a further 150 mounted archers under the leadership of an esquire of the household, John Hide.[91] A little over a quarter of the total number of mounted archers on this campaign had been recruited in Cheshire. Many of those summoned from Essex and London had arrived without horses and served as foot archers, while other counties provided small numbers. The next largest contingents were to be found in the retinues of the magnates, where a group of sixty mounted archers served under Sir Henry Percy, and groups of fifty served, respectively, in the retinues of Henry, Bishop of Lincoln, Henry of Grosmont, William de Bohun, William Montagu and Sir Walter Mauny.[92] Clearly, therefore, the county of Cheshire was playing a vital role in the early provision of mounted archers alongside the retinues of the magnates.

In Scotland during the winter of 1341 Cheshire again provided the largest individual contingents of mounted archers: fifty king's archers serving under John Ward, and another 195 mounted archers under the leadership of John Grey and Alexander Wastenays.[93] The county's pre-eminence was to be shortlived, however, and in Brittany in the following year the eighty king's archers under Ward were overshadowed by the retinues of the magnates, the earls of Northampton, Derby,

Warwick and Pembroke each contributing groups of between 100 and 200 mounted archers to the army of Edward III.[94] The closeness of the relationship between the crown and the county of Cheshire in the patterns of military recruitment would not be repeated, and only then under rather different circumstances, until the reign of Richard II.

Meanwhile, the years of Ward's service between 1334 and 1343 have clearly raised a number of important questions, not least as to the reason why Cheshire proved so important in the early provision of mounted archers. An initial difficulty, however, is that it is only in 1334 that Ward's archers are explicitly mentioned as having been recruited in Cheshire. Thereafter they are normally described simply as 'the king's mounted archers'. Is it possible, therefore, that these groups, initially recruited in Cheshire, were later transformed into a household force raised from a variety of territories, while the county itself was providing independent contributions from 1337 onwards? This is perhaps suggested by the recruitment of the king's archers in Radnor in 1334, in Knaresborough and the March in 1337, and by the status of Ward and the other leaders in the king's household.[95] However, the names of those archers who occasionally appear in the wardrobe accounts in receipt of gifts and rewards do suggest Cheshire origins for many of them. The behaviour of wage rates during the campaign of 1341 would also suggest that the royal archers were predominantly of Cheshire origin. Hitherto the king's archers had served alongside those raised in Cheshire on only a single occasion, in Flanders in 1338, where all the mounted archers were paid, as would become the custom on continental campaigns, at the higher rate of 6*d* a day. In 1341, however, the retinues of the magnates in Scotland had reverted to the lower rate of 4*d* a day, the higher rate being reserved for the king's archers, hobelars and mounted archers recruited in Cheshire.[96] If preferential rates of pay were offered to the archers from Cheshire, it can only have been because those in the king's guard were themselves raised in the county.

The significance of the service of these Cheshire men is perhaps more complex, and is to be seen in the context of the political crises of Edward III's minority and in the light of developments in retaining. It has often been suggested that English armies at the beginning of the Hundred Years War were recruited mainly by contract, and that the contribution of the magnates, who had strengthened their hold on the leadership in war, was furnished largely by means of the indenture.[97] Historians have, moreover, sought in the written and oral contracts which provided much of the non-feudal military service at the end of the thirteenth century the origins of the life indenture itself. The retinue, in its widest sense, had origins far more diffused than the demands of war and, whilst the development of the indenture may have progressed quickly after the 1280s, it is apparent from the terms of the earliest military indentures that there was seldom any provision for the service of mounted archers or other troops below the status of the knight. A large number of the earliest indentures are indeed little more than agreements for personal service.[98] The grant of fees and robes by a lord to his follower was the expression of much more than the simple obligation of military service and seldom went so far as to involve the provision of mounted archers in war. At first the recruitment of hobelars and mounted archers may have been dependent solely upon the quality of lordship exercised by an individual magnate; upon the power of a lord to compel the service of his tenants, clients and neighbours.[99]

In Cheshire the right of the earl to the military service of his free tenants had been recognised in the charter of 1216, and enforced during the Welsh wars of Edward I, although Earl Ranulph III had earlier been compelled to concede that such service beyond the eastern boundary of the county should only be with consent and at his wages.[100] Meanwhile, public duties came under increasing strain as the counties, burdened by taxation and purveyance, and wary of the rising costs of military equipment, proved steadily less responsive to demands for mounted archers. Opposition to the burdens of war which Edward III now sought to place more firmly upon the local communities would erupt in the crises of 1338 – 41 – a series of disturbances in which the county of Cheshire, insulated by custom and tradition against both purveyance and taxation, and unrepresented in the commons of the medieval parliament, would play little part.[101] Herein, of course, lies the significance of the Cheshire evidence, for Edward III, like the magnates, and perhaps also of necessity, had been forced to employ the resource of personal lordship in the raising of mounted archers, thereby ignoring the rights of his young son Edward who had been created earl of Chester in 1333. Interestingly enough, both Radnor and Knaresborough, the other sources of royal archers, were then also in royal hands as the result of minority and forfeiture.[102]

Thus the employment of Ward's archers may be seen as occupying that interim stage between the decline of unpaid feudal service and the emergence of a fully contractual army recruited through the nobility and funded by parliamentary grant. For a brief moment in the late 1330s, and against a background of mounting tension and criticism in the country and in parliament, personal lordship had become important in the recruitment of Edward III's armies. That lordship had underwritten the precocious development of military service in the earldom of Chester, for what may indeed have been of slight importance in the final elaboration of military organisation under Edward III nevertheless holds an immense significance for the county. The independence of the earldom, as of other franchises, was guaranteed only by the interest and goodwill of the king. The apparent commitment of Cheshire men to warfare was less the product of a live tradition of military service and a propensity for violence, than the recurring price of that goodwill which had sustained the liberties of the county. This is the link between the Macclesfield archers and those under the leadership of John Ward; each was the product of the infrequent exercise of royal lordship.

These observations do not, of course, offer a solution to the origins of the retinue and its relationship to the provision of military service, nor do they comprehend the quality of royal lordship, or reveal the level and character of the gentry contribution to the conduct of war. They do, however, establish the context in which we may approach these questions. What then do we know of the origins of the retinue in Cheshire, and of the careers of those who fostered its development in war?

III. LORDS AND RETAINERS

Nigel Saul's detailed study of the Berkeley retinues during the fourteenth century has revealed the paramount importance of locality and shared interest in the relationship of the lord and his retainer; and the Cheshire evidence, though less complete, would seem to match the pattern on the Berkeley estates in Gloucestershire and Somerset.[103] Much of what we know of the dynamic of retaining in the county in the early fourteenth century concerns the brief lordship of Thomas of Lancaster, who acquired the substantial estates of his wife in Cheshire and the March after the death of her father Henry Lacy, earl of Lincoln, in 1311.[104] Three local families almost immediately figured in Lancaster's household: Robert Prayers as steward of Denbigh, Richard Aston as a fee'd retainer, and Geoffrey Warburton as an estate official called on to muster troops for Lancaster's retinue in Scotland in 1318.[105] Lancaster's influence was more far-reaching than the number of indentured retainers, however, particularly as he had recently acquired the lands of Sir Thomas Burgh in north-east Cheshire and the lordship of Bromfield and Yale.[106] In addition to the three retainers named above, a further fifteen local men were so closely connected with the earl to make it prudent for them to take out pardons for the death of Peter Gaveston.[107]

The management of Lancaster's estates also reveals the ways in which one or two fee'd retainers could be established as patronage-broker acting on the earl's behalf. Thus the manors in north-east Cheshire which had been acquired in 1318 were almost immediately granted to Sir Robert Holland, the earl's favourite.[108] Holland added the resources of office to those of landholding and served as justice on three occasions between 1307 and 1322, engaging retainers among the local Cheshire gentry. In 1309 John Mobberley, who held the manor of Nether Peover of the Lancaster lordship of Halton, served as lieutenant to Holland as keeper of Beeston castle.[109] A close neighbour, Hamo Mascy, also moved into the orbit of Lancashire society dominated by Holland after an indenture with Philip Samlesbury in 1312, chiefly remarkable as the earliest yet found in the county. In return for service in peace and war, Samlesbury received an annual rent.[110] Lancaster's extravagant patronage enabled Holland to win a following in north-west England, but ultimately its purpose was to provide the earl with a dispersed following which would muster under the leadership of his immediate retinue. Clearly, however, those who had shared in the patronage of the earl and of Sir Robert Holland did not view their loyalties in the same fashion and at the battle of Boroughbridge in 1322 barely 700 men mustered in Lancaster's support.

At Gloucester in 1322 Edward II had determined to confront Lancaster before proceeding to Scotland. Among his first moves was the removal of Holland as justice of Chester, and his replacement by a prominent royal servant, Sir Oliver Ingham.[111] Ingham's immediate duties as 'keeper of the county' were to expedite the raising of troops to aid the king. The identity of a large part of that force can be established from a subsequent indictment before the King's Bench in the Lancashire hundred of Salford, which consequently provides the earliest satisfactory 'retinue roll' in the county.

The Cheshire levies were probably aimed at countering Lancaster's musters in neighbouring Lancashire, where 500 men marched from Wigan to Rochdale. The speed of Ingham's movements is impressive, for the king was already moving towards Coventry where musters had been called for 28 February. The earliest skirmishes took place near Burton-on-Trent in Staffordshire, where the baronial coalition broke up. Ingham's levies were ordered to pursue the rebels in their retreat towards the river Mersey, while Edward II continued towards Pontefract. Lancaster was finally defeated at Boroughbridge by Harclay's border levies, whilst many of the troops raised for Edward II preferred to pillage the earl's estates in Yorkshire, Staffordshire and Lancashire.[112]

It is this stage of the campaign that remains most fully documented for Ingham's Cheshire retinue.

The course of events is clear. Sir Oliver Ingham and a force of 105 Cheshire men are reported to have continued their pursuit into south Lancashire where they took 'horses, mares, colts and fillies, oxen, cows, sheep, pigs and goats to the value of 2,000 marks ... from men who had never been adherents of Thomas, Earl of Lancaster, or any of the lord king's enemies'.[113] The pillaging took place over a wide area surrounding the town of Manchester, and was continued by a smaller group of Lancashire men who also figure in the resulting indictments. In a very real sense Edward II's retinue from Cheshire had proved more durable than that of the Earl of Lancaster, and in the event the king suspended proceedings against his following since the charges related to 'aid or maintenance of the said expedition' against Lancaster.[114] Nevertheless, Sir John Radcliffe, whose manors had been pillaged, continued legal action against Ingham and his retinue, and not until 1326 were the proceedings brought to a final close after a petition to the king from Sir Hamo Mascy and Sir Geoffrey Warburton.[115]

Radcliffe's complaints were by no means disinterested, for he had already made a fine with the king as a rebel and is known to have been with Holland at Ravensdale where some equally casual pillaging had followed the desertion of the earl.[116] When the retinue was highly localised such events were perhaps inevitable, and it is not surprising that independent gentry felt aggrieved at their treatment. The widow of Adam Prestwich, who had taken refuge at Chester, complained that 'the men of Cheshire care nothing for outlawry or any other processes made against them in any other part of England'.[117] The conflict of loyalty between king and magnate also prompted several defections, and among those who joined Ingham's retinue were several of Lancaster's tenants and at least one retainer, Robert Prayers.

The organisation of recruitment in Ingham's retinue cannot be established solely on the evidence of the indictments, although many of those who are named were clearly men from the hundred of Bucklow in the north-east of the county. Sir Hamo Mascy and Sir Geoffrey Warburton appear to have been the most prominent members of the force, but members of other local families, the Mobberleys, Baguleys and Davenports, were also present, together with men who appear in deed-collections as witnesses and pledges. For a number of reasons it is tempting to regard the force raised by Ingham as typical of the retinues of mounted archers recruited in the county in this period. Certainly Sir Geoffrey Warburton and Peter Thornton were ordered to raise 120 archers and 100 hobelars in the same year '*armes montez et apeiller a lour droit face venir a nos au dit lieu de Portesmuth*'.[118] One wonders whether that force would have been vastly different from the one which the same men had led under Sir Oliver Ingham.

The events of 1322 show the ways in which the retinue in its widest sense might find itself called upon to provide military service for its lord. It is possible also that the retinue in the locality formed the basis of the military retinue of men-at-arms and mounted archers which was to achieve prominence in the patterns of military recruitment in the 1330s. At a time when the crown was to be conspicuously unsuccessful in broadening military obligations, the nobility, it seems, were able to compel the military service of their retinues and of those who fell within the web of baronial influence in the localities.

Some of these developments are visible in the career of Sir John Ward, who as the leader of the archers in the royal household, was to occupy an important role in the pattern of military recruitment in Cheshire at this date. John Ward held a fourth part of the manor of Sproston near Middlewich which he had leased from the lord of Kinderton, Sir Hugh Venables, in or before 1311.[119] In the next few years he had expanded his holdings in the area, acquiring the dower lands of Margery of Sproston and Cecilia of Sproston.[120] Some years earlier, although the exact date is not known, he had been retained by Venables and granted robes and an annual fee of 100s, although these had fallen into arrears after Venables' death and were quitclaimed to his heir in 1329 in return for licence to extend an enclosure in the vill of Sproston.[121]

Further details of Ward's early career and service with Venables remain obscure, and it is not known by what route he had entered royal service in 1334. Sir Hugh Venables had served in Edward of Caernarfon's household in 1301, and in 1308 was commissioned to raise 400 foot soldiers in Cheshire; each was a commitment in which Ward, as his retainer, may have shared, and this seems the likeliest route by which Ward was able to attract royal patronage. The only demonstrable personal connection with Edward III is an improbably distant link through John Paynel, the king's tutor, who was parson of Rostherne, the advowson of which belonged to Venables.[122] Nevertheless, in May 1334, now described as a king's archer, Ward was granted the office of rider in Delamere forest, and appeared on the winter campaign of that year as the leader of the king's archers raised in Cheshire.[123] Unlike the Cheshire archers employed by Edward II, these men returned home between campaigns, and it was not until 1336 that Ward figured in the liveries of the king's household as a sergeant-at-arms.[124] In company with the knights, the sergeants-at-arms formed the essential military element in the household, although frequently employed in a variety of more mundane tasks. Here Ward's career followed a traditional pattern, and in the early 1340s he was often occupied with royal commissions elsewhere in England for the collection of fines and the arrest of those summoned to appear before the king and council. Earlier, in 1337, he had incurred the displeasure of the recently appointed treasurer of the exchequer, William de la Zouche, following an assault on the latter's manor at Whissendine in Rutland, probably as a result of purveyance for the royal household.[125] His patent as a sergeant was renewed at Antwerp in 1339, and he continued to serve in the household until the close of the Breton campaign in 1343. Shortly thereafter he assumed the rank of knight and served at Crécy with a retinue of three esquires and two archers.[126] In 1347 he was granted 2*s* a day in order better to support himself in that rank.[127]

Like others before him Ward's long service in the royal household had brought him honour and promotion but no riches. The attractions of the king's retinue, and the military service which seems to have been the price of membership, were clear enough, however, when the retainer's title to land was challenged in the courts of the lordship. The course of the dispute between Ward and Sir Hugh Venables of Kinderton is clear in outline, complex in detail. In June 1344, probably in anticipation of the campaigns in France, Ward had granted his lands in Sproston to his son in return for a life interest in a moiety of the estate. At this point, and perhaps on the basis of the original lease, Venables challenged Ward's possession in the county court.[128] Whatever the legal strength of Venables' case his position was subverted by the action of royal patronage. In 1345 Edward III had written to the justice of Chester in favour of 'nostre bien ami', requesting that no further plea should be heard as Ward was about to embark in royal service.[129] At the same moment Ward had himself written to the Earl of Chester asking that his lands be seised into the earl's hands.[130] There indeed they remained until at least 1351, during which time both Ward and his heir had been able to draw the issues of the manor.[131] Ward himself died in 1347, but the protection of the earl continued to support the son. In 1367 an inquisition recorded that Sir John Ward, during his absence in the Calais garrison, and for the 'saving, preserving and support of his estate', had again been able to grant seisin of his lands to the earl whilst retaining the profits of the estate.[132] The attractions of military service as an insurance against a litigious neighbour were, it seems, quickly recognised; and indeed possession of the lands in Sproston continued to elude Venables and his heirs.[133]

The small retinue which Ward led on the Crécy expedition was almost certainly a muster of his own close family.[134] The retinues which he had led in the household of Edward III on earlier campaigns were, as we have suggested, the product of royal lordship exercised in the county of Cheshire. We are ignorant both of their composition and of the ways in which they may have been raised within the local community. It does not seem likely that Ward had himself been an intermediary in their recruitment; the size of his retinue in 1345 and his minor role in local society militate against such a proposition. Furthermore, the value of Ward's example as an indicator of the gentry commitment to warfare is limited by the range of relationships in local society which we may reconstruct during his career. Few such relationships other than that between the king and his sergeant, and to a lesser extent between lord and tenant, respond to historical enquiry. Royal service had perhaps provided the opportunity for honour and promotion, and also a real degree of protection for Ward's estates, but otherwise we can no more discern the springs of his action than the aggregate rewards of that service.

It seems likely that the service of John Ward predated that of his class as a whole, and that such martial experience was not common among the Cheshire gentry outside localised conflicts such as that of 1322. The argument e silentio is strong and is supported by comparison of the details of the service of Cheshire men in the royal household and the further demands of the crown as revealed in writs of military summons. The full development of a contractual army did not immediately attract the support of middling landowners any more than distraint of knighthood had coerced them into military service; it simply removed to the localities and to the noble estate the burdens of recruitment which the crown now found it impossible to shoulder alone. Men served not simply because they were now paid, but for the old reasons that they were impressed and bullied by the force of lordship, and attracted by the hope of promotion, favour and reward. The inducements of pay, the issue of charters of pardon, and the degree of protection against litigation would undoubtedly assume an important role in the attractions of military service, but until the conflicts in France had established their momentum and dynamic the relationship of a lord and his follower was paramount in the formation of the retinue.

Such links are visible in the documentation which now survives, although some of the best regional examples come from the Stafford affinity in neighbouring Staffordshire. In 1297 Philip Hardeshull had undertaken to serve Edmund Stafford in Flanders largely because he was the tenant of Madeley and Stafford was his lord.[135] Later of course Ralph Stafford would lay the foundations of comital power and title in the king's wars and at the court, although in common with many of his contemporaries he owed his greatest promotion to the support he had given to Edward III in the overthrow of Mortimer.[136] The instrument of that support had been the gentry of north Staffordshire, who formed the largest element in the Stafford retinue, and to whom Ralph was now able and required to transmit the fruits of royal patronage. Roger Swynnerton received several lands and rents from the forfeited estate of the elder Despenser, including the manor of Barrow in Cheshire.[137] To the relationship of lord and tenant had been added that of local connection, for the retinue in peace and war was the most direct way of maintaining support among the local gentry, and the ideal means of distributing the patronage essential to the maintenance of a lord's position and dignity. Indeed the retinue was often little more than a reflection of the framework of county society, a continuation of social intercourse and command by other means.

This is apparent in an episode involving the marriage of Elizabeth Beek, one of Stafford's granddaughters, to Robert Swynnerton which had been arranged 'on the advice and counsel of the earl and others of his cousins and friends'. Later, as the earl was leading his retinue through Kent en route for France he had enquired of Swynnerton whether he had fulfilled the terms of his marriage agreement. Having received an unsatisfactory reply, the earl had ordered two members of his council to accompany the knight on a return journey where they were to supervise completion of the contract before allowing Swynnerton '*aller à la bataill*'.[138] The incident is a telling example of local society at war.

Although those bound by indenture would form only the very small nucleus of the lord's civil and military administration, the permanent retinue was the tuber of a more complex root system of kinship, mutual support and informal association which reached a great way into the organisation of local society. Those who received fees and robes were often simply the men of substance in the locality whose service guaranteed a wide, if dispersed following to the lord and gave the greatest value to his patronage. In Gloucestershire only between a third and a half of the local gentry were retained by magnates; common interests brought the loyalty of many others.[139] In Staffordshire the Swynnerton family, who had been retained by Stafford, stood among the wealthier gentry just below baronial status, prominent in county society and able to muster an impressive following in their own right.[140] The economics of retaining enabled John, Lord Talbot, to maintain a widespread and permanent following among the Shropshire gentry in the 1390s through the service of thirteen knights, whom he had retained for life.[141]

The formation of such links in gentry and noble society owed little to the progress and conduct of war. It simply reflected their assimilation into military usage. But the vitality of the retinue in the early fourteenth century had contributed greatly to the ease with which the nobility were able to assume the burdens of military recruitment in the 1330s. In Cheshire these relationships were confused and distorted by the structure of county society, and by the position and status of the earl. The county had no resident nobility, and not since 1272 had there been an earl of full age. Successive minorities and the retention of the earldom by the crown had interrupted the continuing of comital lordship. Under such circumstances those who looked to the king as their lord often found themselves isolated from his patronage by the demands and actions of kingship itself, and those opportunities which elsewhere might visit a minor knight or landholder in the service of his lord were depressed in Cheshire. Beyond a handful of knights few could hope to enter the royal household at other than an inferior level, perhaps as a royal archer or sergeant-at-arms. Furthermore, in a region dominated by minor landowners the leadership of gentry society lacked any clear focus or centre from which the king might have benefited. The irony is that although the county had been prominent in the changes in military usage, it remained backward in the development of retinues. The quality and character of lordship itself were crucial factors in determining the military opportunities and organisation of any local society, and it is to the structure of that lordship and its connection with military service that we must now turn.

NOTES

[1] *Annales Cestrienses*, ed. R. C. Christie, LCRS, xiv 1897, *passim*.

[2] D. Knowles & R. Neville Hadcock, *Medieval Religious Houses*, 1971, pp. 118, 123.

[3] *Annales Cestrienses*, cited in R. V. H. Burne, *The Monks of Chester*, 1962, p. 34.

[4] R. Allen Brown, *The Normans and the Norman Conquest*, 1969, p. 215.

[5] *Domesday Book, f.* 269 a,b.

[6] G. Barraclough, *The Earldom and County Palatine of Chester*, 1953; J. W. Alexander, 'New Evidence on the Palatinate of Chester', *EHR*, lxxxv, 1970, pp. 715–29; A. N. Palmer & E. Owen, *A History of Ancient Tenures of Land in Wales and the March*, 2nd edition, 1910, pp. 140–53.

[7] P. H. W. Booth, 'Taxation and Public Order: Cheshire in 1353', *Northern History*, xii, 1976, p. 23. See below p. 48.

[8] The succession of the earldom is as follows: Edward I (1254–1301, 1272–1301 as king); Edward of Caernarfon (1301–07) and as Edward II (1307–12); Edward of Windsor (1312–27), and as Edward III (1327–33); Edward, the Black Prince (1333–76); Richard II (1376–99).

[9] *The Chartulary of Register of Chester Abbey*, ed. J. Tait, Chet. Soc., New Series, lxxix, 1920, pp. 101–9.

[10] *Chartulary of Chester Abbey*, pp. 103, 105; M. Powicke, *Military Obligation in Medieval England*, 1962, p. 62; Alexander, op. cit., p. 723.

[11] J. R. Maddicott, 'The English Peasantry and the Demands of the Crown, 1294–1341', *Past and Present Supplement*, 1, 1975, pp. 35–6.

[12] *Liber Quotidianus Contrarotulatoris Garderobae*, ed. J. Topham, Society of Antiquaries, 1797, p. 246.

[13] H. J. Hewitt, *The Organization of War under Edward III*, 1966, pp. 40–1.

[14] J. Tait, 'Knight Service in Cheshire', *EHR*, lvii, 1942, pp. 26–54.

[15] *Cheshire in the Pipe Rolls, 1158–1301*, ed. R. Stewart Brown, LCRS, xcii, 1938, p. 101.

[16] *Ibid.*, pp. 127–8.

[17] *Calendar of County Court, City Court and Eyre Rolls of Chester, 1259–1297*, ed. R. Stewart Brown, Chet. Soc., New Series, lxxxiv, 1925, pp. 108–12.

[18] G. Ormerod, *History of Cheshire*, ed. Helsby, 1888, I, pp. 707–8 prints a feodary of Halton from the reign of Edward II.

[19] Prestwich, op. cit., p. 91.

[20] E372/124. In 1282 the king specifically observed that the Cheshire foot, unlike those raised in Lancashire, were not to be paid for their service, *Calendar of Ancient Correspondence concerning Wales*, ed. J. G. Edwards, 1935, p. 202.

[21] *Parliamentary Writs and Writs of Military Summons*, ed. F. Palgrave, Record Commission, 2 vols in 4, 1827–34, I, p. 252.

[22] J. E. Morris, *The Welsh Wars of Edward I*, 1901, pp. 115, 118, 127, 130, 154.

[23] *Ibid.*, pp. 92–4; Prestwich op. cit., p. 103; Maddicott, op. cit., p. 37.

[24] Morris, op. cit., pp. 128–31.

[25] *Ibid.*, p. 190.

[26] Palgrave, *Writs*, I, p. 252; E101/4/16.

[27] E101/5/16.

[28] E101/3/11 m. 1.

[29] T. P. Highet, *The Early History of the Davenports of Davenport*, Chet. Soc., 3rd Series, ix, 1960, p. 10.

[30] Morris, loc. cit.

[31] The suggestion that Richard's archers were composed of Macclesfield men is discounted by J. L. Gillespie, 'Richard II's Cheshire Archers', *THLC*, cxxv, 1975, p. 26. On the archers of the crown in the fourteenth century, see J. L. Gillespie, 'Richard II's Archers of the Crown', *Journal of British Studies*, xviii, 1979, pp. 14–29.

[32] Palgrave, *Writs*, I, p. 305. The sources for the campaign of 1296 are not complete but a contingent of 1,000 foot under John of Merk may have been raised in Cheshire. Morris, op. cit., pp. 272–3.

[33] Morris, op. cit., p. 285.

[34] E101/12/17 m. 1.

[35] *Liber Quotidianus Contrarotulatoris Garderobae*, p. 246.

[36] Palgrave, *Writs*, I, pp. 219, 258, 280 – 1, 330, 341.

[37] Prestwich, op. cit., pp. 88 – 9.

[38] E198/3/10.

[39] A brief biography from calendared records can be found in C. Moor, *Knights of Edward I*, Harleian Society, lxxxii, 1930, pp. 127 – 8.

[40] *CPR, 1292 – 1301*, p. 324; Palgrave, *Writs*, I, p. 305.

[41] *Scotland in 1298: documents relating to the campaign of Edward I in that year*, ed. H. Gough, 1888, pp. 139 – 57.

[42] Palgrave, *Writs*, I, p. 359.

[43] A. MacKay, *Spain in the Middle Ages*, 1977, pp. 47 – 50.

[44] *Two Estate Surveys of the Fitzalan Earls of Arundel*, ed. M. Clough, Sussex Record Society, lxvii, 1969, introduction; R. R. Davies, *Lordship and Society in the March of Wales 1282 – 1400*, 1978, pp. 77 – 8.

[45] *Two Estate Surveys*, p. 84.

[46] CRO, Leycester-Warren of Tabley MS DLT/B2 f. 208.

[47] *Calendar of Inquisitions Post Mortem*, HMSO, 1906, II, pp. 181, 460, 749.

[48] *Calendar of County Court, City Court and Eyre Rolls of Chester, 1259 – 1297*, p. 56.

[49] CRO, Cholmondeley of Cholmondeley deeds, DCH/A/15.

[50] Eaton Hall, Eaton charter 107.

[51] Chester 25/4 m. 21.

[52] *Calendar of Entries in the Papal Registers*, W. H. Bliss & J. A. Twemlow (eds), III, 1900, pp. 166 – 7.

[53] J. E. Morris, 'Mounted Infantry in Medieval Warfare', *TRHS*, 3rd Series, vii, 1914, p. 85.

[54] J. C. Russell, *British Medieval Population*, 1948, p. 43.

[55] J. C. Russell, op. cit., p. 144; J. Cornwall, 'English Population in the Early Sixteenth Century', *Econ. H. R.*, xxiii, 1970, p. 40.

[56] Michael J. Bennett, *Community, Class and Careerism. Cheshire and Lancashire Society in the Age of Sir Gawain and the Green Knight*, 1983, pp. 54 – 60.

[57] See for instance the letter of Llywelyn in 1276 complaining of the damage done in Bromfield by the men of Cheshire and Shropshire, *Calendar of Ancient Correspondence concerning Wales*, p. 162.

[58] Michael Prestwich, *The Three Edwards: War and State in England, 1272 – 1377*, 1980, pp. 63 – 70.

[59] J. F. Lydon, 'The Hobelar: An Irish Contribution to Medieval Warfare', *Irish Sword*, 2, 1954, pp. 12 – 16.

[60] J. E. Morris, 'Cumberland and Westmorland Military Levies in the Time of Edward I and Edward II', *Transactions of the Cumberland and Westmorland Architectural and Archaeological Society*, New Series, II, 1903, pp. 307 – 27.

[61] BL Stowe MS 553 f. 80d; Natalie M. Fryde, 'Welsh Troops in the Scottish Campaign of 1322', *Bulletin of the Board of Celtic Studies*, xxvi, 1975, pp. 82 – 9.

[62] S. Andreski, *Military Organisation and Society*, 1968, pp. 33 – 4.

[63] L. White, *Medieval Technology and Social Change*, 1962, p. 28; G. Duby, *The Early Growth of the European Economy*, 1974, p. 167.

[64] J. R. Maddicott, 'The English Peasantry and the Demands of the Crown,

1294–1341', *Past and Present Supplement*, 1, 1975, pp. 41–5; Michael Prestwich, op. cit., p. 68.

[65] E101/24/20; Maurice Keen, *Chivalry*, 1984, p. 224.

[66] M. Powicke, *Military Obligation in Medieval England*, 1962, pp. 52–3; Robert Hardy, *Longbow: A Social and Military History*, 1976; J. F. Verbruggen, *The Art of Warfare in Western Europe during the Middle Ages*, 1977, pp. 105–7.

[67] W. Stubbs (ed.), *Select Charters*, 9th edition revised H. W. C. Davies, 1913, p. 364.

[68] M. Prestwich, op. cit., pp. 68–70.

[69] A. E. Prince, 'The Army and Navy' in J. F. Willard & W. A. Morris (eds), *The English Government at Work, 1327–1336*, 1940, I, p. 339; W. Hudson, 'The Norwich Militia in the Fourteenth Century', *Norfolk and Norwich Archaeological Society*, xiv, 1901, p. 285; CRO, Vernon deeds, DVE/CVIII/17, seal of Kenric Lee, 1379; Probate 11/2a f. 57, will of Robert Winnington, 1404.

[70] A. E. Prince, op. cit., p. 358; H. Ellis (ed.), *Original Letters Illustrative of English History*, 1846, I, pp. 33–9.

[71] M. Powicke, *Military Obligation in Medieval England*, 1962, pp. 182–210.

[72] *Ibid.*; Maddicott, op. cit., pp. 66–7.

[73] See below p. 108.

[74] M. Prestwich, *War, Politics and Finance under Edward I*, 1972, p. 91.

[75] K. B. McFarlane, 'Bastard Feudalism', *BIHR*, xx, 1945, pp. 163–8; G. A. Holmes, *The Estates of the Higher Nobility in XIV Century England*, 1957, pp. 58–84.

[76] Nigel Saul, *Knights and Esquires: The Gloucestershire Gentry in the Fourteenth Century*, 1981, pp. 83–9.

[77] A. E. Prince, op. cit., p. 354.

[78] BL Cotton MS Nero C VIII f.253d.

[79] *Ibid.*, f. 252.

[80] See above p. 32.

[81] E101/376/7 f. 27d. There were 42 Welsh and 32 English archers in 1320, BL Additional MS 17362, f. 20; 25 archers in 1321, *ibid.*, f. 58d, and 56 archers in 1322, BL Stowe MS 553, f. 34d.

[82] BL Additional MS 17362, f. 41–f. 42d; BL Cotton MS Nero C VIII, f. 255, f. 268.

[83] E101/378/4, f. 28, f. 38; E101/14/21; BL Additional MS 17362, f. 58d.

[84] A similar theme is taken up again in the discussion of the bodyguard of royal archers who figure in the household of Richard II between 1397 and 1399, and who likewise were recruited principally in Cheshire, see below pp. 199–201.

[85] G. L. Harriss, *King, Parliament and Public Finance in Medieval England to 1369* (1975), pp. 231–69; Maddicott, op. cit., p. 45.

[86] In Cheshire purveyance seems to have reached its own lower peak in the early years of Edward II's reign, P. H. W. Booth, *The Financial Administration of the Lordship and County of Cheshire, 1272–1377*, Chet. Soc., 3rd Series, xxviii, 1982, p. 78.

[87] BL Cotton MS Nero C VIII, f. 255.

[88] BL Cotton MS Nero C VIII, f. 259; *ibid.*, f. 261.

[89] *Ibid.*, f. 263; E101/388/5, f. 16.

[90] A. E. Prince, op. cit., p. 362.

[91] E36/203, f. 139, f. 140d.

[92] *Ibid.*

[93] E36/204, f. 101.

[94] *Ibid.*, f. 103, f. 104.

[95] Ward and Pledour were both sergeants-at-arms, BL Cotton MS Nero C VIII, f. 228; Hide a royal esquire, and Tyrel a yeoman of the household who received many commissions in Wales and the March, *CCR, 1333–1337*, pp. 39, 539, 571; *CPR, 1338–1340*, pp. 207, 399, 409–10.

[96] Michael Powicke, op. cit., pp. 210–12; E36/204, f. 101, f. 102.

[97] A. E. Prince, op. cit., pp. 346–50; Nigel Saul, op. cit., p. 83.

[98] G. A. Holmes, op. cit., pp. 58–84; see above pp. 18–19, and below p. 50 for two early examples with Cheshire provenance.

[99] See for instance the discussion in R. R. Davies, *Lordship and Society in the March of Wales, 1282–1400*, 1978, pp. 80–5.

[100] See above p. 29.

[101] G. L. Harriss, op. cit., pp. 231–69.

[102] G. A. Holmes, op. cit., pp. 10, 15; B. P. Wolffe, *The Royal Demesne in English History*, 1971, pp. 59–60.

[103] Nigel Saul, op. cit., pp. 69–72.

[104] See below pp. 72–4.

[105] DL28/1/13, m. 3.

[106] G. A. Holmes, op. cit., p. 138.

[107] *CPR, 1307–1313*, pp. 21–5.

[108] J. R. Maddicott, 'Thomas of Lancaster and Sir Robert Holland: A Study in Noble Patronage', *EHR*, lxxxviii, 1971, p. 456.

[109] Chester 2/1.

[110] LRO, de Trafford deeds, DDTr/bundle 5/3 (Additional); Maddicott, op. cit., p. 450.

[111] *CPR 1317–1321*, p. 72.

[112] J. R. Maddicott, *Thomas of Lancaster 1307–1322*, 1970, p. 311.

[113] KB27/254 printed in G. H. Tupling, *South Lancashire in the Reign of Edward II*, Chet. Soc., 3rd series, i, 1949, pp. 63–5.

[114] *CCR 1323–1327*, p. 425.

[115] JRL Arley charter box 22/7.

[116] Tupling, op. cit., p. 81.

[117] *Rotuli Parliamentorum*, I, p. 407.

[118] C47/2/23 (29).

[119] This account of Ward's career is based largely on the small deed collection in the CRO, Vernon deeds, DVE/SIII/17–34.

[120] *Ibid.*, DVE/SIII/17–18.

[121] *Ibid.*, DVE/SIII/20.

[122] BL Harley MS 4304; Palgrave, *Writs*, II, p. 376; T. F. Tout, *Chapters in the Administrative History of Medieval England*, iii, 1928, p. 25.

[123] *CPR, 1330–1334*, p. 544.

[124] BL Cotton MS Nero C VIII, f. 228.

[125] *CFR, 1337–1347*, p. 343; *CPR, 1334–1338*, pp. 509–11; *CPR, 1340–1343*, p. 210; *CPR, 1343–1345*, p. 392. The assault had taken place within the verge and was heard in the court of the Steward and Marshal, which customarily dealt with acts of trespass by royal officials in obtaining provisions

for household, *Select Cases in the Court of the King's Bench under Edward I*, ed. G. O. Sayles, Selden Society, 58, 1939, lxxxiii–lxxxviii.

[126] *CPR, 1338–1340*, p. 401; G. Wrottesley, *Crécy and Calais*, 1898, p. 200.

[127] *CPR, 1345–1358*, p. 228.

[128] CRO, DVE/SIII/25–7, 31; Chester 24/2.

[129] Chester 1/1, box 1/8; Chester 23/3 m. 4.

[130] SC1/54 no. 58.

[131] *Accounts of the Chamberlain and other officers of the County of Chester 1301–1360*, ed. R. Stewart Brown, LCRS, lix, 1910, pp. 150, 203.

[132] CRO, DVE/SIII/31; *BPR*, III, p. 49.

[133] In 1375 the lands passed to Hugh Coton by grant of the younger Ward's daughter, CRO, DVE/SIII/32–4.

[134] John Ward, his son and Adam Ward each held protections, Chester 23/3 m. 4.

[135] See above pp. 18–19.

[136] K. B. McFarlane, *The Nobility of Later Medieval England*, 1973, pp. 201–2.

[137] R. H. Hilton, *The English Peasantry in the Later Middle Ages*, 1975, p. 224; CRO, Cholmondeley of Cholmondeley deed, DCH/G 28.

[138] *Ibid.*, DCH/G 67, 69. A papal dispensation for the marriage in July 1363 survives as *ibid.*, DCH/H 10.

[139] Nigel Saul, op. cit., p. 97.

[140] Hilton, op. cit., pp. 218, 224. Swynnerton had led a retinue of 20 men-at-arms and 20 archers in Scotland in 1334, BL Cotton MS Nero C VIII, f. 233d.

[141] A. J. Pollard, *The Family of Talbot, Lords Talbot and Earls of Shrewsbury in the Fifteenth Century*, University of Bristol PhD, 1968, p. 215.

CHAPTER II

LORDSHIP, SOCIETY AND MILITARY RECRUITMENT

The history of land, its ownership and use, still lies at the heart of much research on medieval England; not simply because the means of production remained predominantly agricultural, but because land was the root of lordship and exemplified the power and attractiveness of individuals and classes to one another. At the close of the thirteenth century military service was still an obligation deriving from land, a tenurial responsibility to be exercised either in person or by proxy. Even a century later, when Jean, Duke of Bourbon, could embark on the foundation of a military order, 'desirous of avoiding idleness and wishing to employ our person to advance our good name by profession of arms', the ownership of land remained an important element in the character of military service. As K. B. McFarlane has pointed out, 'the captains were also lords of land; most of them by inheritance, some by purchase'.[1] Whether military service can be seen to have grown out of a tenurial responsibility, the social milieu of a violent age, or economic speculation and necessity, land shaped its character, and the noble retinues of the fourteenth century continued to be shaped by the estates and tenants of their leaders. In any local community, therefore, the pattern of landholding might exercise a profound influence on the development of military service.

The power of lordship in attracting men into service did not spring only from control of land. It could also spring from the powers of command and governance which were part of all lordship in the middle ages. Edward I's employment of a guard of archers raised on his demesne lands in Macclesfield was, therefore, closely related to his position as Earl of Chester and to his political role as leader of a Marcher coalition. When that particular connexion between tenurial and political circumstances ceased to operate, as it did after 1283, royal wages from the household ceased to be paid to the guard of Macclesfield archers, and they found no further service. The continued employment of Cheshire troops in Scotland had other causes. In this context the relevance of politics and faction in the formation and character of military retinues, not merely under Edward I, but throughout the fourteenth century, cannot be sufficiently emphasised. It has already been suggested that there was little difference between a force raised for service in France and one used to bully a pliant king. Ultimately these two functions were to separate, and during the fifteenth century a noble's retinue in Normandy might be recruited on the spot and bear little relation to his domestic affinity.[2] Before the reign of Henry V, however, the direction and traditions of military service had a magnitude and rhythm which were directly responsive to political change and expediency.

I. THE LORDSHIP OF THE EARL OF CHESTER

The political and tenurial pattern in Cheshire may be seen to have embodied features not commonly found in the rest of England. The primacy of the earl was already well established before the rule of the Lord Edward, and Margaret Sharp commented that by 1236 the earl was 'virtual king of Cheshire'.[3] Recognition of the county's palatine status is the subject of some debate, but the regalian rights of the earl clearly fluctuated according to political circumstance and royal power, as did regalian rights in the palatinate of Durham. From the mid-thirteenth century the government of the county was based upon the earl's household. The earl enjoyed the rights of trial and pardon within the county and, except for certain isolated instances, exercised complete judicial supremacy within the shire during the fourteenth century. Courts were summoned in the earl's name, and Cheshire was subject neither to the general eyre nor to the operation of the royal courts. For much of the fourteenth century neighbouring counties found it difficult to cite Cheshire men in their courts, and protests against this legal immunity reached a peak during the later parliaments of Richard II's reign.[4] The problem was, however, already of long standing, and examples may be cited from the late thirteenth century, as in 1296 when Hamo Mascy petitioned against a summons before the King's Bench in Lancashire, claiming that he ought to answer before the justice of Chester.[5] Control over local government appointments might be exercised by any lord whose landed position gave him a dominant role in local society, but in Cheshire the right of pardon for murders and felonies and the power to grant exemptions from jury and other judicial services entrusted the earl with a fund of patronage that was not readily available to other lords.

The earl maintained his own chancellor and treasurer, both functions vested in the office of chamberlain of Chester, and as the universal landlord in the county he drew the income from escheats, marriages and wardships which elsewhere in England accrued to the crown. Within the limits of the county, therefore, the earl enjoyed the same sources of revenue and patronage as did the crown in the rest of England. These rights were matched by those exercised by the bishop of Durham, but they were radically altered by the personal status of the earl. As king or the king's eldest son, the earl was rarely expected to live of his own in Cheshire, and on occasion the entire revenues of the county could be directed to a particular project. Between 1278 and 1280 the chamberlain of Chester was also keeper of the works at Vale Royal abbey, to which much of the revenue of the county was directed.[6] From 1281 to 1284 those revenues were similarly directed towards payment of wages and expenses during the second Welsh war.[7] These precedents from the reign of Edward I were followed by successive earls, and the Black Prince devoted much of the income of Cheshire to the maintenance of English lordship in Aquitaine and the patronage of his retinue.[8] Cheshire's financial resources could thus be diverted to suit the interests of the earl, wherever those interests might happen to lie. The converse was also possible, and the earl could bring the patronage and power of his position outside Cheshire to bear on county society. In this way, for instance, Richard II sought to re-establish his position in the county during the 1390s by use of a reward of 4,000 marks, raised through forced loans in the rest of England, granted to the participants at the battle of Radcot Bridge.[9] Other lords in the county could only challenge comital supremacy within Cheshire when their own political influence exceeded that of the earl, or when the earl was a minor or showed little interest in his earldom.

The power of the earl's governance extended also to the organisation of military service in the county, as we have seen in the employment of Cheshire troops in Wales and Scotland under Edward I. While military service remained a tenurial responsibility within local society, as expressed in the charter of 1216, the earl remained the dominant employer. Recruiting was led by the justice of Chester, an official who enjoyed a dual military and judicial role, and to whom writs of military summons were addressed. The justice was clearly expected to initiate independent military action in the event of necessity on the Welsh border, and the *Annales Cestrienses* make frequent mention of expeditions so mounted. After the campaigns of the early fourteenth century the direct military role of the justice declined, and the delegation of his responsibilities figures more often in the surviving record.

After 1346 writs were issued to knights and esquires in the county who were responsible for arraying men in the various hundreds. In practice these 'hundredal' levies were shaped by the estates and influence of their gentry leaders, although they may earlier have been more closely related to the administrative divisions of the county. Infantry and cavalry troops appear separately in the records of Edward I's armies, and members of the knightly class are seldom found leading infantry levies. The Macclesfield archers were led by a man who later held a place in the local administration of the lordship, but Henry Davenport's example is unique, and it is probable that levies were raised within the several hundreds by local officials of the justice.[10]

The sheer weight of the earldom's lands and institutions, together with the financial resources available to the king or his heir, were to impose on Cheshire a degree of political and military uniformity that has few parallels elsewhere in England. Knightly families who sought a leading role in the political and military life of the county were inevitably drawn into the orbit of the earl's patronage. While in theory the earl's command of the military resources of Cheshire was complete, in practice his capacity to deploy those resources and to command the loyalty of the gentry of the county was determined by the vagaries of national politics. At crucial points during the century other lords successfully challenged the single faction of the earl, exercising a control over regional politics and recruiting among the knightly class. The influence of these lords was often ultimately based upon a landed presence in the county, and there is a clear need to identify those who were able to compete with the earl.

Regional politics were not always characterised by competition for exclusive control, and the history of Cheshire does not move from one crisis in patronage to another. It should be borne in mind that the earl could, but did not need to, exercise a monopoly on recruitment, and of the fourteenth century earls only Richard II sought to claim exclusive rights of recruitment in the county. The cordial relations between the Black Prince and the rest of the nobility under Edward III encouraged recruiting by other lords, while the factional politics of Richard II's reign served to introduce royal or noble favourites into the political and military life of the county.

These considerations serve to indicate the major directions of recruitment and patronage in the county, but we remain interested in the details of local organisation in the raising of men-at-arms and archers. Such issues cannot be followed in the documentation of the Edwardian campaigns in Wales and Scotland, in which the anonymity of the

Cheshire retinues is maintained; but as the personnel of the military community passes into sharper focus an attempt may be made to relate the details of local organisation to the local tenurial pattern within the county.

II. THE PATTERN OF LORDSHIP

H. J. Hewitt's judgement on the tenurial pattern of Cheshire, that 'the land was for the most part held by lords whose estates were considerable enough to give them local importance, but narrow enough to confine their interests to the county' has recently been confirmed by Michael Bennett's valuable study of the structure of landed society in Cheshire at the end of the fourteenth century.[11] Nevertheless, it is worth remembering that the historian is ill-served by the absence, in the case of Cheshire, of contemporary surveys of landholding, the survival of which provides the basis of research on land tenure elsewhere in England. There are, for instance, no hundred rolls, or lay poll tax returns, or the kind of survey which illuminates the pattern of landholding in neighbouring Staffordshire.[12] The regular taxation of the county, in the form of the Cheshire mise, dates from the mid-fourteenth century, but no returns survive until the early years of the fifteenth century.[13]

For secular lordship the nearest to an official survey of landholding in the county is the series of writs for the performance of military service and distraint of knighthood discussed above. These sources deal only with those landowners who held in chief of the earl and record the transmission and fragmentation of the original Norman *servitia debita*. The distraint of forty librate landholders for the campaign of 1300 adds only a handful of names not to be found in the 1288 inquest of service, and it seems likely that these sources accurately reflect the higher ranks in landed society, a body of some sixty landholders who, as we have seen, were deeply involved in the Welsh wars of Edward I.

Inquisitions *post mortem* survive in some quantity from the mid-thirteenth century, among the records of the royal exchequer until late in Edward I's reign, and then among the evidences of the Chester exchequer.[14] Although their value declines with the growth of enfeoffments to use, they contain important illustrations of the nature of agricultural production, particularly during the mid-fourteenth century crisis in population. There are few chronological series of manorial accounts in the county, saving those for the demesne manors of the Earls of Chester and Dukes of Lancaster, and few records survive from local courts to illustrate the operation of lordship in the localities. Isolated surveys and rentals, and a number of accounts, survive among the inquisitions *post mortem* and within private deed collections, and in one instance an unusual early fifteenth century cartulary of secular origin provides an invaluable picture of the shape and character of lordship in the Macclesfield area.[15] In assessing the value of such evidence it is useful to identify those aspects of the tenurial pattern which are germane to a study of developments in military service.

Initially we are interested in the connexion between landed society and the military community, the relationship between lordship patterns and the organisation of military recruitment. The tenurial relationship clearly shaped the service of an important part of the military community, although it is necessary that we attempt some qualitative appreciation of its relative importance within the hierarchy of the military community. The complexity of relationships within the retinue of Sir Ralph Mobberley, for example, suggests that the purely tenurial bond was an important element in the formation of his affinity in peace and war.[16] At a higher social level the extent of noble landowning and its relation to military recruitment and the organisation of political affiliations reveals a close correlation. Changes and developments in the interest of the Earls and Dukes of Lancaster in their lordship of Halton were clearly responsible for fluctuations in military recruitment there.[17]

The extent of landholding, both by secular and ecclesiastical lords, reveals one element in the formation of the military community and is to be related to the social and economic opportunities available to the prospective military population in Cheshire. The extent of forest, the organisation of agricultural production, or the percentage of free and villein tenures, may also each provide a valid explanation of the origin and development of military service.

The Domesday inquest is the earliest and the most comprehensive survey of landholdings in the county. In 1086 all land, except that of the Bishop of Chester, later (in 1102) of Coventry and Lichfield, and of the abbey of St Werburgh, was held of the king by Earl Hugh. The county of Chester occupied a subsidiary role in the ambitions of the Norman Earls of Chester, who held extensive lands elsewhere in England and sought to expand their territorial interests outside Cheshire. The earl did, however, retain some forty-nine manors in demesne and was the county's largest landholder. Eight lords held most of the remaining land and served in the earl's household. The pattern of lordship was, however, already well established and, as in the rest of north-west England, was characterised by compact lordships taken over

Cheshire *c.* 1360

by incoming Norman tenants, rather than by the dispersed and fragmentary holdings more familiar elsewhere in England.[18] In several instances, therefore, the Domesday hundreds and baronies were almost co-extensive, and many of the earl's major tenants held large and compact estates within the county.[19] By the fourteenth century the most obvious changes in this tenurial pattern were the decline in the size of the earl's demesne, the gradual break-up of the Norman baronies, with the exception of the lordship of Halton, and the maintenance of continuity in ecclesiastical landholding. But the earl remained the largest individual landowner in the county.

The demesne lands of the earl lay in three main concentrations: the hundred of Macclesfield, the valleys of the Dane and Weaver, and the environs of Chester itself.[20] The government of the city was early vested in the hands of the mayor and its citizens, but the earl's interest was maintained in two respects: at the castle and in the operation of the Dee mills. Chester Castle, in the south-west corner of the medieval city, lay at the heart of the administration of the earl's lordship as the site of the exchequer and the county court, and remained essentially an administrative and military centre.[21] Elsewhere in west Cheshire the manors of Frodsham and Shotwick were the sites of Norman castles. Frodsham included a borough granted by Earl Ranulph III at the beginning of the thirteenth century and remained a port of limited importance.[22] Shotwick was enclosed as a comital park in 1351, and the Prince and his council hunted there in 1353 during a brief visit to the earldom. In 1398 its castle was repaired as part of the ring of fortifications garrisoned by Richard II to defend the newly created Principality of Chester.[23]

In east Cheshire the earl held the lordship of Macclesfield, although after 1270 it was frequently the dower portion of royal widows. The demesne lands included the manor and forest of Macclesfield, and there was also the lordship of the hundred with its administrative centre in the town.[24] For much of the fourteenth century, however, the largest element in the comital demesne was not in the earl's hands. When the Black Prince first acquired the lordship in 1347 a commission was set up to enquire whether 'the lordship of Macclesfield was or ever had been part of the county of Chester'.[25] Administratively, Macclesfield was not within the competence of the county court at Chester; the tenants at Bollinton, for example, complained in 1359 that they had been impleaded 'in the county court of Chester whereas they ought to be impleaded in the hallmoot of Macclesfield'.[26] The partial independence of the lordship within a society that was already insular in character created several problems, many of which have a bearing on the military recruitment of the earl. For example, in 1346 the men of the lordship refused both to contribute to a subsidy raised for the campaign in France, and to array men for service in the Prince's retinue.[27]

The remainder of the earl's demesne lands were concentrated in the valleys of the Dane and Weaver in mid-Cheshire, although the manors of Weaverham, Over, and Darnhall had been granted to the new monastic foundation at Vale Royal in 1277. Nevertheless, the earl retained important estates, notably the two salt towns, Northwich and Middlewich, and the waste of Rudheath. Here the Prince established the manor of Drakelow in 1347, after recovering land which had been newly assarted.[28]

The resources of comital lordship within the county of Cheshire were important in three ways. In the first place the income from rents and the farm of manors, and the profits of justice, were devoted to the maintenance of the earl's retinue. The keeping of lands and offices were seldom granted to knightly retainers, whose fees and rewards were commonly paid from the Chester exchequer, rather than by the bailiffs of distant manors. In 1369, for example, a total of £1,537 7s 6d was being disbursed in annuities, fees and wages to members of the earl's retinue, the majority of whom had little active interest in or association with the county.[29]

The Cheshire members of the retinue also benefited from the grant of annuities and fees, although more commonly they were granted the income of lands and wardships or the keeping of offices in the county. Within a familiar local society the payment of fees, often in arrears, was less important than the grant of offices or lands which allowed the individual to exploit the resources of comital lordship. No less important than the rewards granted to the knightly members of the retinue were those offered to individual archers on their return from campaigns. If we take the aftermath of the Poitiers campaign as a base, it is clear that the rewards and grants made to individuals were of several types, although they commonly involved no capital outlay on the part of the earl.

Two categories dominate the distribution of largesse: the suspension of legal proceedings and services, and grants of timber or pasture rights within the forests or on the waste of Rudheath. The latter category, which involved little capital outlay or loss of income and services, dominates the management of comital resources of lordship in the development of military service, and represents the distribution of comital largesse at the base of the social and military pyramid. Resources on this scale were not normally within the control of other lords.

Table 2   *Rewards to the Cheshire retinue*
1357

Type of Grant	Number Recorded
Land	8
Money	17
Office	10
Trade Licenses	3
General pardon of all felonies and trespasses	31
Pardons for specific offences	22
Exemptions from judicial services	14
Comital enquiries into legal disputes and claims	16
Grants of timber, pasture and other materials	52

(Source: *BPR*, III.)

Nevertheless, in 1357 the tenants of the Earl of Chester's demesne manor at Frodsham had petitioned against their neighbouring townships, complaining that 'the lords of the said townships are great men and have a great connexion throughout the country, so that the petitioners cannot obtain a fair panel [of jurors]'.[30] Their observations were accurate enough, for Frodsham was then almost encircled by the demesne lands of the Duke of Lancaster, the Earl of Arundel, and their prominent gentry supporters. The complaint is also an instructive one in any discussion of the impact of secular lordship on the development of military service, for often the particular extent of land held remains less important than the ambition, on the part of the retainer, to progress beyond the more limited resources of lordship in the immediate locality. Moreover, a noble captain offered to his retainers, in addition to land and income, the possibility of access to royal patronage. For their part, lords were often anxious to establish an affinity geographically more extensive than their estates. The effect of noble lordship on the county often far exceeded the limited extent of noble landholding within it.

The number of noble captains who held land, and later the office of justice of Chester, offered the military population a multiplicity of potential employers which both complemented and challenged the established traditions of recruitment by the earl, and added a competitive element to the distribution of patronage and rewards for service. Some of the noble captains owed their position in Cheshire society solely to the operation of faction. It was in this way, for instance, that Robert de Vere, Thomas of Woodstock and Thomas Mowbray came to recruit in the county during the reign of Richard II.[31] These men held no land in Cheshire and exercised their lordship through the patronage and favours of office. A longer tradition of military recruitment did, however, belong to those secular lords who held land in the county. In the 1300 list of £40 landholders two earls, Henry de Lacy and Richard Fitzalan, held land in Cheshire; the Audleys of Heleigh held estates which straddled the Cheshire border with Staffordshire; and both Reginald Grey and John Orreby, who had prospered in the administration of the county during Edward I's Welsh campaigns, were lords of land.[32] If the majority of the county's larger landholders were men with few if any landed interests outside Cheshire, there were notable exceptions.

Between 1292 and 1294 the daughter of Henry de Lacy, Earl of Lincoln, had married Thomas of Lancaster; and the death of the earl in February 1311 made his son-in-law the richest of the English earls and, in the words of J. R. Maddicott, 'placed him in a position of economic strength from which political strength almost inevitably followed'.[33] To his lordships in the county of Lancaster Thomas added the lordship and castle of Halton, the town of Congleton, and the hereditary constableship of Cheshire – an agglomeration of lands and privileges known collectively as the Honour of Halton. For much of the century the lord of Halton was the county's largest landholder other than the earl himself, and one whose own political standing and influence might compete there with those of the Earl of Chester. Moreover, the inheritance which Alice de Lacy brought also included the lordship of Denbigh, and in 1318 Lancaster himself added the lordship of Bromfield and Yale, acquired in an agreement he forced upon John Warenne, Earl of Surrey. The method of acquisition could leave little doubt that Lancaster intended to expand and consolidate his holdings in north-west England and the Welsh March.[34] Earl Thomas's entry into Cheshire society was, however, brief; and, notwithstanding some early retaining among the gentry of Halton and a muster of tenantry in the Scottish campaign of 1318, he failed to establish himself as a military employer in the county.

The forfeitures of 1322 interrupted the continuity of lordship within the honour of Halton for much of the first half of the century. Earl Thomas's brother and heir, Henry of Lancaster, was restored to the county of Lancaster and the honour of Leicester by 1324, but clearly had no legal claim to Halton, although he was to petition for its return in 1326.[35] It was in fact not until 1348 that Earl Henry's son and heir, Henry of Grosmont, acquired those lands in Cheshire which had been held by his uncle, Thomas of Lancaster. Like Thomas, Henry of

Grosmont also began to expand his territorial interests, and in the same year he purchased the manors of Dunham Massey, Kelsall, and Bidston from Hamo Mascy, thus extending his holdings in the county from their relatively narrow focus in Halton itself.[36]

Henry of Grosmont (created Duke of Lancaster in 1351) was perhaps the leading soldier of his generation, and now also the greatest secular lord in Cheshire next to the earl himself. It was a role that soon fostered a variety of relationships with the Cheshire gentry, on whose behalf Henry's patronage was soon exercised. In the trailbaston hearings in 1353 judgements against eleven of the duke's tenants and officials were set aside at his request, and a near neighbour, Laurence Mobberley, complained that he could not obtain a fair judgement in a case of novel disseisin because the panel of jurors consisted of men 'some of whom are kinsmen of Sir John [Legh], leagued with him, or free tenants of the Duke of Lancaster and at John's mercy, he being the earl's steward in those parts'.[37]

It remains difficult to assess the extent of military service associated with Duke Henry's landed presence in the county, although at least two of the men pardoned before the trailbaston hearings were about to go overseas with him, and protections are recorded for others on the French rolls of the royal chancery.[38] In the same year the Black Prince issued a general protection to Cheshire men who had been raised in the county for service in Normandy with the duke.[39] Such service was, however, not simply a muster of tenurial support from the demesne. Much of the lordship of Halton was in fact leased out to tenants who might look for service under a variety of lords. The Warburton family at Arley, for instance, were variously to be found in the service of the Earls of Gloucester, Arundel, Chester and Lancaster, as life retainers and demesne officials.[40] Much, it seems, depended on the political stature of the lord and the enterprise of individual knights.

The long rule of Henry of Grosmont's son-in-law, John of Gaunt, as lord of Halton from 1361 to 1399 provides a case in point, for as an important and influential figure at the royal court and elsewhere in England the duke continued to attract the support and service of gentry affiliations in Cheshire. Richard Clerk of Whitley had, for example, frequently passed information on deceased landholders to the duke whilst serving as a juror, and had acted as counsel to the duke in matters concerning the liberties of Halton. On other occasions he had concealed information from the Earl of Chester's escheator during inquisitions *post mortem*, and allowed a felon to escape. Clerk had indeed long been a life retainer of the duke, and in 1354, somewhat ironically, had obtained a pardon for acquiring land from Henry of Grosmont 'for good and long service under the sheriffs of Cheshire'.[41] In addition, the physical decline of the Black Prince after 1370 enhanced the attractiveness of Gaunt's service, and for much of the remainder of the century the duke was able to recruit extensively among the Cheshire gentry.[42]

At much the same time Richard, Earl of Arundel (d. 1397), had also begun to recruit among the gentry of west Cheshire, notably in the hundred of Broxton which bordered on the earl's land in the March, although he also held the manors of Trafford and Dunham near Chester.[43] Many of the Fitzalan's more important estates were to be found in neighbouring counties, and the earl's treasury was occasionally lodged at the castle at Holt on the Dee. Not surprisingly, therefore, the earl is known to have attracted the service of a number of Cheshire men in those of his expeditions for which retinue rolls survive, notably between 1377 and 1389.[44]

The measure of military recruitment within Cheshire exercised by Richard, Earl of Arundel, betwen 1377 and 1388 was unusual. There is no reason to believe that his father (d. 1376) had set much store upon recruitment in the county. The rather limited extent of the Fitzalan demesne, with its high percentage of villein tenure, had brought little contact with the local gentry affiliations which might have been attracted into Fitzalan service. The events of 1377 to 1388 were rather a reflection of temporary political circumstance than evidence of any continued Fitzalan interest in Cheshire lordship.

Retaining in the county by other lords was not normally a contentious issue, although in 1355 proclamations were issued prohibiting archers from taking service until the Prince's own needs had been met.[45] In general, relations between the Black Prince and other landowners in Cheshire were remarkably cordial, and on occasion that relationship encouraged the employment of Cheshire men in the retinues of the Prince's familiars. Such potential employers were the Earls of Salisbury.

In 1337 William Montague acquired the Cheshire manors of Lea, Neston, and Bosley, at the end of a period of territorial expansion in the March which had followed his support of Edward III in the palace revolution of 1330.[46] His son William, Earl of Salisbury (d. 1397), was one of the most active noble captains in royal service and enjoyed particularly close relations which the Black Prince. In the 1350s he was able to borrow substantial sums against the reversion of the lands of Joan, countess of Warenne, and had arranged a *cydfod* under which officials in Cheshire and Moldsdale would assist in the capture of felons who fled in either direction across the boundaries of the two lordships.[47]

A growing interest in Marcher lordship no doubt encouraged recruitment from the earl's Cheshire manors, and in 1351 he petitioned that archers who had been chosen for the Prince's service from Lea, Neston and Bosley be discharged in his favour as he had great need of their service.[48] It remains difficult, however, to document the extent or regularity of any Cheshire contribution to the earl's retinues, although a few Cheshire men were to figure in that of 1377, and others were later employed in the garrison of Carisbrooke castle (Isle of Wight).[49] In all probability his interest in the area may have declined when he 'lost' the lordship of Denbigh in 1354 after failing to secure the continuing support of the crown, though it may have revived when Cheshire played a central role in the politics of Richard II's reign.[50]

Much of our knowledge of the local recruitment patterns of noble captains is inevitably derived from the nomenclature of incomplete series of retinue lists, although from the examples studied it is clear that a variety of factors, from even a limited landed association and the recommendation of the Prince to the drawing power of a military reputation, may have operated in isolated instances. The association of lordship and military service might, however, be even more pronounced in the retinues of captains whose landed interests were restricted to the locality.

In this way indeed were Cheshire men to find themselves in the retinues of Sir James Audley during the major campaigns of the Hundred Years War. The greater part of the Audley lands lay in Staffordshire, around Heighley castle, but the family also held a third of the barony of Nantwich, the manor of Newhall, and lands in Weston, Chorlton, Stapeley, Tatton and Wirswall.[51] In 1353 James Audley had been the only one of the 'great men' of Cheshire to be named in a general accusation of official corruption and maintenance.[52] As holder of a part of the Nantwich barony, Audley was entitled to appoint a sergeant of the peace, and he had himself served as sheriff of the county. In this respect he was a member of local gentry society on whom the maintenance of law and order devolved. It was, however, Audley's lands and position outside the county which were to provide the resources of patronage and influence with which he attracted the military service of local gentry. The Black Prince had himself stayed at Heighley on his way to Chester in 1353, and Richard II was also to stay there on a similar occasion in 1387.[53] These were connections which no other member of local society could emulate.

Nicholas, Lord Audley, had served with Thomas of Lancaster early in the reign of Edward II; and his son, James Audley, was to serve as a banneret in Scotland in 1335, and with Henry of Grosmont in Gascony in 1345.[54] As much as 50 per cent of the retinue of forty men-at-arms and forty mounted archers which mustered at Heighley on 25 April 1345 was raised among the gentry families and tenantry close to the Audley lands. It was to serve at the siege of Bergerac and at the battle of Auberoche, but returned to England in November. Audley again took out letters of protection in March 1347, but unfortunately no retinue roll survives to illuminate the pattern of recruitment on his lands.[55] In 1353 he was granted respite from further service in parliament and on military campaigns outside the realm, although as late as 1377 he was to retain Sir John Mascy of Tatton in peace and war in return for an annual rent in Tatton and two messuages and thirty-six acres in Wrenbury.[56] The indenture must surely exemplify the relationship of land, lordship and military service which had shaped the formation of retinues raised on the Audley lands over a period of perhaps forty years.

If, however, military service is to be construed as a relationship between tenants and lords, or between neighbours at a fairly exalted level in the social scale, then clearly the extent of ecclesiastical lordship in Cheshire is an important consideration. The religious houses were no less the lords of land, but few could be seen as potential military employers. In addition the extent to which ecclesiastical lords sought to restrict the spread of leasehold tenure and to strengthen the bonds of customary holdings might often limit the available sources of potential soldiers.

The county of Cheshire supported relatively few religious foundations during the medieval period, and the two largest ecclesiastical land-holders, the abbeys of St Werburgh and Vale Royal, could not approach in wealth or landed endowment the status of foundations elsewhere in England.

The abbey of St Werburgh in Chester had been founded originally in 904 as a college of secular canons, but was refounded and endowed by Earl Hugh as a Benedictine house in 1092. Even in 1525 the net income of the house was estimated at no more than £1,000, substantially below that of the more important Benedictine houses in the south of England. A monk of the abbey, Ranulf Higden, produced the most popular world history of the middle ages but, aside from sparse topo-graphical entries, it shows little of the regional concern which marks the chronicles of St Albans or Leicester.[57]

The most comprehensive account of the abbey estate during the four-teenth century appears in a rental of abbot Henry of Sutton in 1398 which lists holdings in some forty-five Cheshire vills. In addition to extensive possessions in the city of Chester and its environs, the abbey also dominated the tenurial patterns of the Wirral peninsula. Michael Bennett has estimated that the Abbey held some 37 per cent of the manors in this area.[58] The 1398 rental reveals a high proportion of customary tenure, with few tenants holding more than half or quarter virgate. The abbey's defence of the restrictions of customary tenure had in fact earlier provoked a brief 'rising' in the Wirral in July 1381, when villeins were reported to have assembled in the forest and collected money in order to pay for legal advocates.[59]

It has been argued that from 1335 the cost of equipping a mounted archer for service in France restricted military service to that section of the population above the peasantry.[60] The extent of the estates of St Werburgh's in the Wirral and the character of ecclesiastical lordship there clearly restricted the distribution of individual wealth, and perhaps also the pool of potential military recruits. Certainly in 1355 the Black Prince had found it difficult to recruit in that area and had complained that 'there are few archers in the forest of Wirral'.[61]

The theme of peasant discontent at the restrictions of customary tenure had also characterised the management of the demesne lands at Vale Royal abbey. Here Edward I had founded a Cistercian house and endowed it with lands, mainly in the Weaver valley, which were valued at £180 in 1291.[62] Despite royal and comital patronage, the house remained chronically underendowed, and the monks proved to be zealous in the assertion of customary rights over the villein population of their demesne manors. Nevertheless, between 1307 and 1336 the bond tenants of Darnhall and Over repeatedly challenged the abbot's claims to villein services, and in 1328 they refused to grind their corn at the lord's mill, asserted the right to be punished only on the assessment of their neighbours, and claimed the right to lease their lands without licence for up to ten years. In 1336 the men of Darnhall even journeyed to Scotland in order to petition the king, although in the end their protests came to little in the face of the abbot's rights of lordship.[63] The Vale Royal estate failed, however, to dominate the pattern of local tenurial relationships, and the persistence of customary tenures on the manors of Darnhall, Over, and Weaverham can have had only a minimal effect on the local pattern of military recruitment.

The extent of landholding by other ecclesiastical foundations was confined to single or dispersed groups of manors which exercised a limited influence on local social patterns. Such manors mostly belonged to houses which lay outside the county and which had, therefore, been leased out at an early date. The bishop of Coventry and Lichfield held a number of Cheshire manors – at Tarvin, Burton, Farndon and

Wybunbury.[64] For much of the fourteenth century, however, the fiscal, military, and legal insularity of the county adversely affected its relations with the bishop who was seldom a figure in local society.

The Cistercian house at Dieulacres in Staffordshire had until 1214 been located at Poulton on the Dee, and the abbey retained lands around the city of Chester at Pulford, Poulton and Dodleston.[65] The manor of Dodleston was leased to a Chester citizen for forty-five years in 1299, but a series of early fifteenth century deeds provides evidence of a continuing interest on the part of the abbey in Cheshire affairs.[66] This is also clear in a chronicle written at the abbey early in the reign of Henry IV by two authors of opposing sympathies, which provides a unique insight into events in Cheshire and the March during the deposition of Richard II.[67] Two other Cistercian houses, at Combermere and Whalley (Lancashire), the latter originally founded at Stanlow, complete the picture of ecclesiastical landholding in the county, but neither controlled extensive estates.

The restricted pattern of landholding by religious houses extended also to the patronage of parish churches, few of which lay in their gift. In 1379 nearly 80 per cent of the beneficed clergy were resident, and there were few clerical careerists or graduates. The resident body of beneficed clergy was overwhelmingly local in character, and the high percentage of younger sons and other kin reflects the patronage of secular manorial lords.[68] Ecclesiastical lordship, no less than that of the Earl of Chester, reinforced the insular character of local society. The religious houses were part of local society, and on occasion could be well informed and sympathetic observers of its actions, but the extent and character of landholding, with perhaps the exception of the Wirral, imposed few restraints on the levels of manpower demands which local society might support.

III. ECONOMY AND SOCIETY

The pattern of lordship in Cheshire was clearly an important element in the development of military service, but the nature of the medieval economy and of county society provided the limits within which that development occurred.

Geographically, the county of Cheshire enjoys no uniformity of physical feature. Indeed, the terrain is characterised by distinct variations which inevitably imposed constraints on the nature of medieval settlement patterns. In the north, only with difficulty could the river Mersey be forded or bridged between its estuary and Stockport in the east, where the uplands of the Pennine massif hem the county in from Derbyshire. To the west, the boundary is less clear, and the mountains of North Wales are punctured by major river valleys which allow a deep penetration from the English plain and vice-versa. The later medieval boundary with Wales, although for the most part following the course of the river Dee, is the product of resistance to English incursions and the expulsion of the Norman settlements from the plain of North Wales during the late eleventh century. In the south, the Cheshire plain runs gently into Staffordshire and Shropshire. Within these bounds the structure of the medieval economy and the character of local society clearly affected the development of military service, determining the levels of available manpower and the economic attractions of warfare relative to other opportunities in the locality. It is to this relationship between the social and economic configuration of the county and its impact on military recruitment that we now turn.

The extensive colonisation of the English landscape before 1086 had, in Cheshire, fallen well short of the possible limits of settlement; and wide areas of waste, woodland and marsh continued to dominate the medieval countryside. The Cheshire woodland, later the forests of the Wirral, Delamere and Macclesfield, stretched almost continuously across the county, and the labour of clearing had clearly inhibited the spread of early settlement. Parishes, their size an early indicator of low population densities, remained unusually large throughout the middle ages, and in 1086 population in the county had seldom exceeded a density of 2.5 quintiles, well below the median in the rest of England.[69] It has been suggested, however, that the county may have been over-populated in relation to the resources of a predominantly pastoral economy during the later fourteenth century, and that this imbalance increased, and to a large extent fuelled, the attractiveness of military service.[70]

The clearest restrictions on settlement had been imposed with the creation of comital forests in the county by the Norman earls. In 1086 Earl Hugh had afforested the woodland of twenty hides, stretching from Chester along the south of the Dee estuary, 'whence the manors have greatly deteriorated'.[71] In Eddisbury hundred, five manors were reported to be in the earl's forest, later called Delamere, which was created soon after the Conquest.[72] During the course of the twelfth century Earl Hugh's successors had afforested both the Wirral and Macclesfield, and by 1181 as much as 30 per cent of the surface of the county lay within the competence of the forest law, the extension of arable cultivation closely controlled as a result.[73] Elsewhere in the county tracts of waste survived, at Rudheath and Hoole, which were not colonised until the late thirteenth century.

Much evidence therefore suggests that by the early thirteenth century there remained within the county significant reserves of potentially fertile arable land. In the Cheshire charter of 1216 Earl Ranulph III conceded the right to assart within the arable area of the forest, and to cultivate lands which had previously (that is before the date of afforestation) been ploughed without payment of herbage.[74] In another section the earl recognised the right of his barons to maintain avowries on their lands.[75] The system is described in an early fourteenth century inquisition into the earl's own avowry at Overmarsh: 'that it was of old appointed and assigned for the dwelling-place of foreigners, of any country, seeking the protection of the Earl of Chester or coming to his aid in time of war, where they might remain for a year and a day'.[76] The liability of the earl's avowrymen to military service and the attractiveness of the avowry system to felons outside the county has been suggested as an important element in the later development of military service, although the value of avowrymen is perhaps confined to the Welsh campaigns of the thirteenth century. Of equal importance as an explanation of the avowry system is the need felt by the Cheshire barons to attract settlement to their demesne lands perhaps as early as 1120.[77] Neither the clause referring to assarting, nor that dealing with avowrymen, has a direct counterpart in Magna Carta, and each indicates that the low population densities suggested by Domesday Book had been maintained during the twelfth century. At a time when landlords were coming to recognise the value of customary labour services and the direct exploitation of arable lands, the earl was willing to allow free assarting in the forest, and the community of Cheshire was concerned to attract settlement to the wastes of the county. At the end of the thirteenth century payments from avowrymen to the earl were between £30 and £40, while the individual annual fine was usually 4d.[78]

Within the national time-scale of rising population and the colonisation of marginal lands Cheshire appears to conform to the patterns which have been observed elsewhere in the March, in Devon and Cornwall, and in the forests of the Midlands and southern England. In Cheshire colonisation appears to have been late and to have continued extensively well into the fourteenth century, whereas in the rest of England the limits of settlement and population growth were being reached at the end of the thirteenth century. H.J. Hewitt has suggested that the major impetus to colonisation in Cheshire followed the acquisition of the earldom by the crown in 1237, although most evidence would now favour a peak in expansion in the later thirteenth century. Assarting on a large scale, often in conjunction with the erection of wind and water mills, is clearly visible in the pleas of the forest during the 1280s.[79] The process did, however, also continue well into the fourteenth century; Robert Grosvenor ploughing 453 acres on Rudheath in 1315, abbot William Bebington 400 acres in the Wirral in 1330. In the reign of Edward II William Lancelyn granted licence to a kinsman to erect three new messuages 'wherever he wished' in Lower Bebington.[80] Many of the clearest signs that the limits of expansion were being reached – including the partitioning of waste and common, and the appearance of tenements in neighbouring villages in the boundary clauses of deeds – do not occur until well into the 1340s.[81]

A number of sources suggest that landlords in the county were aware of the profits of demesne cultivation, and that population, while failing to press against the limits of settlement, had continued to rise until the eve of the Black Death. Even if we assume a rapid replacement rate for the population after 1349, it seems probable that later levels of military recruitment fell on a population established well within the limits of settlement available to medieval agriculture. The themes of rising population and the colonisation of waste and woodland within the modes of agricultural production in the Cheshire countryside are indeed of crucial significance. Earlier writers have suggested that the lower manning levels required by livestock farming, which had developed early in Cheshire as a result of the poor quality of the local soils for the cultivation of wheat as a cash crop, released surplus manpower into military service. Here, they suggest, is a major reason for Cheshire's prominence in the pattern of military service in the later medieval period.

The surviving evidence relating to the character of the rural economy in Cheshire is fragmentary and heavily dependent on the records of the demesne lands of the earl and the chronicles on which H. J. Hewitt based his original judgements. The comital studs of cattle and horses at Macclesfield to which livestock were moved from the other demesne manors have, as a result, bulked large in surveys of the rural economy in the county. However, where the ownership of land in the county was vested in the hands of a multiplicity of minor local lords it is their approach to the problems of agricultural production which will determine the character of rural society. What, then do we know of agricultural production on the estates of these local lords?

Few sources deal comprehensively with the management of a single estate during the fourteenth century, and it is only rarely possible to form an accurate judgement on changes and developments in agricultural production on secular or ecclesiastical lands. In 1403, however, a series of inquisitions *post mortem* and forfeitures which followed the battle of Shrewsbury record in detail the household possessions, livestock and acreages of growing crops in the lands of thirty-three soldiers, ranging from the holders of single messuages to important knightly families.[82] The information recorded reflects the kind of agricultural production on the estates of men who took part in military activity.

If we may take the figures of this sample as representative, it would seem that although oats were the dominant grain crop, wheat was grown on the majority of holdings, with other crops at much lower levels. The acreage of legumes, at seldom more than half an acre on many holdings, suggests their use as fodder for plough beasts, and in only three instances are numbers of livestock in excess of that consistent with their use for arable agriculture. Sir Hugh Browe forfeited 76 cattle and 39 horses, William Crue of Sound 21 cattle and 8 horses, and Sir William Legh 12 cattle and 8 horses. Some at least of Browe's cattle may have been collected as booty during the campaigns of the earl in Wales in 1402 and 1403, although a regular trade in cattle across the border was an important element in livestock farming in the county.[83] Some of the large number of horses may perhaps be regarded as mounts for men-at-arms and archers as well as evidence of widespread livestock farming. What does emerge is the mixed character of agriculture over a wide area, a suggestion which is confirmed by the few surviving manorial accounts of the period and by recent research on the earl's demesne manor at Frodsham.[84]

Amongst the manorial accounts of minor lords, that of Newhall in 1386 is particularly instructive.[85] As one might expect at this date, there is a low level of entry fines and an increased percentage of income drawn from rents and leases of demesne land and rights. On the remaining lands of the manor the bailiff accounted for 81 quarters and 4 bushels of grain, mainly oats with smaller amounts of wheat, barley and rye. In addition, 26 cattle were taken to the fair at Nantwich and sold for £15, and a further 24 Welsh cattle raised £8. This juxtaposition of arable cultivation and the raising of cattle appears to characterise the organisation of agricultural production on manors in the county for which accounts survive.

Clearly, however, the extent of pastoral farming had been closely related to the operation of market forces throughout the fourteenth

Table 3: Agricultural production on the estates of the military community, 1403

Holder	Livestock			Arable acreages			
	Oxen, Cows & Bullocks	Horses & Mares	Pigs	Wheat	Oats	Peas	Barley
Ranulph del More	4	3	5	3	1	–	–
Robert Boydel	4	2	–	2	3	–	–
David of Tiverton	6	–	–	6	5	1	1
Thomas Sparke of Wettenhall	8	5	2	4	4	–	2
Peter Carter	2	–	–	–	1	–	–
Thomas of Hassall	2	–	–	–	1	–	–
Thomas Bendebowe	2	2	2	1	2	1	1
Nicholas Pemberton	–	–	–	–	2	–	1
William del Yate	1	–	–	–	1	–	–
John Hobson of Wettenhall	5	1	2	4	1	–	–
Sir Hugh Browe	76	39	–	–	–	–	–
Thomas of Huxley	6	1	–	6	6	–	–
John Knight	3	1	–	(4)		(3)	
John Dod	–	–	–	2	–	1	–
Hugh Wreskhomes	2	–	–	2	2	1	–
John Heth of Oldcastle	3	6	–	4	3	1	–
John Madocson of Newton	4	1	–	1	2	–	–
Philip Hobbecliffe	2	–	–	–	1	1	–
Robert, son of Robert of Salghton	1	–	–	3	3	1	–
Richard Knight	2	2	1	1	–	–	–
William Pallehare	4	–	1	1	1	–	–
Peter, son of Robert Brundeley	2	2	2	4	6	–	–
Hugh of Bickerton	4	3	2	1	3	–	3
Richard Venables of Kinderton	7	–	–	12	24	–	3
				5	10	4	
Roger de Hyghfield	2	2	2	1	3	–	–
John of Overton	–	2	–	–	–	–	1
Henry Crue of Aston	–	3	2	2	2	–	–
William Crue of Sound	21	8	4	8	20	2	2
John of Beeston	–	1	–	6	1	1	2
Sir Richard Vernon	–	12	8	6	23	2	4
Sir William Legh	12	8	–	12	8	–	–
Hugh Legh of Legh	–	1	–	8	21	9	1
Henry of Bebington	–	–	–	5	10	5	1
				3		3	3
Totals:	185	105	32	113	170	36	26

(Source: Chester 3/21)

century. The Audley account at Newhall reveals the profitable management of livestock farming; and in an extent of the lands of Richard Minshull in 1360 the 40 acres of demesne at Aston-juxta-Mondrem are described thus, 'each acre being worth 12d if it could be let for sowing, but if not the herbage is worth 13s 4d'.[86] At Oulton Lowe the seven demesne fields, several with names suggesting recent assarts such as 'Newmore' and 'Newmarlemore' were each valued for their herbage alone; and at Bollin in 1395 autumn works had been commuted and the demesne lands leased for pasture.[87] From the research so far undertaken, most notably by Paul Booth, it seems likely that the scale of livestock farming had increased dramatically after the plagues of the mid-fourteenth century. The nomenclature of earlier extents and inquisitions reveals a clear commitment to arable agriculture which is replaced in later documents by the valuation of demesne lands in terms of pasture.[88] This suggestion too is confirmed by recent work on the earl's demesne lands in Frodsham where the abandonment of demesne arable and meadow to pasture can be dated to the late 1350s and 1360s as a result of a fall in population.[89] The extent of pastoral farming in Cheshire, visible in the documentation of the later fourteenth century, was, therefore, a response to a decreased population and a decline in the income from arable cultivation rather than a historic feature of local agricultural production. The county had only briefly experienced a period of relative over-population, and thus any theory of local over-population as a factor in the development of military service ignores the difficulties faced by lords in leasing arable land after 1349, and must as a result be discarded. It is not with the fortunes of the villein and tenant population and the character of agricultural production that the roots of military service must be sought, but in the fortunes of the landholding classes and the fluctuations in income from land.

At the time of the Domesday survey a small number of baronial families had dominated the pattern of landholding in the county, but few had retained that influence into the fourteenth century. As we have seen, there were then few significant monastic estates and no resident nobility, with the result that the leadership of landed society was vested in the local gentry who held land in the county and wielded local political authority in the earl's name. Few families held lands which would grant them a degree of unopposed local influence.

The process of change is exemplified in the decline of the barony of Dunham Massey during the late thirteenth and early fourteenth centuries. In 1288 Hamo Mascy held five knights' fees, although the establishment of cadet branches during the twelfth century had already reduced the extent of the Dunham Massey estate. By the early fourteenth century the income from the manors of Dunham Massey, Kelsall and Bidston and other lands had failed to meet the increasing costs of service in Edward I's Welsh wars. A large part of the estate lay in the hands of free tenants, and Mascy was dependent on a small unexpandable income. In 1309 he sold the reversion of his lands to Sir Robert Holland and moved within the orbit of Lancashire gentry society, retaining among Holland's affinity and forming part of the extended retinue of Thomas of Lancaster.[90] Notwithstanding his success in the pursuit of Lancaster's army from Boroughbridge, when like many others he changed sides, and the plundering of south Lancashire which followed, Mascy's financial resources continued to decline, and in 1325 he was pardoned for debts of £82 in the county. In the same year his son had sold the reversion of Dunham Massey to the justice Sir Oliver Ingham for 1,000 marks and an annual rent of 40 marks. In 1347 Henry of Grosmont bought out the co-heirs, and the lands eventually passed to the Lestranges of Knockin.[91] The ultimate failure of the male line had, however, been prefaced by a long period of decline during which Mascy's position had been bolstered by loans and service under Thomas of Lancaster's favourite. Following the withdrawal of royal service and patronage after 1301, and in the absence of monastic purchasers, the noble retinues offered the clearest opportunities to members of the knightly class in financial difficulties. During the same period Sir Thomas Burgh had granted the manors of Mottram, Tintwistle and Longdendale to Thomas of Lancaster in return for a re-enfeoffment for life and an annuity of £40.[92] The financial pressure on many of Lancaster's retainers to seek service with the earl has not been sufficiently explored, but is evident in several of the indentures between the earl and members of the lesser gentry.[93] The intervention of noble patronage was, however, seldom permanent, and Lancaster's purchases, like those of others, were quickly granted away, thus contributing to the subdivision of gentry lands in the county.

Cheshire was not highly manorialised, and the extent of free tenure and leasing lay at the heart of problems of landholding in the county. On the earl's demesne manor at Frodsham labour services had been replaced by money rents by the end of the thirteenth century, and leases are recorded as early as 1281.[94] A similar chronology is to be found on the estates of other lords. On the Earl of Arundel's manors in the west of the county no attempt was made to enforce labour services on newly assarted lands in 1301, and by 1398 the whole of the demesne was itself leased out.[95] Inquisitions *post mortem* on prominent landholders at the end of the thirteenth century reveal the fragmentation of earlier military responsibilities among an array of leaseholders and tenants, whilst the earliest series of manorial extents likewise indicates a preponderance of free and leasehold tenure on local gentry estates.[96] At Barthomley and Crewe, for example, the bailiff recorded the decline in the value of the two manors as a result of the deaths of the tenants-at-will who held the greater part of their lands.[97] In general, the fourteenth century saw a gradual blurring of the status boundaries between free and villein tenure in the county, with profound consequences for the development of military service in local society.[98]

Although the population of Cheshire was to grow dramatically in the centuries after the Domesday survey, the late colonisation of waste and woodland and the high percentage of free and leasehold tenure suggest that opportunities for profit from direct arable cultivation were not as widely available in Cheshire as elsewhere in England. Faced with the reality of military commitments in Wales and the March, landholders were constantly under pressure to maintain their incomes either through the exploitation of the resources open to local society or through military service and its rewards. In that sense, service at royal wages in Scotland or membership of a noble retinue offered a supplementary income to a harassed landed population. At the same time, the emergence of a middling class of landholder between the peasantry and the armigerous ranks of gentry society perhaps allowed a greater section of the local population in Cheshire to maintain the equipment of a man-at-arms or mounted archer.

Within Cheshire society during the fourteenth century no single family would seem to have replaced the baronial class which had been established under the Norman earls, and the intervention by the earl and by other noble lords was sporadic and partial. As a result local society operated in a web of overlapping gentry affiliations, each acting as a focus for gentry aspirations. Competition for the limited resources of local society was insistent and often violent; land ceased to be a major instrument of political power and was replaced by the control and abuse of office-holding and membership of local confederacies. The development of military service during the fourteenth century took place against a background formed by the operation of these groups of gentry support. Within them were forged the bonds of association, often remote from the tenurial relationship, which shaped many of the retinues of the Hundred Years War: they represent the ties of mutual support and locality which characterise this insular and border society.

Resentment at the operation of these affiliations in the maintenance of law and order and the exercise of comital authority were articulated in complaints before the trailbaston judges in 1353. Overlaying the traditional patterns of assault and petty crime are specific accusations of corruption and maintenance on the part of the earl's officials such as William Stanley, forester of the Wirral, Richard Done of Utkinton, forester of Delamere, Adam Mottram, revenue collector and gaoler of Macclesfield, and Sir James Audley, a former sheriff.[99] The evidence of oppressions and evil deeds, the taking of bribes, packing of juries, biased judgements, and levying of unwarranted fines and payments may be given a minimal rather than a maximal interpretation; the records of medieval courts cannot easily be used to demonstrate that society was non-violent and equitable in the maintenance of law and royal authority. The demands of war and the distribution of pardons to returning soldiers have been seen as a causative factor in the county's reputation for lawlessness and disorder, the rewards of military service subverting the operation of law in the locality.[100] The intervention of comital patronage and favour is, however, far from being a wholly convincing explanation of the levels of crime in Cheshire society, although it clearly contributed something to the difficulties of maintaining order. As Michael Clanchy has observed, 'ultimately good order did not depend on law courts of any sort but on people's attitudes to their neighbours'.[101] Where the operation of the local courts, on which the keeping of good order depended initially, fell under the control of particular affiliations, the fabric of law and order lay under threat. Complaints of this nature preface the indictments of 1353 – witness the 'jury of foreigners and strangers' controlled by Richard Done – and find echo in later petitions attesting the difficulties of obtaining fair panels of jurors.[102]

In Cheshire the lack of capital and an inability to increase customary rents and services in a period of rising population meant that knightly families were increasingly likely to have recourse to violent assaults and the abuse of office in the maintenance of their incomes and status. In that respect the evidence of the trailbaston hearings of 1353, showing the importance of gentry affiliations and mutual support groups at the apex of social relationships, illustrates clearly both the threat to order and the motive forces behind the operation of local society on which the patterns of military service were based.

In 1353 one of the largest affiliations was mustered in support of the master forester of the Wirral, William Stanley, and pledges for the payment of fines reveal an elaborate framework of mutual support among the lesser officials of the forest of the Wirral.[103] The operation of the Stanley interest in the Wirral was to be of long duration, and a study of the family during the fourteenth century exemplifies the organisation of gentry society.

In 1284 William Stanley of Stanley in Staffordshire married Joanna Bamville and thereby acquired a third of the manor of Storeton and the hereditary forestership of the Wirral.[104] Another two daughters of Philip Bamville were married to members of local gentry families, William Laken and John Becheton, who received the remaining two thirds of Storeton. The earlier widespread leasing of Bamville's lands gave Stanley a widespread group of tenants and clients in the Wirral, but the source of his local power was not so much the extent of his landed presence or influence, which was rather small, as the exercise of authority as master forester. Although the order issued by the Prince in 1351 concerning the ordinances of the forest that were to be observed and Stanley's own claims in a writ of *quo warranto* in 1362 may be regarded as ambitious claims rather than statements of self-evident usage, the forester remained an important force in local society.[105] The early ferocity of forest law had greatly diminished, but its operation gained an added impetus during the period of rapid population growth from the mid-thirteenth century.

By the early years of the fourteenth century the forests represented the last important reserves of land available for cultivation and settlement, and the insistent pressure and competition of colonisation by lord and peasant created impressive opportunities for peculation and the misuse of authority by the foresters. In 1353 Stanley was accused of taking bribes from a former prior of Birkenhead to allow assarting in the forest, and of impressing labour from several villages to work in his fields during the harvest. In addition to other petty assaults and high-handed behaviour attributed to the foresters there was a general indictment, that 'while exercising their official positions, [they] have repeatedly oppressed the common people of the Wirral by many crimes to their grave damage. Furthermore, the same men have openly issued threats against the said common people so that none of the community dared complain about their behaviour or prosecute them'.[106] Although much of the indictment may amount to little more than ritual gestures before a judicial enquiry, the reality of Stanley's authority in the Wirral is clear enough; indictments may indeed be unproved allegations, but they are seldom aimed at those without a clear and pervasive local influence. At a time when other local gentry like Sir Hamo Mascy of Puddington could 'only feign to be sergeant of the peace' in order to cloak their assaults, Stanley could muster official support in his capacity as master forester.[107]

Complaints against the undue rigour of forest law and the influence of the Stanley family as foresters re-emerge in 1376 when the community of the Wirral paid a fine of £400 for a charter of disafforestation.[108] There appears to have been little direct pressure on land at this date, and a petition to Edward III, after the death of the Black Prince, mentions in general terms the damage done to the community by the beasts of the forest and the destruction of parish churches as a result of forest regulations.[109] The charter of disafforestation, however, makes clear that resentment at the undue influence of forest officials and the enforcement of forest law lay behind the community's willingness to contribute a fine of £400.[110]

A central element in the operation of Stanley's influence had been a system of puture for the maintenance of the foresters, which had attracted complaints as early as 1353.[111] In 1377 he had not been compensated for the loss of rights and privileges as master forester, and as a result continued to enforce forest law and exact puture. The extent of this semi-official perambulation and the level of exactions and distraints provide eloquent testimony to the power of the office as late as the 1370s.[112] The exercise of authority in the earl's name and the income from arbitrary fines and oppressions insulated the family from the economic pressures on landholders and gave it a base of power and income not usually available to the local gentry. At the same time Stanley was negotiating quitclaims of his rights to puture with local landholders, and eventually he received an annuity of 20 marks and the office of keeper of the earl's avowries in recompense for his loss of office as forester.[113]

From the evidence of indictments in 1353 and 1377 it seems clear that Stanley had been able to exercise an unprecedented measure of control over local society, acting as a focus of gentry aspirations and offering protection against redress for petty crime and violent assaults. The level of lawlessness and disorder resulted not from the intervention of comital favour or the character of the law itself, but from the actions of those charged with its maintenance. The authority which successive members of the Stanley family had wielded was directed towards the establishment of a local system of allegiance and support, and the advance of the family's landed possessions.

William Stanley I (c. 1284 – 1320) had arrived in the county, probably as a client of Adam Hoton, and had acquired a third of the manor of Storeton. By 1400 his great-grandson had acquired the Hoton lands through marriage and the remaining two-thirds of the Bamville inherit-ance by purchase. Their land dealings, visible in the deeds and charters of the family, do not obviously reveal the economic and financial pressure that the family were able to exert on local society. Between 1363 and 1369 William Stanley III (1337–1398) had acquired that part of the Bamville inheritance which had passed to the Becheton family, and after 1377 the lands which had gone to the Laken family.[114] In both instances the various leases, grants and quitclaims which appear in the deed collection had been prefaced by the murder of the male heirs. In 1355 Richard Becheton was murdered during the period of the Black Prince's campaign in Gascony, and William Stanley was arrested and his bailiwick confiscated.[115] In the event, however, he was released and compensated for loss of revenue, while Becheton's uncle was to complain that 'he had been imprisoned at Chester, harshly, maliciously, unlawfully, unreasonably and undeservedly, so that he is ruined by the enmity that certain persons have against him on account of William Stanley'.[116] In 1376 Thomas Clotton, who had married the daughter of William Laken, was murdered by John Stanley and Henry Harper of Wervin, who both received royal pardons at the supplication of Sir Thomas Trivet, in whose company both were about to embark.[117] The murder had taken place during the course of William Stanley's brief campaign to continue the enforcement of forest law and the exaction of puture in which John Stanley, his younger brother, had been prominent. In both instances the impact of wealth and position in the locality had served to safeguard the family against the customary processes of law and order.

It would be unfair to suggest that in either instance the motivation behind the murders had been merely the mundane acquisition of land. The family deed collection, although it shows the painstaking reconstruction and extension of the Bamville inheritance, is important less as a measure of landed expansion than as an illustration of the dominant position in landed society held by the Stanleys. In 1376 William Stanley was in a position to double the patrimony through the simple expedient of the marriage of his son William (1368–1436) to Margery, the daughter and heir of William Hoton. For more than forty years, however, the family had occupied a dominant role in the framework of local society, attracting the support of local families and exercising authority as master foresters. A measure of their success may still be seen in the remains of Storeton Hall, built by William Stanley III c. 1373. It consisted of a great hall with a wing containing service chambers, solar and chapel.[118]

The history of the family reveals an independent success based on the actions of a local grouping of gentry support and the misuse of office in the administration of the Black Prince. Comital service and favour played little part in that success and, indeed, illustrates the imperfect control exercised by comital lordship in the locality. The rise of the family was seldom unopposed, and some success of the opposition to its pretensions is apparent on several occasions, not least in the negotiations for the disafforestation of the Wirral. Thereafter an essential element in the Stanley influence was absent, and they failed to maintain the dominant role that had previously been theirs. The example of the Stanleys is not unique, although few areas came under such exclusive control as did the Wirral. Cheshire society as a whole did, however, operate under the same web of interlinked affiliations of gentry support. When the aspirations of such families turned towards warfare, as they did notably in the years of the Prince's lordship, the character and organisation of such affinities explains in large measure the development of the patterns of military service.

The monopoly of influence on local society held by such affinities often encouraged men to seek alternative careers, and the opportunities for advancement in royal service were greater even than those provided by service to the Earl of Chester. The military career of Sir John Stanley, for example, pursued in the households of Richard II, Henry IV and Henry V, has overshadowed the early success of the family.[119] The intervention of royal servants in local society, another feature of the pattern of lordship, has been followed in a number of careers. Of these John Macclesfield, clerk and later keeper of the signet under Richard II, was perhaps the most successful.[120] From 1387 he had pursued a policy of acquiring lands in and around the town of Macclesfield, constructing an imposing town house and, by 1414, holding twenty-four of the one hundred and twenty Macclesfield burgages. In 1396 he purchased the manor of Bosley from William Montague, Earl of Salisbury, and later acquired the manors granted to John Mainwaring after the forfeiture of Sir Hugh Browe in 1403. The success of his purchases and the extent of his rise in importance in east Cheshire are revealed in a cartulary, compiled to safeguard the transmission of his estates to his illegitimate family in the early fifteenth century.[121] The financial pressure on many of those who sold lands to him is apparent and reinforces assumptions made earlier concerning the fortunes of many landholders in Cheshire.

Military service might spring from a number of concerns – as furnishing a supplementary income or statement of social status. Equally important, however, was that it provided an escape from the control of local affiliations within which advancement was limited and restricted.

During the fourteenth century the organisation of war mirrored the forms of domestic social relationship which we have described here. In Cheshire the strength of gentry society within the overall pattern of lordship and the high percentage of free and leasehold tenure each lay behind the levels of manpower demand sustained during the campaigns of the Hundred Years War.

NOTES

[1] C. T. Allmand, *Society at War: The Experience of England and France During the Hundred Years War*, 1973, p. 25; K. B. McFarlane, *The Nobility of Later Medieval England*, 1973, p. 41.

[2] See for example A. J. Pollard, *John Talbot and the War in France, 1427–1453*, 1983, pp. 75–101.

[3] M. Sharp, *Contributions to a History of the Earldom of Chester*, University of Manchester PhD, 1925, p. 35. This remains the best general introduction to the administration of the county, although superseded in part by P. H. W. Booth, *The Financial Administration of the Lordship and County of Chester 1272–1377*, Chet. Soc., 3rd Series, xxviii, 1981.

[4] See below p. 208.

[5] SC8/323.

[6] R. Allen Brown, H. M. Colvin & A. J. Taylor, *The History of the King's Works*, I, 1963, p. 249.

[7] *Cheshire in the Pipe Rolls, 1158–1301*, ed. R. Stewart Brown, LCRS, xcii, 1938, p. 147.

[8] See below pp. 126–8.

[9] See below p. 189.

[10] T. P. Highet, *The Early History of the Davenports of Davenport*, Chet. Soc., 3rd Series, ix, 1960, p. 10; J. R. Maddicott, 'The English Peasantry and the Demands of the Crown, 1294–1341', *Past and Present Supplement*, 1, 1975, pp. 37–8.

[11] H. J. Hewitt, *Medieval Cheshire: An Economic and Social History of Cheshire in the Reigns of the Three Edwards*, 1929, p. 27; Michael J. Bennett, *Community, Class and Careerism. Cheshire and Lancashire Society in the Age of Sir Gawain and the Green Knight*, 1983, pp. 69, 81.

[12] R. H. Hilton, 'Lord and Peasant in Staffordshire in the Middle Ages' in *The English Peasantry in the Later Middle Ages*, 1975, pp. 215–43.

[13] The returns were in any case arranged by vills; the lords, generally unnamed, were obliged to provide only a portion of the levy, normally a third. An original receipt from Bollin and Pownall in 1374 survives in LRO, de Trafford deeds DDTr, Miscellaneous, bundle 5,1; Michael J. Bennett, op. cit., pp. 51–2.

[14] *Calendar of Inquisitions Post Mortem*, HMSO, 1904–70; Chester 3/1–22. An *index nominum* appears in an appendix to the *25th Report of the Deputy Keeper of the Public Records*, 1864, pp. 32–60; Michael J. Bennett, op. cit., pp. 84–5.

[15] BL Cotton MS Cleopatra D VI, (The Macclesfield Cartulary). It is discussed in J. L. C. Bruell, *An Edition of the Cartulary of John of Macclesfield*, University of London MA, 1969. See below pp. 91–2.

[16] See below pp. 150–2.

[17] See below pp. 72–4.

[18] G.W.S. Barrow, 'The Pattern of Lordship and Feudal Settlement in Cumbria', *Journal of Medieval History*, 1, 1975, pp. 117–38.

[19] B.M.C. Husain, *Cheshire under the Norman Earls*, 1972, pp. 14–19.

[20] M. Sharp, op. cit., pp. 301–24; Anne E. Curry, *The Demesne of the County Palatine of Chester in the early Fifteenth Century*, University of Manchester MA, 1977.

[21] *The History of the King's Works*, II, pp. 607–12.

[22] P.H.W. Booth & J. Phillip Dodd, 'The Manor and Fields of Frodsham', in *Medieval Cheshire*, THLC, 128, 1979, pp. 27–57.

[23] *BPR*, III, 47, p. 115. See below p. 203.

[24] P.H.W. Booth, *The Financial Administration of the Lordship and County of Chester*, pp. 86–115.

[25] *BPR*, III, p. 92.

[26] *BPR*, III, p. 335.

[27] See below pp. 99, 103.

[28] Booth, op. cit., p. 4.

[29] SC6/772/5, Account of the Chamberlain of Chester, September 1369–September 1370, m. 2d.

[30] *BPR*, III, p. 257.

[31] See below pp. 187–8, 194–7.

[32] E198/3/10.

[33] J.R. Maddicott, *Thomas of Lancaster, 1307–1322*, 1970, p. 114.

[34] Maddicott, loc. cit.

[35] SC8/56/2766.

[36] DL42/1 m 44. The manors included outliers in Hale, Altrincham, Ringway, Partington, and Saighton and Moreton in the Wirral.

[37] *BPR*, III, pp. 116, 126, 143, 154.

[38] C76/33 m. 2–4.

[39] *BPR*, III, p. 211.

[40] JRL, Arley Charters, box 4/6a, box 4/35, box 14/5.

[41] Chester 25/4 m. 20; DL29/26/4; *BPR*, III, pp. 285, 293.

[42] See below pp. 161–2, 169, 195.

[43] *Two Estate Surveys of the Fitzalan Earls of Arundel*, ed. M. Clough, Sussex Record Society, lxvii, 1969, pp. 85–8.

[44] See below p. 191.

[45] *BPR*, III, p. 205.

[46] *Calendar of Charter Rolls, 1329–1341*, pp. 431–3; R. Douch, *The Career, Lands and Family of William Montague, Earl of Salisbury, 1301–1344*, University of London MA, 1950; K.B. McFarlane, *The Nobility of Later Medieval England*, 1973, pp. 159–61.

[47] *BPR*, III, pp. 54, 149, 180, 226; *ibid.* IV, pp. 144, 184.

[48] *Ibid.* III, p. 23.

[49] E101/32/30 Richard Weston, Geoffrey Aston, Robert Whitley and Thomas Frodsham; Michael J. Bennett, *Community, Class and Careerism*, p. 76.

[50] R.R. Davies, *Lordship and Society in the March of Wales, 1282–1400*, 1978, pp. 50–1.

[51] *BPR*, III, p. 138.

[52] Chester 29/65 m. 11d. See below p. 87.

[53] *BPR*, II, pp. 98-9; Chester Record Office, Cotton of Combermere deeds, CR72/box 6/1.

[54] G. A. Holmes, *The Estates of the Higher Nobility in XIV Century England*, 1957, p. 141; R. Nicholson, *Edward III and the Scots*, 1965, pp. 246-8; E101/24/20.

[55] Chester 24/2, 21 Edward III, bundle 5.

[56] *Foedera, Conventiones, Litterae etc.*, ed. T. Rymer. Revised edition by A. Clarke, F. Holbrooke & J. Coley, 4 vols in 7 parts, Record Commission, 1816-69, III, part 1, p. 257; CRO, Egerton of Tatton deeds, DET/303/14 (42).

[57] VCH (Cheshire), III, pp. 124-6; R. V. H. Burne, *The Monks of Chester*, 1962, pp. 81-3.

[58] BL Additional MS 36764; Michael J. Bennett, *Community, Class and Careerism*, p. 69.

[59] Chester 25/8 m. 57; Michael J. Bennett, op. cit., pp. 93-5.

[60] See above pp. 39-40.

[61] *BPR*, III, p. 200.

[62] *Ledger Book of Vale Royal Abbey*, ed. J. Brownbill, LCRS, lxviii, 1914, p. 10.

[63] *Ibid.*, pp. 40, 89-90, 124-5.

[64] *Magnum Registrum Album of Lichfield*, ed. H. E. Savage, SHC, 3rd Series, 1925, p. 539.

[65] *Chartulary of Dieulacres*, ed. G. Wrottesley, SHC, New Series, ix, 1906, pp. 294-5.

[66] Eaton Hall, Eaton charters 107, pp. 382-5.

[67] *The Chronicle of Dieulacres Abbey* in M. V. Clarke & V. H. Galbraith (eds) 'The Deposition of Richard II', *BJRL*, xiv, 1930, pp. 125-81.

[68] M. J. Bennett, 'The Lancashire and Cheshire Clergy, 1379', *THLC*, cxxiv, 1972, pp. 1-30.

[69] R. C. Richardson, *Puritanism in North-West England*, 1972, pp. 15-17; H. C. Darby, *Domesday England*, 1977, pp. 90-3.

[70] J. A. Tuck, *Richard II and the English Nobility*, 1973, p. 166.

[71] *Domesday Book* f. 268d.

[72] *Ibid.*, f. 263c,d, 267d.

[73] B. M. C. Husain, 'The Delamere Forest in Later Medieval Times', *THLC*, cvii, 1956, pp. 18-34; J. McN. Dodgson, *The Place-Names of Cheshire*, English Place-Name Society, xliv, 1970, pp. 8-13; VCH (Cheshire), II, pp. 167-87.

[74] *The Chartulary or Register of Chester Abbey* ed. J. Tait, Chet. Soc., New Series, lxxix, 1920, p. 104.

[75] *Ibid.*, p. 103.

[76] Chester 2/6 m. 20.

[77] R. Stewart Brown, 'The Avowries of Cheshire', *EHR*, xxix, 1914, pp. 41-55; G. Barraclough, 'Some Charters of the Earl of Chester', in Patricia M. Barnes & C. F. Slade (eds) *A Medieval Miscellany for Doris Mary Stenton*, Pipe Roll Society, New Series, xxxvi, 1960, p. 35.

[78] H. J. Hewitt, *Medieval Cheshire*, p. 156.

[79] Chester 33/2 m. 4d.

[80] H. J. Hewitt, *Cheshire Under the Three Edwards*, 1967, p. 15; JRL, Rylands charter 1393.

[81] BL Additional charters 66, 279–80, an agreement to partition the waste at Storeton dated 1343.

[82] Chester 3/21.

[83] See below pp. 210–12; C. Skeel, 'The Cattle Trade between England and Wales, 15th to 19th Centuries', *TRHS*, 4th Series, ix, 1926, pp. 135–58.

[84] P. H. W. Booth & J. Phillip Dodd, op. cit., pp. 39–47.

[85] Chester Record Office, Cotton of Combermere deeds, CR72/Box 6/1, (Account of the bailiff of Newhall, November 1386–November 1387).

[86] Chester 3/17 (17).

[87] Chester 3/7, (17); LRO, de Trafford of Trafford deeds, DDTr/Miscellaneous, bundle 5.

[88] H. C. Darby (ed.), *A New Historical Geography of England*, 1973, pp. 207–10; P. H. W. Booth, ' "Farming for Profit" in the Fourteenth Century', *Journal of the Chester Archaeological Society*, 62, 1980 for 1979, pp. 73–90.

[89] P. H. W. Booth & J. Phillip Dodd, op. cit., p. 44.

[90] See above p. 50.

[91] G. Ormerod, *History of Cheshire*, ed. Helsby, 1888, I, pp. 520–9; C. Moor, *The Knights of Edward I*, Harleian Society, lxxxii, 1930, pp. 127–8; DL42/1 f. 45d.

[92] G. A. Holmes, *The Estates of the Higher Nobility in XIV Century England*, 1957, pp. 71, 138–40.

[93] *Ibid.*, p. 73; J. R. Maddicott, op. cit., pp. 65–6.

[94] P. H. W. Booth & J. Phillip Dodd, op. cit., p. 49.

[95] *Two Estate Surveys of the Fitzalan Earls of Arundel*, pp. 85–6; Shropshire Record Office, Powis Estate Roll 56, 552/la/1.

[96] *Calendar of Inquisitions Post Mortem*, II, pp. 181, 213, 460, 493, 749; Chester 3/1.

[97] Chester 3/1 (29); Michael J. Bennett, *Community, Class and Careerism*, pp. 86–7.

[98] P. H. W. Booth, *The Financial Administration of the Lordship and County of Chester*, pp. 2–6. Michael J. Bennett, op. cit., pp. 33–6.

[99] P. H. W. Booth, 'Taxation and Public Order: Cheshire in 1353' *Northern History*, xii, 1977, pp. 16–31 discussing the evidence of the trailbaston roll, Chester 29/65.

[100] *Ibid.*, pp. 27–9.

[101] M. T. Clanchy, 'Law, Government and Society in Medieval England', *History*, 59, 1974, pp. 73–8.

[102] Chester 29/65 m. 6; see above pp. 71–3.

[103] Booth, op. cit., p. 30.

[104] The published accounts of the family are inadequate: J. Seacombe, *Account of the Ancient and Honourable House of Stanley*, 1848; P. Draper, *House of Stanley*, 1864; T. Aspden, *Historical Sketches of the House of Stanley*, 1877. The following account is based largely on the deed collections of the family, BL Additional charters 66, 240–66, 313 and JRL, Rylands charters 1269–1673.

[105] *BPR*, III, p. 34; Chester 29/67 m. 98, m. 99.

[106] Chester 29/65 m. 4; Booth, op. cit., p. 26.

[107] Chester 29/65 m. 10.

[108] R. Stewart Brown, 'The Disafforestation of Wirral, 1376', *THLC*, lix, 1908, pp. 165–80.

[109] SC8/7364.

[110] R. Stewart Brown, op. cit., p. 172; *Calendar of Charter Rolls, 1341 –1417*, v, pp. 230 – 1.

[111] T. P. Highet, *The Early History of the Davenports of Davenport*, pp. 51 – 6; Chester 29/65 m. 4.

[112] Chester 29/81 m. 2d *et. seq.*

[113] *CPR, 1392 –1399*, p. 134.

[114] BL Additional Charters 66, 263 – 4; 66, 283; 66, 286; 66, 291; 66, 295; JRL, Rylands charters, 1, 343; 1, 417; 1, 824 – 6.

[115] *BPR,* III, pp. 217, 357.

[116] *Ibid.*, p. 254.

[117] Chester 29/81 m. 6; Chester 2/51 m. 1.

[118] N. Pevsner & E. Hubbard, *The Buildings of England: Cheshire*, 1971, p. 346. An indenture for the construction of five stone gables in 1373 survives as BL Additional charter 66, 294.

[119] B. Coward, *The Stanleys, Lords Stanley and Earls of Derby 1385 –1672: The Origins, wealth and power of a landowning family*, Chet. Soc., 3rd Series, xxx, 1983, pp. 3 – 6.

[120] T. F. Tout, *Chapters in the Administrative History of Medieval England*, 1930, v, pp. 220 – 1.

[121] J. L. C. Bruell, *An Edition of the Cartulary of John de Macclesfield*, University of London MA, 1969, pp. 73 – 89.

CHAPTER III

THE ORGANISATION OF WAR AND THE LORDSHIP OF EDWARD, THE BLACK PRINCE

In considering the impact of war upon late medieval society, historians have perhaps too readily devoted their attention to those aspects which reflect the growing involvement of the state in its conduct.[1] Nevertheless during the period between 1277 and 1342 the increasing responsibility of the nobility in the recruitment of troops had clearly deepened the relationship between the patterns of lordship and the organisation of war. The bond between a lord and his follower, however constructed or understood, would become the most important single element in the assembling of English armies. Furthermore, the web of loyalties within the retinue was often simply a reflection of the structure of local society, and enjoyed a general validity beyond the particular experience of individual campaigns. The study of war therefore provides a suitable test of the nature of late medieval society. In this respect the experience of Cheshire presents an unusual opportunity, for there was little separation in the county between the role of the state and the functions of personal lordship; the development of war finance, commissions of array and the indentured retinue would each occur firmly in the context of the earl's lordship.

In the early years of the fourteenth century the pattern of military recruitment, in so far as one may discern it in the surviving evidence, had held a magnitude and a rhythm which were closely related to the quality of comital lordship.[2] During the minority of Edward of Woodstock (the Black Prince) the county had contributed mounted archers to the military household of Edward III, reaching a level of 350 men during the Flanders campaign of 1338. Thereafter the retinue led by John Ward had exhibited a marked decline in numbers, although the level of recruitment elsewhere in the county was at first maintained in Scotland. During the Breton campaign of 1342, however, the county was represented solely by the eighty royal archers under Ward's leadership.[3]

Earlier in the same year writs for the archers and foot, who were to be chosen, tested and arrayed in Cheshire and the lands of the earldom in Wales, had been returned with an endorsement observing that the county owed military service only in time of war with Wales.[4] The reluctance of the justice to implement a royal writ, although perhaps far from unique, is nonetheless a signal which directs our attention to the early development of the lordship of Edward, the Black Prince.

I. THE LORDSHIP OF THE BLACK PRINCE

The king's eldest son, born in 1330, had been created Earl of Chester in 1333, although the revenues of the earldom were already devoted to the maintenance of his infant household. Nevertheless, in raising archers in the county under John Ward's leadership, Edward III had clearly not scrupled to intervene in the lordship of the earl, although occasionally his demands were baulked by the action of local officials. In June 1335 the bailiffs of Chester had refused to countenance attempts by Thomas Gairgrave to impress shipping in the port, observing that 'they could not, and would not, listen to the lord king's commission concerning the arrest of that ship without an order of the Earl of Chester'.[5] As with other franchises, however, the independence of Cheshire was guaranteed largely by the goodwill of the crown, and beyond the sporadic rejection of royal writs for military service there is scant reference to any conflict with the earl's interests. Indeed, given the successive minorities of royal earls, the possibility of such conflicts had been avoided in the years after the rule of the Lord Edward in the reign of Henry III. Furthermore, the king now clearly had little concern to diminish the resources of his son's appanage, although from time to time he might find it politic to remind the Prince of his superior lordship.[6] For the most part, however, any difficulty arising between king and earl was resolved on the basis of consent and co-operation, and in Cheshire the regality of the earl was seldom impaired by royal interference.

The quality of the Black Prince's lordship is already established in the work of historians as an increasingly aggressive and expansive power.[7] That reputation perhaps masks the extent to which real authority, at least in Cheshire, had earlier fallen into the hands of local gentry affinities. The rule of Edward of Woodstock, as an order of 1346 succinctly put it, simply served 'to restore the peace and estate of the Prince's lands and lordship'.[8] The organisation of war and the elaboration of military service, to which the Prince's administration would increasingly devote itself, were to that extent merely an aspect of the imposition of an effective and masterful lordship.

The major instrument of that power as it evolved was the Prince's household which, although largely undeveloped until 1343, quickly emerged as a mature and imperious authority.[9] In that year it was reorganised and a central exchequer established within the precincts of the palace of Westminster, a move which recognised the growth of household control over the management of the Prince's estates.[10] In its earliest years it was characterised by its careful scrutiny of the resources of the Prince's lordship, and by a forceful campaign to increase its profitability. Even during his minority the council had written in the Prince's name to his subjects in the county of Flint, that:

inasmuch as on examination before him and his council as to the true value of and profit of all his lands and lordships, the Prince is informed that, in view of the great costs which he has incurred and must needs daily incur, as well as for his present passage to parts beyond the sea in aid of the king's war, as also for the honourable maintenance of the new estate of knighthood which he intends to receive in those parts, reason and justice require that he should be helped and consoled by his subjects, and especially by his people of the said county; he therefore requests them to treat among themselves touching these premises, and to grant unanimously such a contribution in aid of the support of the said charge as shall bind him especially to them in the future.[11]

Here, in terms resonant of that aggressive conceit which marks the quality of an expansive lordship, the Prince's council was turning its ambition to the extensive lands under its authority in Cheshire and the March.

The widespread farming of offices which had characterised the minorities of previous earls was reversed, and measures taken to ensure the probity of local officials. In 1347 a clerk of the household was appointed on a temporary basis as controller of pleas, receipts and issues in the county, and for a time thereafter all fines had to be taken openly in either the great hall or the exchequer of Chester castle. Entry to the earl's treasury could be gained only through a triple-locked door, and required the joint presence of the justice, chamberlain and controller.[12] At the same time the council had undertaken other measures aimed at reversing the decay of comital resources. Rudheath and Overmarsh, where widespread and unlicensed assarting had been in progress from the beginning of the century, were recovered and incorporated in the comital demesne. The lordship of Macclesfield, held in dower by Queen Isabella since 1327, was exchanged for the Wiltshire manor of Mere, and an attempt was made to incorporate it more firmly within the normal administration of the county.[13] Successive minorities and the slack lordship of royal earls had long operated in favour of the local gentry for, as an early commission observed, 'divers damages, oppressions, wastes and destructions were perpetrated in the hundred of Macclesfield while it was in the hands of Queen Isabella, and many men of that hundred are bound to her in great sums'.[14]

The conspicuous consumption of the noble household and the Prince's early role in the military ambitions of his father were similarly responsible for the adoption of a series of measures designed to increase the profit of comital lordship. In 1346 the 'community' of Cheshire was persuaded to grant the Prince a subsidy of £1,000 'in aid of his great expenses in furthering the king's war'. As yet, however, the ambition of the Prince's lordship was seldom its own guarantee of success, and in the event that sum proved to be extraordinarily difficult to collect. In April 1347 the council reported that no money had yet been received, and in May writs addressed to the hundred of Macclesfield were returned with an endorsement noting that the coroners had been unable to collect the amounts due.[15] Money did not begin to reach the Chester exchequer until the close of the year, and its collection was not finally completed until 1349.[16] A system of taxation was not fully developed until the years after 1368 and, among the lord's casual revenues, might often prove the least responsive to the urgency of political crises.

In Cheshire, however, the dispensation of justice, which might elsewhere operate solely to the advantage of the crown, remained a valuable perquisite of the earl's lordship. The county court, with competence over civil and criminal actions, was also the lord's court; and under the hand of the Prince the manipulation of judicial sessions to produce an immediate income quickly assumed an important role in the exaction of comital revenues. The management of the earl's judicial lordship is closely associated with the royal justice Sir William Shareshull, who had been in the Prince's service since 1338.[17] In the autumn of 1347 he heard pleas of *Quo Warranto* at Caernarfon and Chester, although sadly the detailed record of the latter sessions does not now survive.[18] At the same time he had presided over the first forest eyre to be held in the county, the severity of which later persuaded the communities of the Wirral and Delamere to proffer fines of £3,000 to redeem a second eyre in 1357.[19] In 1353 the Prince visited his lordship for the first time to view those matters 'which cannot be fittingly redressed without his presence'. In the county court at Chester he accepted a communal fine of 5,000 marks to remit a proposed general eyre, although sessions of trailbaston were immediately commissioned in its place and raised some £1,200 in fines.[20] Even by the crudest measure the yield of the Prince's lordship had risen dramatically over the decade between 1347 and 1357, for these were not inconsiderable sums when set against the annual income from the earldom itself.[21]

Much of this narrative is indicative of a revival of comital lordship which did not, however, pass without opposition, and which was not restricted solely to the lands of the Earldom of Chester. Edward of Woodstock was at the same time Duke of Cornwall and Prince of Wales; and these lordships, no less than the county of Chester, had felt the renewed weight of lordly rule. In 1354 the Prince's perambulation of his lordships, which had begun at Chester, continued in the Duchy of Cornwall where Sir William Shareshull again presided at sessions of trailbaston. Here some £2,500 in fines were delivered to the royal exchequer and immediately assigned to the Prince.[22] In Wales the pressure of the Prince's lordship had perhaps been even more insistent, although the appeal of the Marcher lords against the expansiveness of the Prince's rule had quickly attracted royal intervention.[23] Even in the locality the impact of lordly rule was often tempered by the action of the 'community', and occasionally by resistance of the type which had delayed collection of the 1346 subsidy.[24] The doomsmen and suitors of the county court retained an important role in the framing of legal judgements, and the occasion of county court sessions often embodied an element of consultation. In 1342 Sir Thomas Ferrers had returned the king's writ for the service of archers in Brittany after discussion *en pleyn contee*, and in 1351 the men of Cheshire had succeeded in restricting the competence of the Prince's exchequer at Westminster.[25]

These were perhaps small triumphs, but the presentments to the sessions of trailbaston in 1353 introduce a variant picture of the Prince's lordship, in which the substance of comital power remained widely devolved upon local gentry affinities who wielded authority in their own interest. As one indictment observed, 'the lord earl has been lord in name only, up to the present day, while they [the earl's officials] have taken the revenues which belonged to him, and kept them for their own use'.[26] One wonders, however, to what extent this degree of corruption and peculation among office holders was not typical of most lordships. In a real sense effective government was invariably exercised by those who retained a close and vested interest in the locality. This fact was clearly appreciated by the Prince's council, for the revelations of the trailbaston hearings produced no widespread administrative purge. Indeed it is perhaps not unreasonable to view the large fines paid by the *great men* of the county on that occasion as virtually a system of licensing. The Prince's lordship had striven to be effective where it mattered most: amongst those who led the gentry affinities.

Such considerations are a firm reminder that the Prince's lordship was above all a lordship of men. Indeed, lordly rule is to be measured less in terms of the financial income which it generated than in the control of local society which it conferred. In an era of falling demesne profits that control had nevertheless prospered. This was partly a result of the elaboration of resources of judicial lordship and the expansion of casual revenues in general, but perhaps more importantly a consequence of the wealth which passed into the hands of the nobility in the form of wages of war.[27] As an instrument of social command the conduct of war could boast few equals.

II. THE DEVELOPMENT OF RETINUES

> C'est du fait de chivalrie:
> En sa persone fuist norie
> En le quele il regna trente ans.[28]

Writing after his death the Chandos Herald had composed a conventional portrait of the Black Prince for the court of Richard II which may nevertheless have matched the reality of the Prince's life. Edward of Woodstock had joined his father on the expedition which landed at St Vaast-la-Hougue on 11 July 1346, and at the age of sixteen took part in the battle of Crécy and the siege of Calais. From then until his death in 1376 he was perhaps the most active of the English noble captains in the Hundred Years War, and by that date had spent no less than ten years either in France or Spain. In 1350 he led a minor expedition to Calais, and between 1355 and 1357 served as the king's lieutenant in Gascony where, at the battle of Poitiers, he was responsible for the capture of King John II. In 1359 he joined Edward III on his last campaign, and in the 1360s pursued an active military role as Prince of Aquitaine, intervening also in the civil war in Castile. These were the major investments of the Prince's lordship, in which 'reason and justice' required that his subjects of the county of Cheshire should play a significant role; and it was in the pursuit of these ambitions that the militarisation of Cheshire society was grounded.

Somewhat earlier, in the spring and summer of 1345, Edward III had commenced preparations for a three-pronged invasion of France. The Earl of Northampton was to land in Brittany with the support of John of Montfort, and the Earl of Lancaster in Aquitaine, while the king himself returned to Flanders. The Prince, who was to accompany him, was then the same age as his father had been on his own first campaign in Weardale in 1327. In the event, however, the initial unity of the king's plan had collapsed with the murder of the Flemish rebel leader, James van Artevelde, and Edward returned from Sluis in late July after little notable military activity. Not until the following year, at Crécy and Calais, did he succeed in effecting a co-ordinated effort between himself and the two earls.[29]

Meanwhile, as a result of his indenture with Lancaster the king had agreed to provide 1,500 men for the earl's retinue in Aquitaine, including some 600 foot archers who were to be raised in Staffordshire, Derbyshire, Lancashire and Cheshire.[30] Although commissions of array were employed for the recruitment of the infantry, it is hardly surprising that these counties were also those in which Lancaster was the single greatest lord. In Cheshire, where Alice Lacy held the lordship of Halton in dower, the king's writ was re-issued in the Prince's name, and Sir John St Pierre, John Legh, Peter Ardern and the sheriff, Ralph Oldyngton, were commissioned to choose 125 archers at royal wages. At the beginning of May 1345, Ardern was appointed as their leader and granted 20 marks for the expenses of the journey to Southampton in order to avoid delay. Neither payment nor the later threat of distraint appears to have expedited the muster, and on 23 June Ardern was ordered to repay his expenses to the chamberlain.[31] The arrayers had met with particular opposition in Macclesfield, where the men of the lordship had refused to sanction the earl's demands in spite of the agreement of Queen Isabella, who still held the manor and hundred in dower.[32] Sir John St Pierre did himself join the earl's retinue; but it seems unlikely that any of the archers had also found their way into Lancaster's service during his two Gascon campaigns.[33] The retinue did, however, include some eighty men-at-arms and archers raised by Sir James Audley of Heleigh on his lands in north Staffordshire and south Cheshire. Few were in any strict sense his tenants, although Audley had clearly had little difficulty in meeting the demands of warfare from within his own widespread affinity. In 1353 he would be one of the 'great men' of the county charged with the distribution of fees to office holders, and with usurping the resources of comital lordship.[34] To be fully effective, therefore, the earl's military lordship had to secure the loyalty of these members of local society as well as seeking to compel the service of its subjects.

The progress of the Prince's own demands are less than fully documented, although it seems probable that compulsion was also initially the major means of recruitment. In April 1345 the justice of Chester, Sir Thomas Ferrers, was ordered to join the Prince at Sandwich with his retinue and 100 archers; and later in the same year, after Edward III's return from Flanders, a royal writ called upon the Prince to provide some 3,500 Welshmen and 100 archers from Cheshire.[35] In 1353 an indictment at the sessions of trailbaston recalled that Sir John Hide had been commissioned to choose and lead archers in the Prince's company, but that nevertheless he had accepted bribes and chosen less suitable men.[36] A later petition from Thomas Crewe also records how he came upon the Prince's ship off the Isle of Wight during the voyage to St Vaast-la-Hougue and was taken aboard to serve in Hide's company.[37] In many respects Hide was indeed the obvious choice for the leadership of the archers recruited in Cheshire. He had earlier served in the household of Edward III and, as an esquire, had led 150 archers from the county in Flanders in 1339. At Crécy, however, his retinue may have been made up of as few as 71 men.[38]

A sluggish response to demands for military service was not, it seems, restricted to the Earl of Lancaster's retinue, nor indeed to the lordship of Macclesfield. Many of the Welsh had either ignored the musters altogether, or else deserted at Portsmouth; and almost immediately the Prince had to demand that a further 300 archers be raised in Cheshire.[39] On 8 August, less than a week before Crécy, Sir William Brereton was commissioned to choose and lead 100 of the best of them and to 'make as long marches as possible, for the day of the passage is soon'.[40] Later in September, as the army took up its station before Calais, the Prince again called for more Welshmen and reminded the justice 'not to be so negligent or tardy in this matter as he was in the last array of archers of Cheshire'.[41] As with the subsidy of 1346 the ambition of the Prince's lordship may initially have overreached its powers of compulsion.

As a measure of that ambition, however, archers raised on the Prince's lordships in Cheshire and North Wales were to be equipped with uniforms of a short coat and hat in green and white cloth.[42] In 1346 the archers would appear to have been issued with finished uniforms, although later it became customary for them to be responsible for making them up themselves. In 1355 Welsh deserters were indicted for taking 'cloth and wages', while in the following year Richard Norton of Broxton, having failed to join the retinue at Bordeaux, was later accused of taking two ells of green and white cloth and four shillings from the Prince.[43] The provision of uniforms for the shire levies had become widespread during the 1330s, and clearly added considerably to the rising costs of warfare which preceded, and may in some part have brought about, a decline in the military role of the local community.[44]

An expedient originally adopted to improve the quality of infantry levies quickly acquired a heraldic purpose, however, as the responsibility of the nobility for the recruitment of troops widened. As early as 1321 Roger Mortimer of Wigmore had mustered his following in London, 'all clothed in green with their arms yellow', and it is likely that other noble retinues were soon to be seen in similarly distinctive liveries. In 1342 red and white cloth was provided for the Earl of Arundel's Welsh troops, and later, in 1355, the same colours, although not perhaps in the same pattern, were employed by the archers of Norwich.[45] In Cheshire the heraldic purpose of the Prince's green livery extended even to the decoration of the exchequer. A room in the Prince's palace at Westminster was early described as *'la verte chambre de la receyte'*, and in 1359 when the exchequer table at Chester was re-covered, green cloth was employed for the purpose.[46] Such displays were a fundamental element in the non-literate modes of communication: they proclaimed the identity of the lord in whose service these men had mustered and under whose lordship they fell.[47]

The progress of recruitment in the county during the final years of the Prince's minority had nevertheless fallen well below the levels which the demands and ambition of that lordship had perhaps envisaged. Commissions of array issued to the justice of Chester had invariably produced forces which lacked any element of cohesion beyond the common bond of service with the earl; and clearly a reliance upon communal obligations and the traditional avenues of recruitment could not now be made to operate successfully in meeting the claims of an active lord. Individual commissioners were often amenable to bribery, and local communities could clearly prevaricate over their musters for as long as they did over the collection of subsidies. In this form lordship had often to rely ultimately upon a display of force to compel the service of its subjects. Little wonder then that the military administration of the county had appeared so slow and cumbersome in ordering its response to the Prince's urgent demands for more troops in Normandy during 1346. At the same time the formation of 'bastard feudal' relationships between lords and their more important tenants and neighbours, which elsewhere supported the increasing weight of noble recruitment, was in Cheshire inhibited by the peculiar status of the earl and the long succession of comital minorities. Nevertheless, as the example of Sir James Audley's retinue would suggest, the root system of gentry affinities which made such arrangements so attractive to a lord was widely present in the county. What was missing was that connection between the earl and the leadership of gentry society which would make military service the expression of more than the customary constraints of tenurial loyalty. The county of Cheshire had perhaps fared no worse from the minorities of its earls and the arrangements made for dower than several other noble estates; its custody, however, was never granted to others who might at least have maintained the firm hand of seigneurial control.[48] The only enfeoffment-to-use widely practised in the earldom was that which had committed the reality of social command and the substance of political authority into the hands of the local gentry. This was the 'problem' of Cheshire society in the mid-fourteenth century, and one which soon attracted the unremitting effort of the Prince's administration.

Meanwhile, some elements of the army besieging Calais appear to have dispersed during the winter of 1346, and the Prince's retinue in particular seems to have been greatly weakened.[49] When military activity was resumed in the spring of 1347, however, a number of innovations had been introduced. On 6 March commissions of array had again been issued in Flintshire and north Wales to raise some 200 Welsh foot, and later the newly appointed steward of the Prince's lands, Sir Richard Stafford, was sent a copy of the retinue roll and ordered 'to arrange that the retinue needed be quickly made up, and to make personal survey that the array of the Prince's men of North Wales and the counties of Cheshire and Flint be made in accordance with what the Prince has written'.[50] In the minds of the Prince's council the imposition of household influence over military recruitment can have been scarcely less significant than the recently-established household control of the financial resources of the Prince's lordship. Indeed in Cheshire the local administration now played little active part in these new musters. On the same day that commissions of array had been issued in Flintshire and North Wales, Sir Thomas Danyers was ordered to come to Calais with all haste 'according to his retainder', and with 100 archers at the Prince's cost. The terms of the indenture were not immediately known to the chamberlain of Chester who initially refused payment to Danyers' three esquires; and indeed they do not now survive.[51] Later in the month, however, Sir John Hide was also retained for one year with two esquires, taking 'the king's usual wages, and for the mounted archers provided by him 6d a day for their wages when the king and other great men give so much to archers of like condition'.[52] The two agreements mark the first efforts in the county to delegate the work of recruitment into the hands of indentured retainers, and are indeed among the earliest of the Prince's indentures of war now extant. In general, however, the practice of retaining among the Cheshire gentry was not yet widespread, and a number of other cancelled bills had simply stated that should the recipient 'come to Calais apparelled for war, the Prince will act towards him as towards others of his estate'.[53] Neither it seems were such agreements immediately successful in expediting the progress of recruitment, for Hide's retinue had still not reached Calais by early June.[54]

The ensuing years of relative military inactivity may perhaps mask this early development of retaining in Cheshire, and there is in fact scant evidence which bears on the contribution of the county, either to the Calais expedition of 1350, or to the naval battle of Winchelsea. Some 276 ells of green and white cloth were purchased for the Prince's expedition in 1350 and would have equipped somewhere in the region of 138 archers, but there is little further information as to the ways in which these groups may have been raised.[55] During the years between 1346 and 1353 it is perhaps the relentless pressure of judicial lordship which is more accurately a reflection of the relationship of the Prince and local society. Nevertheless, the success or failure of that pressure and its culmination in a gratuitous display of comital force at Chester, reminding the county of the mastery under which it lay, would also have greatly influenced the subsequent development of military service during the Prince's later campaigns.

On 10 July 1355 the Black Prince had formally agreed to serve in Gascony as the king's lieutenant, and under the terms of his indenture was to provide a retinue of 433 men-at-arms, and 400 mounted and 300 foot archers. Recruitment had in fact already been in progress for some months, and its success may as a result have borne some actual relationship to the terms of the contract.[56] In London the Prince had discussed the details of his demands upon Cheshire with a group of eight knights and esquires, each of whom was retained for one year.[57] On their advice the lieutenant-justice was ordered to test and array 200 archers from all the hundreds in the county 'in whosoever lordship they be' and, in addition, to array 100 of the best archers that could be found.[58] In June another three Cheshiremen were retained and the demand for the 200 archers was increased to 300.[59] On the same day leaders were appointed for the various hundreds, although the order made no mention of the hundreds of Bucklow and Northwich.[60] The Prince had also been advised that few archers were to be found in the forest of the Wirral, and its contribution was therefore amalgamated with that of the hundred of Broxton.[61] In response to the earlier problems of recruiting which had been faced in 1345 and 1346, proclamations were issued in May and June prohibiting archers from taking service under other lords until the Prince's own requirements had been met.[62] Wages for the journey to the muster at Plymouth were to be paid from the fine which the county had offered in 1353, and on 28 July letters of protection were issued on behalf of those who were to proceed in the Prince's service from Cheshire and Flint.[63]

Military service was still encompassed within a framework of communal obligations which were now supplemented by troops raised by indenture of retinue. Nevertheless, such indentures rarely enumerated the service of mounted archers. Sir John Griffyn had, for instance, been retained with a fee of 40 marks if he was accompanied by two esquires, or 35 marks if he brought only one; earlier, however, Sir John Hide had been promised royal wages for such mounted archers as he was prepared to provide.[64] In 1355, therefore, men served, either in hundredal contingents raised by the Prince and assigned to the leadership of particular indentured retainers, or else were recruited by the retainers themselves, presumably within their own lordships. The divisions of responsibility do not, however, appear to have been governed by the personal wealth or status of the retainer. Such differentiation as each role may have implied is far from clear, and in practice individual companies may not have differed materially in form from each other. The case of Richard Mascy, who had been retained in June 1355, is particularly instructive. Early in 1359 he petitioned the Prince as the leader of the Nantwich archers in Gascony for arrears in the wages of his company, but was initially refused payment by the chamberlain, John Brunham, on the grounds that 'they were Richard's men and not assigned by the Prince to be led by him, and were at his own costs except wages'. It is, however, to be doubted whether the hundredal levies had enjoyed any lesser degree of cohesion than those companies which were led by retainers at their own costs. In any final analysis the distinction may well have been solely a matter of finance, and in the event Mascy was required only to affirm that he had paid his archers what he now claimed from the Prince.[65] In the same year Sir John Fitton, arriving at the Cheshire muster with twelve archers, was simply appointed as their leader.[66] Ultimately the expedient of knights and esquires retained by the Prince and then appointed to be leaders of archers raised either by commissions of array or by the retainer himself, was established as the customary form of military recruitment in the county. In 1359 the Prince retained fourteen knights and esquires and raised some 400 archers for service during a campaign which, it was hoped, would culminate in the coronation of Edward III at Rheims. Robert Legh was again appointed to lead archers from Macclesfield, and other knights were to be chosen to lead the remainder 'as shall seem best to the lieutenant and chamberlain'.[67] In 1363, after his appointment as Prince of Aquitaine, Edward prepared to visit his lordship there, and Sir John Delves was ordered to choose 200 archers and 'to retain certain knights and esquires to be their leaders'.[68] Similar examples can be cited at intervals throughout the fourteenth century as such methods were widely adopted in the elaboration of the earl's military lordship.[69] Commissions of array were to provide a financial and administrative framework within which this system would operate, but often, one suspects, the hundredal companies were effectively the personal follow-ings of their leaders.

It should also be borne in mind, however, that the Prince was never dependent on Cheshire for more than a small percentage of his retinue in war. His own personal status as the king's eldest son and regular doles from the parental purse ensured that his retinue was widely attractive and seldom tied to any particular lordship. In fact comparatively few Cheshiremen figure amongst the Prince's permanent retainers, al-though the county had early come to dominate the household in the provision of mounted archers. Unlike the order of knighthood, it is apparent that recognition as a man-at-arms depended solely upon possession of the necessary equipment, and not upon a particular station or role in local society. In 1345, for instance, Roger Trumwyn had chosen among the Welsh archers several who claimed to be men-at-arms, but advised the Prince that he would 'not find them to be of such condition as they make themselves out to be'.[70] Likewise in Cheshire there were many whose standing, within the context of county society, was analogous to that of men-at-arms raised elsewhere in England, but who took service in the Prince's retinues as mounted archers.

In measuring the level of recruitment in the county we should perhaps treat the evidence of the Prince's register with no less circumspection than that of earlier royal writs of military summons. It should always be remembered that these were not in fact records of service but demands, which in practice may only rarely have been met in full or in their original terms. Sadly, however, there is only a single surviving retinue roll from the Prince's campaigns, and that does not identify individual archers.[71] A variety of other sources can often be employed to fill out the knowledge of particular companies, but one can seldom pretend that the documentation is sufficient to allow accurate statistical comparisons to be drawn.[72] Nevertheless, the survival of the *Journal* of John Henxteworth, the Prince's treasurer of war between September 1355 and July 1356, does allow a unique insight into some aspects of the character and organisation of an expeditionary force. These daily accounts record the payment of fees, wages, gifts and rewards to the retinue amongst a diversity of other more mundane charges which had fallen within Henxteworth's competence at Bordeaux.[73] Its major value rests with the detail it affords of the payment of wages to the Cheshire retinues, often allowing a correlation between archers and their leaders and occasionally enumerating the separate companies. The majority of the entries are, however, rarely explained, and deductions as to the total size of individual retinues, based on the comparative value of payments, may be wildly inaccurate. The rather spare detail of Henxteworth's disbursements, often explained simply as '*pro denariis sibi debitis sicut patet libro memorandorum*', satisfied his own accountability, but could not be used to verify the full settlement of army wages, which were in most cases several years in arrears.[74] In 1359, for example, when a general order on the settlement of arrears was issued, Richard Mascy provided his own schedule of the archers in his company, claiming wages for twelve, although Henxteworth had recorded payment of only eight at Bordeaux in September 1355.[75] Clearly the production of an archive did not immediately facilitate its continuing use. Treated with suitable caution, however, Henxteworth's record may be used to frame a number of propositions as to the relationship of the Prince's demands to the actual service of the Cheshire retinues.[76]

The English fleet had reached Bordeaux by September 1355 without incident, although at least one ship had needed repairs and several horses were lost from the companies of Hamo Mascy and Robert Brown.[77] In the following week several companies received their first payment of wages, and twenty-four archers under John Hide and John Danyers were granted 40s towards their expenses in the city.[78] While the Prince took the homage of the Gascon lords, more commonplace concerns occupied the interest of the Cheshire retinues. A white horse was sold by William Brown, an archer in Robert Brown's company, and the Prince made a gift of shoes and hose to William Lawton, an archer in Ralph Mobberley's company.[79] When the army finally left the city on 5 October, archers from Cheshire were employed ahead of the main body at Bazas and in the purveyance of food supplies at La Réole.[80] Thereafter the entries in Henxteworth's record abate, and there are few reports of such domestic incidents until the return from Narbonne in November, when several archers sold horses to the Prince for the carriage of bread and perhaps also of booty.[81] The payment of

Table 4   The Cheshire retinues in Gascony, 1356

Payment of wages, 2 January 1356

Hamo Mascy	63 archers	£11 18s 6d
John Danyers	18 archers	£ 4 1s 0d
Ralph Mobberley	32 archers	£ 7 4s 0d
Hamo Ashley	2 archers	9s 0d
Robert Brown	28 archers	£ 6 6s 0d
John Hide	37 archers	£ 8 6s 0d

Payment of wages, 14 May 1356

Thomas Stathum	5 archers	£ 1 1s 0d
Hamo Mascy	15 archers	£ 2 12s 6d
John Danyers	10 archers	£ 1 15s 0d
Ralph Mobberley	11 archers	£ 1 18s 6d
Robert Brown	13 archers	£ 2 5s 6d
John Griffyn	5 archers	17s 6d
John Hide	5 archers	17s 6d
William Carrington	9 archers	£ 1 11s 6d

Payment of wages, 30 June 1356

William Golborne	43 archers	£31 10s 0d
Robert Legh	108 archers	
Adam Mottram	127 archers	£80 7s 0d
Ralph Golborne	49 archers	£35 14s 0d
Hamo Mascy	28 archers	£89 12s 0d

(Source: Duchy of Cornwall Office, *Journal* of John Henxteworth.)

wages was resumed in December as the army settled into its winter quarters, and on 2 January 1356 the leaders of the archers from Cheshire were paid for nine days, the disbursements noting the size of their companies.[82] The five large companies, who presumably accounted for the core of the Cheshire strength, were normally paid on the same day and at regular intervals during the ensuing months, although by the beginning of May their number had declined dramatically from around 180 archers to a little over 50.[83] Part of the missing complement may undoubtedly be accounted for in the division of the companies which had taken place along the Gascon March, these smaller groups being employed in the intermittent skirmishing which punctuated the long period of military inactivity during the winter and spring.[84] It is more likely, however, that withdrawal or desertion had also been responsible for the depletion of the Prince's retinue during that same period.

On 19 January Henxteworth recorded a gift of 24s to six archers who had been allowed to return to England, and a licence for William Jodrell, 'un de nos archers', sealed on paper with the privy seal of the Prince and dated 16 December, does indeed still survive.[85] The Jodrell pass itself is unique, although transcripts of seven others, all apparently sealed on paper in the same fashion, were made by the Cheshire antiquarian Randle Holme III in 1640.[86] Five were dated on 16 December, and two of these were issued in favour of more than one archer, presumably to small groups who intended to return to England together; the remaining two, issued in April and June 1356, omitted the phrase 'un de nos archers' from their terms, but were in every other respect identical.[87] Holme also transcribed a single example which, dated at La Neyte in February 1364, was sealed on parchment rather than on paper, and issued to William Warde of Bickerton, 'un de nos archers de nostre comte de Cestre', allowing him to return to England to attend to his own affairs.[88] It appears likely that such arrangements may have been more widespread than the surviving examples would suggest, and that licence to leave the army may regularly have involved the issue of letters patent.[89] That such innovations may also have originated in the household of the Black Prince suggests a growing sophistication in its approach to the details of military administration. At the same time, however, it is apparent that the issue of such passes was a response to the problems of desertion which had characterised both this and earlier expeditions.

Heavy losses through desertion had been a persistent problem among the poorly equipped infantry levies of Edward I's armies, and were met with severe penalties.[90] The emergence of contractual armies ought perhaps to have obviated the need for such harsh measures and reduced the levels of desertion, although some wastage during the early part of campaigns was probably inevitable. In September 1355 the Prince had excused a small number of archers who were judged to be too ill to embark, and issued writs against others who had deserted before the fleet left Plymouth. Richard Wistaston, one of the four Cheshiremen who were included in the indictments, was reported to have absconded with £6 in wages for himself and his companions.[91]

Nevertheless these remained minor irritants compared to the losses which continued to affect armies, particularly in the intervals between campaigning seasons. In some cases archers may have been reluctant soldiers who had served solely for the benefit of letters of protection, and who now saw little virtue in prolonging that service; in others the value of booty already won, an imagined threat to unguarded lands, or simply the rigours of a winter campaign may have acted as equally powerful impulses.

On 6 March 1356 the Prince issues writs to the Lieutenant-Justice and the Chamberlain of Chester ordering them to arrest those archers who had returned to England without licence, and to distrain their goods until they returned to Gascony. The enclosed schedule named some forty-three archers in the five companies who had deserted, although five of the names were endorsed with a note that they held passes.[92] If we include those who had earlier been granted licence to leave Libourne it is apparent that somewhere in the region of sixty-four archers had returned to England, either under the protection of passes or as deserters. Any calculation as to the percentage loss from the Cheshire retinues which this figure represents may be rather misleading, although, even if we assume only light casualties during the first *chevauchée*, it becomes clear that the Prince's forces had been greatly reduced by the beginning of the new campaign season in 1356.[93] In order to make up these losses the Prince had at first ordered that some 200 archers be raised in Cheshire, but later increased his demands to 500 archers.[94] H.J. Hewitt doubted whether such a large number of mounted troops could be mustered in the county at that date, particularly as Henry of Grosmont was also recruiting archers for his own expedition to Brittany.[95] Nevertheless, amongst his last payments John Henxteworth recorded the issue of wages to over 300 Cheshire archers who had been sent from England in the early summer.[96] Several men who had deserted during the winter returned to take part in the Poitiers campaign, although these new musters did not escape the now traditional bout of desertions. Some fourteen archers were later indicted for taking cloth and wages from the Prince, including one, William Warburton, who achieved the dubious distinction of having deserted twice in the same year.[97] Stringent measures were taken to discourage desertion, and later to verify the service of those who claimed pardons or rewards. John Baguley, who had earlier been pardoned for his desertion, was mistakenly prosecuted to the point of 'outlawry' in the aftermath of the campaign; others were subject to rigorous examination of their claims, or else required to submit proof of their service at Poitiers before the issue of pardons.[98] A certain level of desertion and peculation remained as a continuing problem, and probably lay beyond effective solution.[99]

Many of these developments had occurred against a background of growing military activity in England and France, to which the administration of the Prince's lordships had quickly and aggressively responded. During the period between 1346 and 1359 the resources of county society had been fully mobilised, and a sophisticated military administration created to meet the demands of an active lord. Military service had moved from the muster of indifferent infantry troops and the recruitment of small specialised groups to become a widespread social phenomenon. Sir John Ward had been a minor tenant; his successors as leaders of archers were recruited among the major landed and office-holding families in the county. In a simple and direct way the change is marked in 1346 by the appearance of the novel excuse '*quia in servicio domini regis*' enrolled on the essoin rolls of the county court.[100] Military service had begun to interrupt the business of an increasingly litigious landed society to an extent that had not been true of the county under Edward I. In a real sense therefore the lordship of the Black Prince had marked the earliest experience of county society at war.

III. THE PATTERN OF LAWLESSNESS AND THE CONDUCT OF WAR

We have established a strong case for regarding the rule of the Black Prince as the period in which the militarisation of Cheshire society was founded, and in which the leaders of that society were first fully involved in its captaincy in war. Earlier conceptions of a region brutalised by the cumulative martial demands of a succession of its earls have been shown to be largely without foundation. Nevertheless, it has been argued elsewhere that the experience of warfare, and more especially the operation of the Prince's military lordship, contributed greatly to a breakdown of law and order in the county in the later years of the fourteenth century.[101] The Cheshire evidence does indeed add to that 'contemporary sense of crisis' already identified 'in the language of royal statute and late-fourteenth-century ballads, in the works of polemicists and contemporary chroniclers, and in successive novel procedures for law enforcement'.[102] Much of the argument has centred somewhat unreally on the initiative of royal and comital justice, although initially the tempering of violence in medieval society was clearly dependent on the action of the local communities where attitudes to law and order were formed. As we have observed, in Cheshire the community operated through a web of overlapping gentry affiliations, each acting as a focus and ultimately as the major restraint on the intense and occasionally forceful competition of locally expansive groups. Violence there was, and much of it was undoubtedly perpetrated by those charged with the administration of justice in the earl's absence and with the operation of his military lordship; but whilst it is apparent that no satisfactory explanation of these attitudes can ignore the often close association of war and lawlessness, it remains true that individual acts of violence often had deep and traditional roots within local society. An understanding of criminality therefore demands far more than simple knowledge of a crime or why it was committed, and it is proposed rather that we examine these issues through the evidence of a number of gentry affinities active in the years between 1290 and 1380.

In the first years of the thirteenth century Augustine of Breightmet had granted a life interest in a moiety of his lands in Mobberley to his brother Patrick with permission to endow a house of Augustinian canons. It seems likely that the priory survived only until Patrick's death and was then annexed to Rocester abbey which continued to maintain canons in the church.[103] Augustine's heirs, having taken the name of Mobberley, had limited status in local society but do not figure greatly in the palatinate records, although Ralph Mobberley was able to secure the intervention of the Lord Edward in a dispute over the patronage of the church during the latter's visit to Chester in August 1260.[104] By the close of the century, however, William Mobberley had begun to extend his landholding, acquiring an interest in both Nether Peover and Tatton. In 1308 his son William was able to share more fully in the growing economy of the area when he acquired the borough of Knutsford from William Tabley at an annual rent of 50s.[105] These transactions doubtless form part of the customary framework of tenurial relationship in many local societies within which there was perhaps a continuous exchange of fortunes between rising and declining families. Nevertheless Mobberley's example does form part of a discernible pattern of landed success amongst the minor gentry of Cheshire, many of whom had clearly been able to profit from the decline of the 'baronial' class in the county.[106] Their success is evident in the quality and range of archives which were formed by many families at this date, and in which one may witness the creation of a patchwork of contiguous estates.[107]

Whilst the scope of this landed expansion is often apparent from the sheer volume of deeds and charters, the means of its achievement is less intelligible and remains a matter for conjecture. In some instances an increasing role in local office-holding may have been a significant factor, for in a crowded landscape men had already begun to measure their status less in terms of the land which they owned than in the wealth of offices which they exercised. John Mobberley had, for example, held Beeston castle for Robert Holland in 1309, thereby securing access to the patronage of Thomas of Lancaster; and as the expansion of the estate continued, William Mobberley took the sheriffdom of the county at farm for £200 a year, an office which brought opportunity for peculation and a role as the familiar of leading members of county society.[108] On a broader basis, however, such gentry also enjoyed a closer and more direct relationship with the rising population of their lands and were able to profit from the management of relatively small estates. Nevertheless, as the points of contact between such estates increased, so did opportunities for conflict, and throughout the fourteenth century relationships between such families hovered uncertainly between demonstrations of group unity, aggressive litigation and outright violence; and such a situation was made even more complex when a period of political crisis provided cover for acts of aggression on purely domestic issues.

In that part of east Cheshire the expansion of landholding under William Mobberley was matched on the estates of other neighbouring lords. Less than a mile distant, John Legh I had completed his purchase of the manor of Knutsford Booths from William Tabley and Reginald Grey between 1294 and 1297, and in the first years of the century his additional purchases had marched alongside those of his nearest neighbour.[109] The family, unusually responsive to the economic opportunities presented by a period of demographic expansion, had invested heavily in the improvement of the estate, notably in the purchase and construction of corn mills and in the setting up of a weekly market at Knutsford Booths.[110] In 1302 contacts between the two families grew even closer when Legh secured the hand of Sir John Ardern's daughter and acquired the remaining third of Mobberley itself.[111] John Legh I had thus established himself within the ranks of the minor gentry, and thereafter assumed a position which is readily apparent from his frequent appearances as a witness to local charters. In 1322 both he and William Mobberley were present on that other demonstration of the cohesiveness of gentry society when they joined Sir Oliver Ingham during the pursuit of Thomas of Lancaster's shattered retinue. Although the two men had been frequent witnesses to each other's charters and, in 1304, had reached agreement in a potentially violent dispute over the joint ownership of Knutsford Booths' mill, a narrow range of shared ambitions clearly favoured a somewhat volatile relationship.[112] In fact, late in 1326 Legh's eldest son, John Legh II, and Sir William Chetulton, the latter having figured in south Lancashire in 1322 'cum societate sua ignota', were indicted for the murder of William Mobberley and several members of his following, although all were later pardoned in return for military service in Scotland.[113] The immediate cause of the conflict appears to have been the purchase by Mobberley of the wardship and minority of Legh's close kinsman, Hugh Venables.[114] Certainly, disputes over land appear to have underpinned the majority of gentry feuds in this period, although it is perhaps equally likely that a whole series of unreported provocations on either side had prefaced the crime.[115] That itself was of course by no means unique in any local society at this date or indeed at any other in the fourteenth century, nor should such crimes always be given a moralistic interpretation by historians. Thus the later murder of Peter Ardern, who had similarly established himself as a notorious criminal in the 1330s, by his kinsman Sir John Ardern clearly added to rather than detracted from the maintenance of a form of law and order in the locality.[116] The regulation of inter-personal relationship, to which legal records can only provide an imperfect and often inadequate guide, cannot be judged on solely the counting of 'criminal' deeds. Nevertheless, the inducements for Legh's crime remain clear, for the murder would have effectively removed the power and influence of the Mobberley family from the area for a generation, during the minority of the heir.

At the same time Legh's heir had continued his close association with Sir William Chetulton and in the early 1330s was prominent in a number of assaults outside the county.[117] At Carlton-in-Lindrick in Nottinghamshire he was accused of attempting to abduct the widow of Sir John Orreby, custody of whose lands had only recently been granted to Sir Geoffrey le Scrope, chief justice of the King's Bench. The details of John Legh II's brief criminal career do not, however, differ greatly from those of the Folvilles and the Coterels, although it is perhaps worth stressing of many such criminal bands that these were not men operating at the fringe of society, but at its very heart.[118] Legh's small affinity, as far as it can now be recognised, drew its core from his kinsmen and neighbours and was established over several years in a variety of roles. A degree of tacit acceptance in the locality is also suggested by Ardern's own somewhat equivocal role in the stewardship of Mobberley's minority and by the presence of his steward, Thomas Danyers, amongst Legh's accomplices.

To this unofficial but wholly pragmatic local approval was also added effective royal sanction, for on several occasions both Legh and Chetulton had been able to escape the legal consequences of their actions as a result of pardons granted in return for military service.[120] Despite the character of his early career, Sir John Legh II soon appreciated the virtue of legal guile built on the initial advantage of brute force, and in the years following his father's death in 1333 he appears to have exercised a close control of local society. During the trailbaston hearings of 1353, which had quickly become a forum for complaints against peculation and maintenance, he had paid a fine of £20 for all the crimes presented against him, none of which as a result appear in the record; but in the following year Laurence Mobberley complained in a case of novel disseisin that he could not have serjeanty or panel 'save of the men of the hundred in which the lands are situated, some of whom are Sir John [Legh]'s kinsmen, leagued with him or free tenants of the Duke of Lancaster and at Sir John [Legh]'s mercy, he being the earl's steward in those parts'.[121] It is an assertion which provides a convincing paradigm of the nature of Cheshire society in the later middle ages, but the conflict of the Legh and Mobberley families is important also because its course can be seen to have had a clear and demonstrable connection with the military retinues of Sir Ralph Mobberley.

William Mobberley's widow attempted unsuccessfully to cite her husband's murderers before the county court and to retain custody of lands held in socage from Sir John Ardern, but she was quickly remarried, first to John Boydell of Lymm and latterly to John Domville of Mobberley, and eventually outlived her son.[122] Ardern had granted the wardship and marriage of the heir to John son of Robert Pulford, and retained possession of the estate himself as late as 1337.[123] Much of the detail remains obscure, but it seems likely that Ralph Mobberley was poorly served by his peers. Lands on the periphery of the estate were soon detached and recovered only after protracted legal dispute.[124] Of his two known wives, one immediately granted a life interest in her estate and lands to Sir John Legh II, and the other makes only a brief appearance in a deed of 1347. Mobberley himself later denied any legitimate issue of these unions, and in his will preferred the heirs of his two sisters.[125] During his lifetime he rarely appears as a charter witness, exercised no local office, and made few if any additions to his lands. The impact of the minority on the position of the family in local society had been little short of disastrous, and following Sir Ralph's own death disputes over the inheritance were directed only at the carcase of the estate; the reality of social command which had been William Mobberley's was long since exercised elsewhere. In the final years of the century, as Richard II looked towards those who exercised that role in the Cheshire local communities, his patronage fell inevitably on John Legh IV of Booths.[126] Nevertheless, Sir Ralph Mobberley had been among that small group of knights and esquires retained in London in July 1355, and had presumably already played some role in the development of the Prince's military lordship. Indeed, in Gascony during the campaign of 1355/56 and thereafter until his death at the siege of Rheims, Mobberley had been among the more important of those military retainers with whose aid and counsel the Prince had mobilised the resources of his lordship in Cheshire.[127] The size of his retinue cannot be explained solely in terms of the strength of the Prince's commission, and indeed detailed study of its composition confirms it as being intelligible only within the context of relationships in local society.[128] In that society there were those like Legh who might trade military service for the pardon of domestic crimes, or like his son James Legh who might as the occasion demanded follow in the service of their lord; but given the emasculated role to which Mobberley was heir, military service had for him clearly provided an alternative career.[129] He remained, of course, a significant landowner whose position might attract the service of men in the locality, but he rewarded that service with the profit of comital patronage and measured his standing in the company of the Prince's familiars.

In the months before his departure on the campaign of 1355 Sir Ralph Mobberley conveyed his lands to a group of feoffees who were to allow him to re-enter them 'on his return in peace' or, in the event of his death, to fulfil the terms of an enfeoffment-to-use. Beyond a small number of annuities, the greater part of the estate was to be divided between his two closest kinsmen, John Leycester and John Domville jr.[130] The arrangement was repeated for the king's campaign in 1359, although on this occasion Sir Ralph died of a sickness before Rheims during the siege of 1360. Thereafter the dispute over land in the Mobberley area reached a new and more violent pitch, although the management of the conflict does in fact also illustrate the variety of responses by which local society sought to maintain a state of peace. In the enfeoffment of 1359 Mobberley had granted the whole of his inheritance to his nephew and fellow soldier, John Leycester, thus ignoring the claims of his brother-in-law and a daughter, Margaret Chadderton, whom 'he held not to be his daughter'.[131] In the months following Ralph's death, Leycester was subject to assault, first by John Boydell of Lymm, and later by Hugh Chadderton and John Domville, who had assembled a large company (larger, it should be said, than many which had fought in the Prince's service in Gascony) and had ejected Leycester from the manor house at Mobberley.[132] Summoned before the Prince's council in London, where it was observed that the Prince had full knowledge of Leycester's 'lawful and ancient entry, and Hugh's later entry by main force', Chadderton agreed to submit his claim to a grand assize, each party nominating eight jurors.[133] Much of the evidence assembled by

Leycester is known, and it included Mobberley's last will, recorded in an affidavit of Sir John Wingfield, who was present at Rheims 'in the beginning of the sickness', and the legal opinions of three friars.[134]

It was with some irony therefore that the verdict of the jurors upheld the claims of the heir; a judgement to which Leycester responded by murdering Hugh Chadderton at Coventry in the following year.[135] He was released into the custody of Thomas Stathum, the Prince's yeoman and an executor of Mobberley's will, under a recognisance of £2,000, but was soon able to attract the intervention of Edward III himself. Having already obtained the support of the earl's tenants-in-chief, among them the Duke of Lancaster and the Earl of Salisbury, the king was persuaded to lend his authority to a writ of right against the judgement of the first assize.[136] Thereafter a somewhat fragile peace was maintained until the close of the reign when John Domville, who was then in possession of the estate, was taken under the Prince's protection and later warned by the vicar of Mobberley church to strengthen his manor house against the threat from his enemies which was 'greater than ever before these hours'.[137] On this occasion, however, the dispute was settled without recourse to violence when a group of local gentry assembled at Knutsford in a public adjuration of the case and Domville agreed to buy out Leycester's claims on the manor.[138] Two years later he had consolidated his hold on the estate by acquiring the interests of Robert Grosvenor, whilst agreeing to maintain covenants established in the will of Sir Ralph Mobberley under which a chaplain was provided to sing perpetually for the soul of William Mobberley, whose murder in 1326 had initiated the feud.[139] It is a convincing epitaph to a period during which a single career had maintained a consistent and pervasive influence on local society.

The various disputes which occupy the history of the Mobberley estate in the early fourteenth century illustrate an established pattern of social behaviour which bore little relationship to military service; indeed the experience of warfare can be seen to have played only a transient role in local society. The issue of pardons in return for service and the intermittent effect of patronage exercised by the crown and the nobility in favour of their military servants were plainly among those factors which undermined the effectiveness of comital justice, although it should be stressed that the courts were seldom the sole arbiters of relationships in the community. The rewards of military service were often a minor element in the success of families like the Leghs of Booths, whose ambitions and disputes had a momentum independent of the chronology of campaigns in the Hundred Years War. Contemporaries were, however, clear about the causes of the county's level of violence, for, as Thomas Walsingham observed 'because of their fickleness the people of those parts are more ready and accustomed to doing such things; because of former wars and local disputes they more readily resort to arms'.[140] The mentality of the county may then indeed have been conditioned by that of an earlier border society, but the behaviour of the Cheshire gentry, although 'unfashionable' in its chronic violence, at least showed evidence of attempts to maintain order on the basis of a consensus among the *élite* of county society. During the same period the privileged viewpoint of the courts provides a picture of increasing maintenance and deepening corruption. It is apparent that whilst military service held a significant role in the development of local society, its characteristics are not to be delineated by crude notions of causal relationships between war and lawlessness under the lordship of the Black Prince. What has emerged from the study of a narrow section of the Cheshire gentry is the variety of individual ambition and experience in war, and it is to that concept that we must now turn.

IV. THE PRINCIPALITY OF AQUITAINE AND THE DEVELOPMENT OF THE MILITARY COMMUNITY

Between 1362 and 1371 the county of Chester had been part of a lordship on which were imposed the twin burdens of war finance and military service.[141] The profits and resources of that lordship in Cheshire and Cornwall, no less than in Aquitaine, were devoted to the maintenance of a court at Bordeaux which sought to compete with those at London, Paris and Avignon. It was also a court, as its most eloquent apologist, the Chandos Herald, reminds us, that was geared for war. The fortunes of that court and its involvement in Spain were the concern of the Prince's 'subjects' throughout his dominions, and in the county of Cheshire we may consider the extent and character of those burdens of finance and military service placed upon the community. In a limited sense the period offers an opportunity to assess the impact of war in a local society.

The creation of the Principality of Aquitaine in July 1362 was not merely the recognition of the territorial gains of the treaty of Brétigny and of the personal status of the king's eldest son. At the same time it represented a response to the growing burdens of war finance in a period when the defence of Gascony had become a regular charge on the incomes of the English exchequer. During the period of heightened military activity between 1348 and 1361 some £86,227 had been paid to the Constable of Bordeaux, the duchy's chief financial official, and even in years of comparative peace the annual cost of garrisons had become an onerous burden. Thereafter, English financial administration was marked by a series of experiments, both in Ireland and Gascony, under which the responsibility for defence was moved from the exchequer to the regions themselves.[142] The independence of provincial France which the rule of the Black Prince was to sustain and strengthen was to be self-financing, and indeed beyond the initial cost of equipping the Prince's retinue there were to be few liveries of money from the English royal exchequer to Bordeaux during his principate.[143]

The creation of the Principality had endowed the Prince with lands which overshadowed his English possessions, and established a lordship which, taken as a whole, stretched from the estuary of the Mersey to the Rouergue. In a series of ceremonies, beginning in July 1363 at the cathedral of St André in Bordeaux, the Black Prince received the homage of 1,747 lords and towns throughout the Principality.[144] The rule of Edward of Woodstock was to be no mere lieutenancy, but a lordship of men and land: a lordship, moreover, which would brook no liberty or franchise, and which recognised no judicial or territorial limitations within its boundary. In the Rouergue, an area which had not figured in the itinerary of 1363, the first action of the English seneschal, Sir Thomas Wettenhall of Dorfold, was to order the erection of the Prince's arms at the gates of Millau and Rodez. Like the public ceremony of homage, it was to be a firm and permanent reminder of the mastery under which the region lay.[145]

While these lands, both in England and in Aquitaine, were characterised by a wide diversity of custom and administrative practice, all were subject to a greater or lesser degree to the political and military ambitions of the Black Prince. These ambitions centred increasingly on the Principality and Spain. The Principality itself bore the brunt of demands for finance and manpower, but few even of the peripheral areas of the Prince's dominions could hope to escape those demands. It is a point which is made forcibly enough in a surviving memorandum from the Prince's council to Sir John Delves of Doddington, who was acting as governor of the Prince's business in 1363. This memorandum represents a single act of lordship in which the concern of the Prince's council moved inexorably from pardons granted in Wales and Cheshire to arrangements made for the Prince's arrival at Bordeaux and enquiries into the ravages of the Free Companies in the Limousin.[146]

It was, however, a lordship that foundered in the aftermath of an ill-judged campaign in support of Pedro I of Castile, on the cumulative

The principality of Aquitaine

financial deficit of the Prince's administration and the collapse of his taxation policy of 1368/9. That failure was underlined and indeed exemplified in the conduct of campaigns undertaken in defence of the Principality during 1369 and 1370. Even before the appeal of the count of Armagnac to the *parlement* of Paris in June 1368 there had been clear indications of a resumption of hostilities in south-west France with the progress of attacks on the Rouergue by Henry of Trastamara, the Castilian usurper, and the activities of mercenary companies in the Périgord. Charles V of France had himself been implicated as early as October 1367 when he retained Jean d'Armagnac, the count's son, with 1,000 men-at-arms and a similar number of auxiliaries, 900 of whom were recruited among the subjects of the Prince's lordship in the Gascon companies.[147] In response to this and further adverse developments in the military situation, the Prince had organised the raising of retinues in England which ultimately found service in Poitou. Elsewhere, however, the Rouergue, the Quercy, parts of the Agenais and the Périgord had been witness to numerous attacks and sieges of a type which would mark the conduct of war over the next decade, and which in 1369 struck a mortal blow at the Prince's lordship in Aquitaine. Without the ultimate sanction of military power and force, men throughout the Principality withdrew from their lord and acknowledged the sovereignty of Charles V.[148]

The first half of the fourteenth century in England saw the growth and elaboration of a national system of public finance based upon the insistent pressure of warfare and which grew from the military and political ambitions of successive kings. From the interplay of interests between the crown and the lords and commons in parliament, and out of the experience of frequent crises over taxation, there developed the characteristic institutions of the early modern state. Within that polity, however, the commons had secured recognition of claims which served to mitigate the effects of war finance and purveyance within the local communities.[149] It is apparent, however, that royal demands, and in particular the taking of subsidies in successive years, often in combination with purveyance, had pressed heavily upon the resources of the peasant population as well as exercising a cumulative influence on economic development.[150] Although the social and geographical incidence of those demands varied widely, few counties could hope to escape from them to the extent that was possible in Cheshire as a result of its independent 'palatine' status.[151] For much of the later middle ages the county is not known to have contributed to parliamentary taxes on the laity, nor indeed was it represented in the commons of the medieval

English parliament. Thus far it was a liberty shared with the March of Wales.

Here, however, a form of lay taxation had developed in response to the pressure of Marcher lordship and appears as an irregular series of aids, gifts, and subsidies exacted in recognition of the lord's superiority or recent succession. Such casual revenues assumed an increasing importance in the income of Marcher lords during the fourteenth century and reached levels comparable to parliamentary taxes.[152] Although a similar development may be followed in Cheshire, the county is not known to have granted or paid such subsidies before 1346. For perhaps as long as fifty years Cheshire had to a large extent been insulated against both the burdens of war finance and the pressures of an aggressive and masterful lordship. It is ironic that an area which is reputed to have been highly militarised should, in that respect alone, have been so protected from the impact of war upon the civilian population.

The relationship of the earldom to the crown as the customary endowment of the king's eldest son had perpetuated and supported the traditions of 'palatine' independence which were asserted with some success against occasional and unwarranted demands for military service.[153] But whereas the independence of the March was dynamic and the product of a developing lordship, in Cheshire it remained an expression of political inertia. From 1301 to 1344 the county was isolated by the successive minorities of Edward of Caernarfon, Edward of Windsor, and Edward of Woodstock, punctuated only by brief periods of royal control which had failed to establish a pattern of comital taxation. In a situation of almost permanent minority, unmatched on few noble estates, the resources of comital lordship were weakened and diminished to the advantage of the local gentry who usurped the leadership of local society.

The long rule of the Black Prince from 1333 to 1376 marks the development of a quality of lordship which had long been absent from the county, and it is in this context that one must view increasingly strident demands for revenue raised on a variety of pretexts or the scale of *Quo Warranto* enquiries during the 1360s.[154] The Prince visited the county on only two occasions, but his was nonetheless a lordship which aimed to be both masterful and enduring, a lordship, moreover, which was firmly geared to the pursuit of military ambitions. As a result, the emergence of a system of public finance in the county was even more obviously related to the exigencies of warfare. In 1346 a mise of £1,000 was granted by the 'community' of Cheshire explicitly 'in aid of his [the Prince's] great expenses in furthering the king's war'. In the event, however, that sum proved extraordinarily difficult to collect. In April 1347 the council reported that no money had yet been received, and in May writs addressed to the hundred of Macclesfield were returned with an endorsement that the coroners had been unable to collect the amounts due within the lordship.[155] Although the success of comital lordship might, as we have already seen, fall below the level of its ambitions, its progress is made apparent in the increasing profitability of the county which had virtually doubled the income of the earl by 1360.[156] The greater part of the increase since 1301, of the order of perhaps £2,000 per annum, came as a consequence of a growing range of novel and arbitrary exactions of a type that mark a domineering and expansive lordship. In 1347 a forest eyre was held for the first time, in 1353 the community of the county offered 5,000 marks for the redemption of a general eyre, and in 1357 the Wirral and Delamere forests offered a fine of £3,000 for the redemption of a second forest eyre.[157] There can be little doubt that the Prince's continuing involvement in the French war had acted as a catalyst in the development of his lordship in Cheshire, for although the king's exchequer was by this date almost wholly responsible for the financing of continental expeditions, warfare remained the principal avenue of lordly expenditure. The payment of annuities and rewards and the provision of uniforms and equipment had all to be set against the value of liveries from the exchequer and the profits of lordship: a relationship which, in the Prince's career, seldom approached a balance. In 1362 he borrowed £1,000 from the Earl of Arundel as a result of 'great need of money for the equipment of himself and his men for the coming expedition to Gascony'.[158] The continuing inadequacy of the Prince's income and the particular circumstances of the Principality of Aquitaine after 1363 had placed a heavier and more enduring burden upon the lordships of Edward of Woodstock than upon those of other magnates.

As we have suggested, the Principality of Aquitaine was expected to be financially independent of the English exchequer, and although Edward III himself invested heavily in his son's rule from the profits of King John's ransom, the Prince was forced largely to rely upon the income of his own lordship. Here the summary account of Richard Fillongley reveals a steady increase of income throughout the Principality of Aquitaine which, in the same manner as Cheshire twenty years earlier, felt the renewed weight of lordly rule.[159] The urge for display in the organisation of the court and the defence of the Principality did, however, bring a corresponding increase in the costs of that rule. The development of the crisis in Aquitaine is well established in the work of French historians, although it is not generally recognised that the Prince's financial demands fell with equal weight upon his English lands. In 1369, at the same time as the Estates met at Angoulême to vote the *fouage*, the 'community' of Cheshire had granted a subsidy of 2,500 marks payable over two years, and in 1373 it added a 'gift' of 3,000 marks.[160] The Prince's subjects in Cheshire, no less than in Gascony, were asked to subsidise the financial deficit of the Spanish campaign of 1367, and the events of 1368 to 1370 in this sense exemplify the unity of the Prince's lordship in England and Aquitaine. In England the development of the casual revenues of the earldom of Chester had taken place over two decades earlier under the rising pressure of the Prince's military ambitions, reaching a peak during the defence of the Principality of Aquitaine. In 1369 almost the entire yield of the subsidy levied from Cheshire was accounted for by wages of war paid to men-at-arms and archers raised in Cheshire for service in Aquitaine, although the Cheshire revenues had in fact long been dominated by the Prince's military commitments.[161]

In the chamberlain's account for 1361 – 2 annuities payable at the Chester exchequer amounted to some £350, for the most part grants of minor offices and small incomes to the lesser members of the Prince's affinity such as his tailor and baker.[162] In 1369 the payment of annuities reached a level of over £1,500, many of them as a result of indentures of retinue entered into during the early years of the Principality.[163] The escalation began at Plymouth in 1363 during the muster of troops for the retinue in Aquitaine, and continued during its service at Bordeaux on a scale which had not marked the Prince's earlier campaigns.[164] For almost a decade the resources of comital favour, the payment of fees and the grant of offices, were governed to an unprecedented degree by considerations of military service in Aquitaine. Robert Mascy received a pardon for abducting the daughter of John Snelson because 'he is in our service'; and Roger Swetenham, John Eton and Roger Page received grants of money, land and minor office, as archers in the Prince's service; and military service clearly determined the grant of pensions and offices to many others.[165] Of the grants enrolled at the Chester exchequer between 1362 and 1369 perhaps as many as 70 per cent may be considered to have been based upon similar considerations.

Of greater significance, the majority of the larger annuities were paid to members of the retinue with little or no demonstrable connection with the county, an arrangement which suggests that the running costs of the retinue in Aquitaine were being paid, at least in part, from the issues of the county of Chester. Sir Robert Neville, whose annuity of 100 marks was paid at Chester in 1361 until he could be found an income elsewhere, had by 1365 deputed his brother, the archdeacon of Cornwall, to act as his treasurer of war in collecting his fee at Chester.[166] In 1367 five life annuities of £40 were granted in return for service in Spain, and by 1369 as many as twenty-five annuities had been granted to men who are known to have been serving in Aquitaine.[167] In the short term not merely were the augmented profits of lordship in the county carried elsewhere, but military service had become increasingly a privileged point, often the sole and necessary point, of access to comital patronage and largesse. When John Holford petitioned the Prince for an office in Newcastle-under-Lyme, and an unknown Cheshireman pleaded for a pardon for the murder of Kenrik of Wirswall, they did so on the basis of service 'in Spain, Guyenne, Brittany and Gascony', as men who had followed their lord.[168] Such claims, from men who had served the Prince, would persist well into the reign of Richard II, when as many as eight annuities granted during the period of the Principality were still being drawn on the Chester exchequer.[169]

In a real and obvious manner the years of the Principality of Aquitaine had brought Cheshire firmly within the orbit of war finance, to which the county had previously been reluctantly and only fitfully exposed. Elsewhere in England the tax on wool exports had become the only regular peace-time levy, and during the period 1362 to 1370 there was no direct taxation of the laity for the needs of war. In a decade of peace, therefore, the county of Chester had for the first time felt the full impact of war.

No small part of this impact had resulted from the recruitment of troops by the Prince, and the levels of manpower demand in Cheshire have already been the subject of extensive comment.[170] In considering the significance of the period of the Principality, however, it is not simply the fact of military service in which we are interested (although the level of recruitment within an essentially agrarian economy was clearly of vital importance) but rather the social context of that service. In a sense the question has already been posed by the experience of Sir Ralph Mobberley, and we need now to know which groups in society formed the military community, and why and under what circumstances they served in the military campaigns of the Black Prince.

As we are concerned with the foundation of a tradition of military service, it has seemed prudent to give attention to a later campaign; and, indeed, of those campaigns mounted in the Principality, that in Poitou during the spring and the summer of 1369 is already known to Cheshire historians from the evidence of a heraldic dispute in 1385.[171] In the most celebrated case heard in the court of chivalry in the fourteenth century, many of the witnesses in favour of the Cheshire knight, Sir Robert Grosvenor, recalled a common bond of service with Sir James Audley '*a Blank* [le Blanc] *en Berry, et al gayne del tour de Brose* [Brux], *et a Issouden* [Issoudon] *et al siège de Rochsirion* [La Roche-sur-Yon] *en Payto*'.[172] The memory of that campaign in Poitou in 1369 was perhaps sharpened by common experience of the recent expedition of Richard II in Scotland during which many had indeed seen Sir Robert Grosvenor bear the arms *azure bend or*, possession of which was then disputed by the Yorkshire knight, Sir Richard Scrope. Earlier campaigns make only a limited appearance in the testimony of the witnesses, for by the 1380s death had greatly thinned the ranks of survivors from Crécy and Poitiers, although several still recalled 'Edward III's last French voyage' in 1359. It is clear, however, that these martial recollections reached a wide and sympathetic audience in local gentry society where the experience of warfare was widespread. The moment when '*dominus Princeps et alii magnates regni Angliae extiterunt ultime cum exercitu suo in regno Franciae*, like the *prima pestilencia*, was instantly recognisable to local jurors, a point as fixed and well known in secular chronology as saints' days.[173] Both events illustrate the formation of a collective memory of already distant campaigns under the impact of another, the Scottish campaign of 1385, which appeared to follow in the same tradition.

In another sense the Scrope/Grosvenor hearings stand as a spontaneous demonstration of a class unity in Cheshire which suggests the operation of a community in a form which is readily apparent to historians.[174] The forms of social cohesion which bound together such local and regional communities are well known, and find confirmation in the evidence of the Mobberley region where we have already identified a wide spectrum of inter-personal relationship based upon a common experience in local society. What has hitherto seemed less intelligible, at least in Cheshire, is the way in which these forms appear to find expression in a high level of commitment to military service.

In part of his testimony in the Scrope/Grosvenor case, Sir Hugh Browe of Tushingham observed that, although he had been armed for twenty years, he could not offer evidence as to the justice of Scrope's claim because he had only served 'during the war in the garrisons and companies in France, and never on the great expeditions'.[175] It was not the fact of military service that was important, but his participation in, or absence from, musters which had a clear social context. In his evidence for Grosvenor, Browe recorded that he had seen him armed in Poitou eighteen years before and again in Scotland in 1385.[176] Within the context of Cheshire society, it was these campaigns which formed the common strand in the military experience of the local gentry. Browe's long service, like that of Sir Hugh Calveley, had taken him outside the confines of local society. The 'great expeditions' to which he referred, and, we may suspect, those of Crécy and Poitiers, exemplify a universal obligation of military service within the county which was neither a muster of tenantry nor, in the contractual sense, the service of an indentured retinue. In Cheshire military service grew from the imposition of a widespread and masterful personal lordship.

In Cheshire, it seems, military service rested upon a personal lordship which underpinned the ordinary recruitment of troops by indenture or was motivated by the promise of pay, rewards or pardons. Furthermore, the leadership of gentry society in peace also provided, within the compass of the great campaigns, its leadership in war. Warfare in that respect simply represented a continuation of established social forms, within which military service was perhaps a conventional experience for the Cheshire gentry. Even in the 1350s, however, the experience of Sir Ralph Mobberley had established a variation from the norm, and certainly by 1385 the career of Sir Hugh Browe had clearly differed in both form and content from that of many of his contemporaries for whom military service may have been an isolated adventure. There is, therefore, a clear need to measure the assumptions of the Scrope/Grosvenor evidence against the records of military service during both the period of the Principality of Aquitaine and earlier.

The escape from the battle of Nájera of the Castilian usurper, Henry of Trastamara, had had immediate consequences in the Principality where Henry's secret treaty with the Duke of Anjou had led to attacks on the Prince's lordship in the Rouergue as early as June 1367.[177] The significance of the breakdown of the peace of Brétigny and the scale of renewed hostilities with France became more clearly apparent during the spring and early summer of 1368, following the appeal of the Count of Armagnac to Charles V. Almost immediately, however, the Prince had undertaken the raising of reinforcements in England which mustered at Northampton in the autumn. The progress of recruitment remains obscure. John Montviron, who was serving as marshal of the Prince's household in Gascony, appears to have supervised arrays held by the justice and chamberlain of North Wales in the early part of 1369.[178] It seems likely that recruitment in Cheshire, however, had been the responsibility of the justice and chamberlain of Chester, perhaps with the assistance of the Seneschal of the Rouergue,

Sir Thomas Wettenhall.[179] More significantly, the retinue proved to be largely a muster of the Prince's lordships, for the royal exchequer had persisted in its notions of military and financial independence for Aquitaine. A retinue led by the Earls of Pembroke and Cambridge which joined the Prince does not appear to have been large, was paid by the exchequer, and was therefore omitted from the Northampton muster roll.[180] This, therefore, was a document of the Prince's household, which retained responsibility for the payment of wages and rewards. Edward III is known to have delivered some £26,000 to the Prince from the ransom of King John in June 1369, some of which may have reached the retinue, but at least £700 and possibly the whole subsidy of 2,500 marks raised in Cheshire appear as wages of war.[181] In military and financial terms the burden of the defence of the Principality fell essentially on the resources of the Prince's lordships in England and Aquitaine.

The Prince's retinue which mustered at Northampton in September 1369 included 369 men-at-arms and 428 archers, of whom 101 men-at-arms and 240 archers were raised in Cheshire and North Wales.[182] Eleven members of the retinue, including Sir Robert Grosvenor, appear as witnesses in the heraldic dispute of 1385, and the service of a further six may be assigned to the campaign which had preceded the battle of Poitiers.[183] Here, therefore, is that tradition of service on the 'great expeditions' suggested in the later testimonies before the court of chivalry. For the most part the remainder of the retinue consisted of men whose association with the Prince was of long duration; many had earlier returned from Nájera and service in the Principality, and as many as eleven held annuities drawn on the exchequer at Chester.[184] The retinue was, therefore, a muster of the Prince's permanent retainers bolstered from his lordship in Cheshire and North Wales. In a limited sense it was a 'Cheshire retinue', raised or at least financed largely from within the county whose contributions to warfare had seldom before reached such proportions. It is not difficult to imagine why for these reasons, if not for those of military success, the campaign retained a hold on the popular imagination.

Protections granted to the retinue are recorded during the late autumn and winter of 1368, although it did not finally reach the Principality until April 1369. The reasons for the delay remain a matter for speculation, but were clearly vital to the survival of the Prince's lordship in Aquitaine. The best account is given in an anonymous newsletter written in March 1369 which describes the impact of French attacks during the year.[185] Since Christmas 'the news had all been bad', and the pressure of the French had kept so many of the Prince's men to their castles that he could not raise an army in the field to meet the threat. The Rouergue and the Quercy were already both all but lost, and Jean de Mauquenchy and Louis de Sancerre were about to enter the Périgord. 'The war is open and the French have already dealt such a blow to the Principality that we shall not be able to recover for a long time'; the tone of despair is punctuated only by astonishment that the greater part of the men-at-arms and archers who had come from England at Christmas had yet to arrive.

Although Sir Thomas Wettenhall and many of the Prince's permanent retainers had left England in the autumn of 1368 and served in the Principality in the campaigns of the winter and spring,[186] the greater part of the retinue which mustered at Northampton, including most of those troops raised in Cheshire, did not in fact reach the Principality until March 1369, under the leadership of the Earls of Pembroke and Cambridge.[187] In the event, many found service with Audley and Chandos on a *chevauchée* through Poitou and Saintonge, the route of which can be identified from Froissart's narrative and the testimony of the Scrope and Grosvenor witnesses. According to the witnesses for Grosvenor, Audley's ride had reached to within twenty miles of Bourges, after taking the castle at Brux as a reprisal against the lord of Chauvigny. Later in the year many were present at the siege of La Roche-sur-Yon where the castellan, Jean Bellon, is reported to have betrayed the castle to the English, and a few witnesses recollected events at Belle Perche early in 1370.[188] It is evident, however, that at least a fair number of Cheshiremen had already returned to England, for at the county court at Chester in December 1369 twelve men-at-arms and forty-four archers were indicted for deserting the army without licence.[189]

That part of the retinue which had been raised in Cheshire appears on the Northampton muster roll in three separate groupings: a group of five esquires described as the leaders of seventy archers chosen in Cheshire; a group of seven knights, each with a small number of men-at-arms, but leading three companies of forty archers each; and finally a group of individual men-at-arms. Four of that second group had served at Poitiers, two as leaders of archers and a third as a deputy. It is likely that, as in earlier campaigns, those four companies of archers represent contributions from the hundreds of Macclesfield, Nantwich, Broxton and Bucklow, raised through an obligation of service to the Prince in those areas where the leaders were important land- or office-holders. In the event those recruited in Macclesfield appear to have joined Wettenhall in the Rouergue before Christmas 1368, while the other companies eventually found service in Poitou.[190]

However they were employed, the question which remains to be answered is to what extent these brief excursions into military service in response to the sporadic demands of the Prince present an accurate picture of the military community in Cheshire and of the impact of war upon the civilian population. Any analysis which concentrates on the 'great expeditions' of Crécy, Poitiers, or the campaigns of 1359 or 1369 may well amount to only a partial selection of military activity on the part of men from the county. The nature of these campaigns, in so far as they represent the military experience of the whole of local society under the lordship of the Prince, may fundamentally distort our view of the character of military service in Cheshire. In short, to what tradition, if any, did the service of Sir Thomas Wettenhall and Sir Hugh Browe belong?

In 1363, as the Prince prepared to visit his new lordship in Aquitaine, the justice of Chester has been ordered to array 200 archers in the county under the leadership of a group of knights and esquires.[191] Similar demands, it seems, were made in the Duchy of Cornwall where the Prince himself was prior to his departure from Plymouth.[192] It seems likely, however, that a substantial part of that whole retinue was disbanded before it had reached the Principality, perhaps even before it had mustered.[193] The reasons were both military and political. Since 1347 Gascon troops had been organised along English lines, with retinues recruited for limited periods of military emergency replacing the permanently garrisoned infantry troops which had characterised an earlier period in the duchy's military history.[194] The importance of these Gascon retinues has been overshadowed by the *chevauchées* of 1346 and 1355 – 1357, although between then and 1361 the greater part of the defensive actions in the duchy were undertaken by a group of some ninety-nine Gascon captains who recruited from among their own feudal dependents. That group also formed the core of the local political community, and up to 50 per cent of the homages received by the Prince at the cathedral of Saint André came from that section of the Gascon nobility.[195] Clearly there was little need for the Prince to be accompanied by the kind of retinue which had been raised for an offensive campaign in France, and that which crossed the channel in 1363 was a personal entourage rather than an English garrison.

The loss of records relating to the Prince's lordship in both Aquitaine and Cheshire tends to obscure the importance of service in the Principality for many members of local society in the county.[196] This is in part made good by the issue of letters of protection enrolled either on the Gascon rolls or the 'recognisance' rolls of the Chester exchequer which identify those serving abroad. At the same time, because of the nature of service in Aquitaine where there was an increasing spate of renewals of letters of protection, there was some awareness of a special problem which such service posed for the operation of law and order in Cheshire and in some instances, therefore, letters were enrolled on the Chester plea rolls alongside cases the hearing of which they automatically suspended.[197] The yield from such sources is, of course, far from comprehensive but, nevertheless, suggests that service in France on a semi-permanent basis had assumed an increasing importance in the period after the creation of the Principality. The evidence is perhaps less than clear-cut but the experience of John Jodrell may not have been untypical of the lesser soldiery in the county. He had served initially on the first *chevauchée* of the Prince in Gascony in 1355, deserting after the return to Bordeaux only to reappear among the reinforcements raised in Cheshire in the spring of 1356.[198] At Poitiers he shared in the day's spoils, picking up a silver salt-cellar belonging to King John which was later bought by the Prince for £8.[199] As a younger son, however, the opportunities for advancement in local society were limited and military service had perhaps suggested itself as an alternative career. He makes a final appearance in Cheshire in a deed of 1362.[200] In 1376, now describing himself as 'Jean Joudrell de Peytowe', he petitioned John of Gaunt and the council for help in raising a ransom of 1,000 francs to secure his release from the custody of Guillaume de Mareuil.[201] Jodrell claimed in his petition to have lost horses, men, goods, houses and rents during the campaigns in Poitou, which had left him without the means to effect his own ransom; losses which nonetheless show the advantages of war gained through service in the Principality and the winning of a landed status that might have eluded him had he remained in Cheshire.

Isolated references of this nature, whether in the form of indentures, petitions or protections, only rarely establish the duration of rewards of the military service performed by Cheshire men when in the Principality. In the administration of the Rouergue and the service of *routier* captains during the Breton civil war, long and unbroken periods of service do, however, figure in the surviving documentation. In May 1365 the Gascon seneschal of the Rouergue, Amanieu de Foussat, was replaced by the Cheshire knight, Sir Thomas Wettenhall, who undertook the organisation of the Prince's lordship.[202] A younger son of Sir John Wettenhall of Dorfold, he is known to have served in Gascony under Sir James Audley of Heighley in 1345, and under the duke of Clarence in Ireland in 1361.[203] The historian of the Rouergue, Abbé Rouquette, suggested that the Prince's rule was here undermined by 'the seneschal and a group of avaricious knights': an opinion that may earlier have been shared by Pope Urban V, whose own Gevaudan origins make a series of petititons to the Prince concerning the exactions of Wettenhall and his retinue an important 'local' source.[204] Whatever the opportunities for peculation, the greater part of that retinue was recruited among the local nobility and eventually found service in September 1366 on the Prince's Spanish expedition.

The defence and administration of the region had fallen to another Cheshireman, David Cradock, who was faced after October 1367 by an escalation of military activity culminating in opposition to the campaign of the duke of Anjou in 1369. Wettenhall had returned from England, where he had been raising troops for the defence of the Principality in December 1368, by which time the situation in the Rouergue was already critical. By March 1369 the anonymous newsletter was unsure whether Wettenhall had been 'captured' or 'killed' in an ambush near Villeneuve, and observed that his lieutenant, David Cradock, had been besieged for over six weeks.[205] The details of a rapidly worsening situation can be recovered from the accounts of the *consuls boursiers* of Millau which report the itinerary of the seneschal, Cradock, and the castellan of Millau, James Mascy.[206] Beyond a small core of English men-at-arms and archers, including the seventy raised in Cheshire, the seneschal was dependent on the faltering resources of lordship in the Rouergue where the pace of defections to the Duke of Anjou had already quickened. A brief and largely unsuccessful campaign following the siege of Compeyre ended during the pursuit of the Count of Vendôme in September 1369. Wettenhall was mortally wounded at Montlaur and carried to a nearby house where he died. The *consuls* organised a remembrance service at Millau in October, less than a week after they had received the sealed opinions of fourteen legists from the university of Bologna on the sovereignty of Aquitaine.[207] The town formally submitted to the sovereignty of Charles V at Rodez in November, although Cradock and his family did not finally leave under a safe-conduct until February 1370.[208]

Others of those who had served during the period of the Principality had not done so as members of the Prince's permanent retinue or as officials in the provincial administration, but in the Free Companies in Brittany, Spain and Poitou. It seems likely not only that these companies were the remnants of earlier campaigns, associations of mercenaries bent upon corporate gain, but that their emergence can be related to a crisis in political authority between 1360 and 1369.[209] Many were those whose service and ambitions went beyond the resources of the Prince's lordship in Aquitaine, and for whom the continuance of conflicts in Brittany and the decay of political authority elsewhere offered prospects of further employment. The springs of their service were simply those of a general commitment to warfare on a semi-permanent basis; those for whom military service had become a career – often, it should be said, an alternative career. This is clearly suggested by the ease with which most were reabsorbed into the traditional military milieu after 1369, finding service in the long rearguard action in defence of English lordship in Aquitaine.[210] In Cheshire the most notable although by no means unique example is provided by the career of Sir Hugh Calveley, whose experience is repeated in the case of a number of lesser known captains.

Among those who are known to have served in Brittany were a number of Cheshiremen including two routier captains, Sir David Hulgreve and John Norbury, both of whom received quittances from Duke John IV in 1368.[211] Hulgreve later reappears in the campaigns in Poitou, first in the garrison of Montcontour, and later at Niort and Chizé where he was captured and ransomed by Du Guesclin.[212] Norbury's presence is not again reported until 1377 when he appears as captain of Libourne.[213] The origins of many of the garrison captains in Gascony during this period do suggest, however, a continuing commitment to warfare among certain sections of the Cheshire gentry which had survived the decay of the Prince's lordship in Aquitaine. In 1373 at least six garrisons were led by Cheshire captains, including that at Derval held by Sir Hugh Browe '*et ses frères*'.[214]

The 'great expeditions' had seen musters of men whose ambitions and position in local society depended on the lordship of the earl, and who therefore responded to irregular demands for military service. The gains of war might also attract the service of local gentry to particular campaigns, as in 1375 when John Leycester led a small retinue under the seneschal of Aquitaine, Sir Thomas Felton.[215] Landed disappointment and a variety of personal circumstances might underwrite the service of other captains like Sir Ralph Mobberley, but it remains true that a general commitment to military service could not easily be reconciled with the necessity of directly controlling small estates. Even among those who made a career of war, many of the 'gains' were those which could not be remitted to England.[216] It is clear that in the conduct of war there was a great variety of individual experience as between those who served regularly and those who served perhaps only once or twice during their lives, either in pursuit of ransoms or booty or in response to the demands of lordship exercised in the county. The tradition of service exemplified by the careers of Wettenhall, Cradock and Hulgreve differed greatly from that which found expression in the heraldic dispute of 1385, in which the testimony of Sir Hugh Browe had sounded a discordant note. What remains to be considered is whether this division within the military community in Cheshire may be expressed in terms other than those descriptive of the quality of martial experience, and whether it corresponds in any degree to an identifiable social stratification. Those who served in the campaign of 1369, and possibly on other occasions and those, like Sir Hugh Browe, who served in the garrisons might belong to the same social stratum, although it does seem likely that there are broad economic and social distinctions which may be drawn.

While the experience of those who served regularly holds its own intrinsic interest, we are perhaps equally concerned with the extent to which they retained links with local society. There is a clear qualitative difference between the impact of military service which merely represents a permanent loss of surplus manpower, a movement beyond the constraints and bounds of the local community, and that which serves to broaden its base and widen the experience of its membership. In that respect the example of John Jodrell is far from characteristic of the fourteenth century experience, and the ties of locality appear to have exercised a vital influence even upon those who found continuous service in the Rouergue, Brittany and Poitou.

In November 1365 Sir Thomas Wettenhall had entertained the retinue of Sir Hugh Calveley at Millau in the Rouergue on its journey to Spain to join Du Guesclin's *routier* army in the conquest of Castile. The two knights belonged to a cosmopolitan world which embraced a variety of social and political experience but, as the account of the *consul boursier* ruefully observed, the town had been burdened because *'Ugo de Carolei dizia que el era cosis del senescalc.'*[217] Within that world the importance of kinship and locality was paramount and found expression in the development of clearly identifiable military fraternities.[218] At Millau, Calveley and Wettenhall were joined by the lieutenant of the seneschal, David Cradock, whose own retinue included at least one son and an uncle, the castellan of Millau, James Mascy.[219] Few of the group, perhaps significantly, are well served by the survival of evidence of a private nature from Cheshire itself, for they were rarely drawn from amongst those who held lands of any importance; but in a small number of extant petitions Calveley's concern for the strength of kinship is made apparent. In 1365 he had petitioned the Pope from the Limousin in an attempt to secure benefices for 'three nephews and one kinsman' who were still minors.[220] In 1378 he petitioned Richard II on behalf of John Calveley, 'his nephew and others of his cousins and friends' who were then accused of an assault at Saint Asaph in support of a clerk, David Calveley, claiming the immunity of the liberty of Cheshire and recalling their service in the garrisons of Calais.[221] In the following year, yet another kinsman, Jenkin Calveley, shared in the grant of the Channel Islands as Sir Hugh's lieutenant.[222] These examples are far from unique and the demands of a kinship society and the enhancement of a military family are repeated elsewhere. In 1380 Sir David Hulgreve's retinue which served under Thomas of Woodstock had included at least three close kinsmen. In the same year a military retinue which rioted in Knutsford included four members of the Masey family and two Vernons, with others of their kin and company (*amitis et societatis*).[223] William Hulgreve had earlier served in the Principality with another brother, and in 1369 appears as a leader of those archers raised in Cheshire who may have reached the Rouergue.[224] Another member of the 1380 retinue, John Hulgreve, could later petition Richard II claiming to have fought for twenty-two years in the earl's service.[225]

Beyond the bounds of kinship lay the ties of locality, and these men shared a common social background among the landless and younger sons of the minor gentry in the Nantwich area. The opportunities in war were greater among that section of the community which could not depend on the income of inherited wealth, or access to the resources of comital patronage except through military service. Notwithstanding the widening of horizons which came from service in Spain or the Principality, these men maintained strong links with the locality, often returning to the county to recruit men for service in France. In 1380 the two surviving muster rolls of Sir David Hulgreve and Sir Hugh Calveley bear all the hallmarks of Cheshire retinues, and indeed Calveley was recruiting in the county at the moment of his death in 1393.[226]

In considering the manpower demands upon Cheshire during the period of the Principality of Aquitaine, it is apparent that military service stands as a response to a complex interplay of differing social circumstance, many of which are not yet fully explained, but which cannot be reconciled to any simplistic view of the nature of war in the later middle ages. If we are to discern those 'calculations of mutual advantage' which K. B. McFarlane felt lay at the heart of military service in the later

middle ages, we must recognise the varieties of individual experience
in warfare and set these against the important realities of local history.

Between 1360 and 1370 the county of Cheshire had for the first time
during the fourteenth century felt the full impact of war which grew from
the claims of a masterful lordship exercised by the Black Prince. Military
service had developed out of customary obligations into the provision
of indentured retinues through which the Prince captured and held the
loyalty of the uppermost of gentry affinities. In the defence of the
Principality of Aquitaine demands upon the resources of that lordship,
both in terms of finance and manpower, had reached a peak. The
insularity and independent development of the county which had
previously been based upon the insecure foundations of political inertia
and royal acquiescence now gained a surer footing in the lordship of
the earl. It is exemplified by the growing use of quasi-parliamentary
assemblies in the granting of the casual revenues of the earldom, and
in the character of military service on the 'great expeditions' which
represent the martial experience of local gentry society under the
dominion of the Prince.[227] Such service had, however, already
undergone a fundamental transformation.

In 1390 John Savage complained at the tournament of Saint-
Inglevert, as he might have done during the defence of the Principality,
that he had not crossed the sea merely to run one lance.[228] The
character of the Prince's lordship in Aquitaine and the development of
individual enterprise in warfare had stretched the bounds of the local
community to the extent that military service was no longer solely an
aspect of a vigorous lordship, but an attractive prospect for a section
of Cheshire society led by the lesser gentry who had now assumed the
command of local society at war during the later fourteenth century.
The retinue of 1369 which was later celebrated in the testimony of
witnesses before a case in the court of chivalry in 1385 marked the end
of a period of large scale musters of the Prince's lordship in Cheshire.
Thereafter it was the garrison captains such as Browe, Hulgreve,
Cradock and others who dominated the organisation of war in the
county. Their importance is understated in the written evidence of
medieval local society, swallowed up by the doings of those with land
and the misdeeds of those without it and, later on, distorted by the
romantic myth of Crécy and Poitiers. Peter Legh, for example, a leader
of archers in 1369 who was later executed by Henry IV, is commemorated on a brass of 1506 in the Legh chapel of Macclesfield church as
having fought 'at the batell of Cressie'. The reference is erroneous, but
for the antiquarians of the early modern period the great expeditions

had become synonymous with military service. Cheshire nonetheless constituted a polyhierarchial society within which the ownership of land and a nobility acquired through military service co-existed in the ordering of gentry affinities.

NOTES

[1] See for instance H.J. Hewitt, *The Organization of War under Edward III* 1966, G.L. Harriss, *King, Parliament and Public Finance in Medieval England to 1369*, 1975, and Sir Goronwy Edwards, *The Second Century of the English Parliament*, 1979, pp. 17–33.

[2] See above pp. 63 *et. seq.*

[3] See above p. 45.

[4] C47/2/34 no. 11. The archers were to be chosen in Cheshire, Englefield, Maelor Saesneg, Moldsdale, Flint and Rhuddlan.

[5] C/47/2/25 no. 12, cited in R. Nicholson, *Edward III and the Scots* 1965, p. 196. Earlier disputes had been fortuitously avoided when the port was declared empty of shipping, see SC1/16 no. 31 and SC1/33 no. 105 and Chester Record Office, Sheriff's files, writs SFW/2.

[6] *BPR*, I, pp. 110–11 (Letter dated 5 August 1347), 'whereupon the king, although owing to the Prince's negligence in the matter he might well *by reason of his superiority* grant justice to the complainants unasked, has thought fit to urge the Prince to appoint some trustworthy men.' The case, involving the diocesan jurisdiction of Chester abbey, is described by R.V.H. Burne, *The Monks of Chester*, 1962, pp. 78–81.

[7] H.J. Hewitt, *Cheshire under the Three Edwards*, 1967, pp. 17–18; Margaret Sharp, *Contributions to a History of the Earldom of Chester 1237–1399*, University of Manchester PhD, 1925, pp. 43–4.

[8] *BPR*, I, p. 29.

[9] The best study remains that of M. Sharp, 'The Central Administrative System of Edward, The Black Prince', in T.F. Tout, *Chapters in the Administrative History of Mediaeval England*, 1930, v, pp. 289–400.

[10] Sharp, *The Administrative System of the Black Prince*, p. 324, and below p. 103. Its location is unclear, see *The History of the King's Works* (ed.), H.M. Colvin, A.J. Taylor and R. Allen-Brown, 1963, p. 537.

[11] *BPR*, I, p. 34. A similar commission was perhaps addressed to the community of Cheshire, but it is not now preserved in the *Register*.

[12] *VCH (Cheshire)*, II, pp. 12, 18–19.

[13] See above pp. 69–70.

[14] *BPR*, I, p. 147.

[15] *BPR*, I, p. 67; Chester 24/2, bundle 21 Edward III. An 'aid for making the king's first born son a knight' was levied throughout England and provoked opposition on a similar scale, see Harriss, op. cit., pp. 410–12.

[16] *Accounts of the Chamberlain and Other Officers of the County of Chester, 1301–1360*, ed. R. Stewart-Brown, LCRS, lix, 1910, p. 122.

[17] B.H. Putnam, *The Place in Legal History of Sir William Shareshull*, 1950, pp. 37, 67–8; *BPR*, I, p. 137.

[18] The record of actions at Caernarfon is printed in the *Registrum Vulgariter*

ORGANISATION OF WAR 141

Nuncupatum 'The Record of Caernarvon', Record Commission 1838, pp. 133–207, discussed by G. A. Usher, 'The Black Prince's Quo Warranto', *The Welsh History Review*, 1974, pp. 1–12.

19 *VCH (Cheshire)*, II, pp. 170–1, 175; *BPR*, III, p. 298.

20 P. H. W. Booth, 'Taxation and Public Order: Cheshire in 1353', *Northern History*, xii, 1976, pp. 21–2.

21 A valor of the Prince's lands in 1376 estimated the Cheshire revenues at a little over £1,000 per annum, C47/17/22 m. 6.

22 Putnam, op. cit., pp. 73–4.

23 R. R. Davies, *Lordship and Society in the March of Wales, 1282–1400*, 1978, pp. 268–73.

24 See below pp. 193–4; J. R. Maddicott, 'The County Community and the Making of Public Opinion in Fourteenth Century England', *TRHS*, 5th Series, 28, 1978, pp. 28–32.

25 *VCH (Cheshire)*, II, pp. 15–18, 23–5; Sharp, *The Administrative System of the Black Prince*, p. 332.

26 Chester 29/65 m. 11; Booth, op. cit., pp. 25–8.

27 K. B. McFarlane, *The Nobility of Later Medieval England*, 1973, pp. 24–6, 59–60.

28 Chandos Herald, *La Vie du Prince Noir*, ed. D. B. Tyson, Beihefte zur Zeitschrift für Romanische Philologie, 147, 1975, ll. 97–9.

29 K. Fowler, *The King's Lieutenant*, 1969, pp. 49–50; *Adae Murimuth, Continuatio Chronicarum and Robertus de Avesbury, De Gestis Mirabilibus Regis Edwardi Tertii*, E. M. Thompson (ed.), Rolls Series, 1889, pp. 244–5.

30 Fowler, op. cit., p. 261 n. 46.

31 BL Additional Charters (Aston Charters), 49, 773–5; Chester 1/1 Part 1 (10).

32 SC1/54 no. 100 (letter of Bartholomew Burgherssh, Constable of Dover, to the Prince, not dated).

33 E101/25/9 m. 2; Fowler, op. cit., Appendix 1.

34 See above pp. 75–6.

35 Chester 1/1 Part 1, (17–18); G. Wrottesley, *Crécy and Calais*, 1897, pp. 76–80.

36 Chester 29/65 m. 3d.

37 *BPR*, III, p. 413.

38 See above p. 45; Chester 2/34 m. 1.

39 *BPR*, I, pp. 7, 9.

40 *Ibid.*, p. 13.

41 *Ibid.*, p. 14.

42 *Ibid.*; H. J. Hewitt, *The Organization of War under Edward III*, 1966, pp. 39–40.

43 *Ibid.*, *The Black Prince's Expedition of 1355–1357*, 1958, pp. 15–16; *BPR*, III, p. 215; Chester 25/4 m. 5d.

44 A. E. Prince, 'The Army and Navy', in J. F. Willard & W. A. Morris (eds.), *The English Government at Work, 1327–1336*, 1940, pp. 362–3; J. R. Maddicott, 'The English Peasantry and the Demands of the Crown, 1294–1341', *Past and Present Supplement*, 1, 1975, p. 36.

45 R. R. Davies, *Lordship and Society in the March of Wales*, pp. 81–4; W. Hudson, 'Norwich Militia in the Fourteenth Century', *Norfolk & Norwich Archaeological Society*, xiv, 1901, pp. 284, 302.

[46] Sharp, loc. cit., p. 332; *Chamberlain's Accounts*, p. 270. Earlier purchases of cloth at Chester had not specified colour, *in tribus ulnis panni stragulati empti pro scaccario Cestrie cooperiendo, ibid.*, p. 105, which recalls the description in the *Dialogus de Scaccario*, 'And there is laid on the top of the exchequer a cloth bought at Easter term, not of any sort, but black divided by laths at intervals of a foot or a span', cited in R. L. Poole, *The Exchequer in the 12th Century*, 1912, p. 85.

[47] A. D. Carr, 'Welshmen and the Hundred Years' War', *The Welsh History Review*, 4, 1968, p. 27, argues that the livery represented a device which allowed the more unruly elements in the army to be marshalled.

[48] For a discussion of the impact of wardships and dower see J. M. W. Bean, *The Decline of English Feudalism, 1215 – 1540*, 1969, and R. R. Davies, *Lordship and Society in the March of Wales*, pp. 40 – 4.

[49] R. Barber, *Edward, Prince of Wales and Aquitaine*, 1978, p. 76.

[50] *BPR*, I, pp. 49, 63; on Stafford's positon see Sharp, op. cit., pp. 386 – 92.

[51] *BPR*, I, pp. 49, 53, 63. Danyers had been present at Crécy and was later rewarded for the capture of the lord of Tancarville and his part in raising the King's standard, R. Barber, *Edward, Prince of Wales and Aquitaine*, pp. 55, 67.

[52] *BPR*, I, p. 127.

[53] *Ibid.*, p. 49. The bills were addressed to Alexander Wastenays, William Tabley, Ralph Oldyngton and Ralph Stathum.

[54] *Ibid.*, p. 84.

[55] SC6/771/17 m. 6. The translator of *Chamberlains' Accounts*, 167, 219 has read *sagitt*(is) for *sagitt*(ariis). The figure assumes a length of two ells for each archer.

[56] H. J. Hewitt, *The Black Prince's Expedition of 1355 – 1357*, 1958, p. 20. I have relied heavily on Dr Hewitt's work in the ensuing discussion of the Prince's campaign, although differing slightly from him in the interpretation of the Cheshire evidence.

[57] For discussion of the recruiting in Cheshire see Hewitt, op. cit., pp. 16 – 19; *BPR*, III, p. 200. Those retained were Sir Ralph Mobberley, Sir John Danyers, William Carrington, Hamo Mascy, John Danyers, Thomas Stathum, Robert Brown and Robert Legh.

[58] *BPR*, III, p. 199. Sir Thomas Ferrers had been the last justice to exercise his office in person, and thereafter commissions were invariably issued to the lieutenant justice, see *VCH (Cheshire)*, II, p. 12.

[59] *BPR*, III, p. 204. Those retained were Sir John Griffyn, Richard Mascy and Hamo Ashley.

[60] *Ibid.*, p. 202. The leaders were: Macclesfield, Sir John Hide and Robert Legh; Eddisbury, Robert Brown; the Wirral and Broxton, Hamo Mascy of Puddington and Hugh Golborne; Nantwich, Sir John Griffyn.

[61] *Ibid.*, p. 199.

[62] *Ibid.*, p. 205. On recruiting by other lords see above pp. 72 – 6.

[63] *Ibid.*, p. 212.

[64] *Ibid.*, p. 202.

[65] *BPR*, III, pp. 43, 327. On the role of the hundred in military recruitment see Michael J. Bennett, *Community, Class and Careerism. Cheshire and Lancashire Society in the Age of Sir Gawain and the Green Knight*, 1983, p. 42.

[66] *BPR*, III, p. 355.

[67] *Ibid.*, pp. 331, 356 – 7.

[68] *Ibid.*, pp. 449, 454.

[69] See below pp. 132, 186–7, 209–10.

[70] *Calendar of Ancient Correspondence Concerning Wales*, J. Goronwy Edwards (ed.), 1935, pp. 246–7; D. L. Evans, 'Some Notes on the History of the Principality of Wales in the Time of the Black Prince', *Transactions of the Honourable Society of Cymmrodorion*, 1925–6, p. 76.

[71] E101/29/24 (Muster of the retinue at Northampton in 1369). Discussed above p. 132.

[72] See above pp. 8–17.

[73] Duchy of Cornwall Office, *Journal of John Henxteworth*.

[74] Hewitt, op. cit., pp. 81–4.

[75] *BPR*, III, pp. 328, 337; *Henxteworth* f. 2.

[76] See Table 4.

[77] *Henxteworth* f. 2, cited in Hewitt, op. cit., p. 42.

[78] *Henxteworth* f. 4.

[79] *Ibid.*, f. 4d.

[80] *Ibid.*

[81] *Ibid.*, f. 5, f. 9.

[82] *Ibid.*, f. 10. See Table 4.

[83] *Henxteworth* f. 22d, see Table 4; Hewitt, op. cit., p. 86.

[84] *Avesbury* 442, pp. 445–7; Hewitt, op. cit., pp. 88–90. In May four archers were sent to Saint-James-de-Beuvron by Sir John Wingfield, *Henxteworth* f. 22.

[85] Hewitt, op. cit., p. 86; M. Sharp, 'A Jodrell Deed and the Seals of the Black Prince', *BJRL*, 7, 1922–8, pp. 106–17.

[86] BL Harley MS 2074, f. 228d.

[87] David Broxton and John Dod received one pass; Richard Mobberley, Thomas Rode and Jenkin Asketon of Mobberley another.

[88] BL Harley MS 2074, f. 229d.

[89] See for instance BL Additional Charter 43217. Licence from Henry V to John Vernon and Ralph More, sergeants-at-arms, to leave the army, dated and sealed at Rouen 16th September 1419.

[90] M. Prestwich, *War, Politics and Finance under Edward I*, 1968, pp. 95–9.

[91] Hewitt, op. cit., p. 18.

[92] BL Harley MS 2074, f. 229.

[93] Sir John Wingfield recorded the loss of only Sir John de Lisle among the knights and esquires, but made no reference to casualties among the archers, *Avesbury*, pp. 439–40.

[94] *BPR*, III, p. 224.

[95] Hewitt, op. cit., p. 92; *BPR* III, pp. 225–6.

[96] *Henxteworth* f. 28d. See Table 4.

[97] Chester 25/4 m. 4, m. 5d.

[98] *BPR*, III, pp. 229, 242, 259, 289.

[99] See below p. 132.

[100] Chester 23/3 m. 1d, m. 3d, m. 4, m. 6d, m. 8d.

[101] H. J. Hewitt, *Mediaeval Cheshire: An Economic and Social History of Cheshire in the Reigns of the Three Edwards*, 1929; P. H. W. Booth, 'Taxation and Public Order: Cheshire in 1353', *Northern History*, xii, 1976, pp. 29–30.

[102] Richard Kaeuper, 'Law, Government and Society: The Evidence of Special Commissions of Oyer and Terminer', *Speculum*, liv, 1979, pp. 735–7; Booth, op. cit., pp. 17–18, and below p. 212. The debate on the causation of

lawlessness in medieval society is to be followed in John Bellamy, *Crime and Public Order in England in the Later Middle Ages*, 1973, and M. T. Clanchy, 'Law, Government and Society in Medieval England', *History*, 59, 1974, pp. 73–8.

[103] David Knowles and R. Neville Hadcock, *Medieval Religious Houses*, 1971, p. 166; BL Additional Charter 72,398.

[104] *Calendar of County Court, City Court and Eyre Rolls of Chester, 1259–1297*, ed. R. Stewart-Brown, Chet. Soc., New Series, lxxxiv, 1925, pp. 11, 13, 31; BL Additional Charter 72399. The following accounts are derived from deed collections in BL Shrewsbury-Talbot MSS. Additional Charters 72,121–74,194 and KUL, Legh of Booths charters, and from transcripts of deeds taken by Randle Holme III in 1658, BL Harley MS 2074.

[105] BL Additional Charter 72,548; KUL, Legh of Booths Charter 26. The purchase at Tatton had already included a fulling mill.

[106] See above pp. 84–5.

[107] See for example KUL, Legh of Booths Charter 326, a roll of copies of some twenty-two contemporary charters recording the formation of the Legh of Booths estate between 1297 and 1310 and expressing the ambition of a rising gentry family to establish its claim to a position in local society.

[108] Chester 2/1 m. 2; SC6/771/9 m. 1 (Account of the Chamberlain of Chester, September 1320–September 1321); CRO, DCH/A/33; *The Ledger-Book of Vale Royal Abbey*, ed. John Brownbill, LCRS, lxviii 1914, p. 123.

[109] KUL, Legh of Booths charters 20–1, 247, 326.

[110] KUL, Legh of Booths charters 231 (Ollerton), 321 (Great Warford), 29 (Knutsford); Chester 29/42 m. 18d.

[111] KUL, Legh of Booths charter 326 (xiv); BL Harley MS 2074 f. 154d.

[112] Mobberley appears in at least nine Legh charters, Legh in seven of Mobberley's; BL Additional Charter 72,404.

[113] Chester 29/39 m. 1; *CPR 1327–1330*, p. 121.

[114] SC6/771/11. (Account of the Chamberlain of Chester, September 1326–September 1327.) m. 1d.

[115] R. H. Hilton, *The English Peasantry in the Later Middle Ages*, 1975, pp. 240–3 draws an interesting parallel for neighbouring Staffordshire at this date; see also the discussion of the Stanley family, above pp. 87–91. Mobberley had already been subject to a violent assault by Richard of Plumpton earlier in the same year, Chester 29/38, m 2.

[116] Details of his assaults at Golborne and Stockport, the latter during Sir John Ardern's absence on the Scottish campaign of 1341, are given in Chester 1/1 part 5, nos. 26–8; Ardern's pardon is given in Chester 29/60 m. 6.

[117] J. G. Bellamy, 'The Coterel Gang: an anatomy of a band of fourteenth century criminals' *EHR*, lxxix, 1964, p. 704 *idem.*, *Crime and Public Order in England in the Later Middle Ages*, 1973, p. 86–7.

[118] *CPR, 1327–1330*, p. 543. Orreby had granted a life interest in lands in Knutsford Booths to the Legh family, KUL, Legh of Booths charter 326 (ii); John Bellamy, *Crime and Public Order*, pp. 69–88.

[119] Hugh Rycroft had been a charter witness *c.* 1318 and was with Legh both in 1322 and 1331, KUL, Legh of Booths charter 6; Danyers is Ardern's steward in BL Additional Charter 72,409.

[120] *Rotuli Scotiae*, I, 312b, 436b.

[121] *BPR* III, p. 143; see above p. 87.

[122] Chester 29/39 m. 1, m. 19d, m. 24d; Chester 29/40 m. 2d.

[123] BL Harley MS 2074 f. 154; BL Additional roll 74131 (Extent of Mobberley, February 1337).

[124] Chester 29/39 m. 9d, m. 11–12, m. 15.

[125] BL Harley MS 2074 f. 155; BL Additional charter 72,416 (Will of Sir Ralph Mobberley, 1355).

[126] The grandson of Mobberley's murderer, see below p. 199 *et seq.*

[127] See above p. 107.

[128] See below pp. 150–2.

[129] KUL, Legh of Booths charter 42 (Letter of protection, dated January 1363).

[130] BL Additional charters 72,415, 72,536. On the significance of uses see J. M. W. Bean, *The Decline of English Feudalism 1215–1540*, 1968, pp. 144–8; K. B. McFarlane, *The Nobility of Later Medieval England*, 1973, pp. 68–76.

[131] George Ormerod, *The History of the County Palatine and City of Chester*, 2nd edition of Thomas Helsby, 1875, II, p. 413.

[132] Chester 19/1 m. 110–11; Chester 29/67 m. 48, m. 61d.

[133] *BPR*, III, pp. 403, 408.

[134] Ormerod, loc. cit. They were copied by Randle Holme in 1658 and by Sir Peter Leycester in 1672, but do not now survive. Both parties in the dispute had originally issued writs against Thomas Davenport for the production of Mobberley's archive.

[135] Chester 29/67 m. 73; *BPR*, III, pp. 447–9; IV, pp. 435–6.

[136] Chester 29/67 m. 73.

[137] BL Additional Charters 72,420, 72,429.

[138] Ormerod, op. cit., pp. 413–4; BL Additional Charters 72,423–72,427. Such assemblies were not uncommon in Cheshire, see M. J. Bennett, 'A County Community; Social Cohesion amongst the Cheshire Gentry 1400–1425', *Northern History*, viii, 1973, pp. 24–8. J. R. L. Cornwall Legh deed 868 records a 'dayhaldying' attended by Richard Mascy of Sale.

[139] KUL, Legh of Booths charter 203.

[140] *John of Trokelowe, Annales* ed. H. T. Riley, (Rolls series, 1866), p. 159 cited by H. J. Hewitt, *Mediaeval Cheshire*, pp. 155–6.

[141] An earlier draft of the remainder of this chapter appeared in P. J. Morgan, 'Cheshire and the Defence of the Principality of Aquitaine', in *Medieval Cheshire*, THLC, 128, 1979, pp. 139–60. I am grateful for permission to reprint it here.

[142] G. L. Harriss, *King, Parliament and Public Finance in Medieval England to 1369*, 1975, pp. 329–32, 476–8.

[143] *Ibid.*, p. 476. Edward III did, however, later make substantial payments to the Prince from the ransom of King John, *ibid.*, pp. 491–5.

[144] J. P. Trabut-Cussac, *Le Livre des Homages d'Aquitaine*, 1959, *passim*.

[145] J. Rouquette, *Le Rouergue sous les Anglais*, 1887, p. 92, pièces justificatives xi.

[146] E30/1647.

[147] Philippe Contamine, 'Les Compagnies d'Aventure en France pendant la Guerre de Cent Ans', *Mélanges de l'École Française de Rome*, 87, 1975, p. 385.

[148] E. Perroy, *The Hundred Years War*, 1951, pp. 158–65.

[149] Harriss, op. cit., pp. 509–17.

[150] See in general J. R. Maddicott, 'The English Peasantry and the Demands of the Crown 1294–1341', *Past & Present Supplement*, 1, 1975; Edward Miller, 'War, Taxation and the English Economy in the Late Thirteenth and Early Fourteenth Centuries', in *War and Economic Development*, ed. J. M. Winter, 1975, pp. 11–31.

[151] See above pp. 28–30, 62–6.

[152] R. R. Davies, *Lordship and Society in the March of Wales*, p. 185.

[153] See above pp. 98–9.

[154] P. H. W. Booth, *Taxation and Public Order*, p. 24; Chester 29/67 m. 98–9.

[155] *BPR*, I, 67; Chester 24/2, bundle 21 Edward III.

[156] H. J. Hewitt, *Cheshire under the Three Edwards*, 1967, pp. 8–9.

[157] P. H. W. Booth, *Taxation and Public Order*, pp. 21–22, 24.

[158] *BPR*, III, p. 482.

[159] E101/177/9 printed in M. J. Delpit, *Collection Générale des Documents qui se trouvent en Angleterre*, 1847, pp. 132–69.

[160] SC6/772/5 (Account of the Chamberlain of Chester, September 1369–September 1370), m. 3; SC6/772/9 (Account of the Chamberlain of Chester, September 1373–September 1374), m. 2.

[161] SC6/772/5 m. 2d; see above p. 70.

[162] SC6/772/3 (Account of the Chamberlain of Chester, September 1361–September 1362), m. 2d.

[163] Chester 2/45 m. 2d. Grant of annuity of £40 to Bertram de Saint Omer dated at Plymouth 4 June 1363.

[164] Chester 2/47 m. 3; Chester 2/48 m. 2d; Chester 2/46 m. 2; *ibid.*, m. 1d.

[165] Chester 2/47 m. 3; Chester 2/48 m. 2d; Chester 2/46 m. 2; *ibid.*, m. 1d.

[166] Chester 2/47 m. 1.

[167] Chester 2/48 m. 2; SC6/772/5 m. 2d.

[168] Ancient Petitions, SC8/333 nos. 1043, 1026. The name in the latter is lost.

[169] SC6/772/6 (Account of the Chamberlain of Chester, September 1389–September 1390), m. 2. See also the references cited in R. R. Davies, 'Richard II and the Principality of Chester 1397–99', in *The Reign of Richard II*, ed. F. R. H. Du Boulay & C. M. Barron, 1971, 262 n. 12–13.

[170] See above pp. 102–14.

[171] N. H. Nicolas, *The Scrope and Grosvenor Controversy*, 1832. Volume 1 contains the testimony of the witnesses, volume 2 a history of the Scrope family and biographical notices of the witnesses in their favour. A projected third volume dealing with the Grosvenor family was never issued.

[172] Nicolas, op. cit., I, p. 82.

[173] The phrase is that of an inquisition *probatio aetatis* in 1374, Chester 3/7 (1). See also CRO, Vernon deed, DVE/11/13.

[174] See the discussion by Michael J. Bennett, *Community, Class and Careerism*, pp. 21–40, and J. R. Maddicott, *The County Community and the Making of Public Opinion in Fourteenth Century England*, pp. 27–43.

[175] Nicolas, loc. cit.

[176] *Ibid.*, p. 256.

[177] The fullest account of the campaign in the Rouergue is given by Rouquette, op. cit., chs. VI–IX.

[178] BL Harley MS 2074, f. 230d. Montviron is described as *nuper mareschallus aulae domini principi* in SC6/772/5 m. 2d.

[179] This had been the arrangement prior to the campaigns of 1355 and 1363, see above p. 107; *BPR*, III, pp. 200, 454. Wettenhall had returned to England after Nájera and appears in the Northampton roll, after which he received £56 for the wages of men-at-arms and archers, SC6/772/5 m. 2d.

[180] J. Sherborne, 'Indentured Retinues and English Expeditions to France 1369–1380', *EHR*, lxxix, 1964, p. 733.

[181] Harriss, op. cit., p. 501; SC6/772/5 m. 2d.

[182] E101/29/24.

[183] William Carington, Richard Mascy, John Griffyn, John Danyers, Hamo Mascy and William Donne. A list of Cheshiremen known to have served at Poitiers is given in H. J. Hewitt, *Cheshire under the Three Edwards*, 1967, appendix 1.

[184] SC6/772/5 m. 2, 2d.

[185] M. D. Legge, *Anglo-Norman Letters*, Anglo-Norman Text Society, iii 1941, pp. 198–202.

[186] Rouquette, op. cit., pp. 148–150.

[187] *Chroniques de J. Froissart*, ed. Siméon Luce, vii, 1878, pp. 116–19.

[188] *Ibid.*, pp. 136–9, 160–1, 216–17.

[189] Chester 25/4 m. 22, m. 29d. They included Robert Grosvenor, Sir William Brereton and Sir John Danyers. On the problem of desertion see above pp. 112–13.

[190] The seventy archers were included under the heading *passerent puis la seint Michel* on the muster roll and were presumably among those accounted for by Wettenhall in his claim to the Chester chamberlain.

[191] *BPR*, III, p. 454.

[192] John Hatcher, *Rural Economy and Society in the Duchy of Cornwall, 1300–1500*, 1970, p. 145.

[193] *BPR*, III, p. 482.

[194] K. Fowler, 'Les Finances et la Discipline dans les Armées Anglaises en France au XIVe Siècle, *Les Cahiers Vernonnais*, 4, 1964, *passim*.

[195] P. J. Capra, 'Les Bases Sociales du Pouvoir Anglo-Gascon au milieu du XIVe siècle, *Le Moyen Âge*, lxxxi, 1975, pp. 278–9.

[196] The accounts of the Constable of Bordeaux do not survive between 1362 and 1372 when it was no longer necessary for them to be submitted to the exchequer in London. The loss is matched by a similar hiatus in the accounts of the Chamberlain of Chester.

[197] Letters of protection enrolled in 1363 were to be invalid on the return of the recipient or in the event of non-embarkation, Chester 29/72 m. 15; *ibid.*, m. 16, m. 19 (William Bulkeley and Hugh Scot) for hearings suspended *sine die*.

[198] BL Harley MS 2074 f. 228.

[199] *BPR*, IV, p. 254.

[200] JRL, Jodrell deed 3a.

[201] SC8/118 no. 5878. Undated but probably *c.* 1375/6.

[202] Rouquette, op. cit., p. 92.

[203] E101/24/20; E101/28/18.

[204] *Calendar of Entries in the Papal Registers*, ed. W. H. Bliss & J. A. Twemlow, iv, 1902, pp. 17–18, 20, 22.

[205] Legge, *Anglo-Norman Letters*, p. 199.

[206] Jules Artières, 'Documents sur la ville de Millau', *Archives Historiques du Rouergue*, vii, 1930, pp. 100–76.

[207] Rouquette, op. cit., p. 207; P. Chaplais, 'Some Documents regarding the Fulfilment and Interpretation of the Treaty of Brétigny 1361–1369', *Camden Miscellany*, xix, 1952, p. 55.

[208] Artières, op. cit., p. 176.

[209] Contamine, op. cit., pp. 376–7.

[210] *Ibid*. A. D. Carr, 'A Welsh Knight in the Hundred Years War: Sir Gregory Sais', *Transactions of the Honourable Society of Cymmrodorion 1977*, pp. 40–53 summarises the details of the campaign. On Sais's recruitment in Cheshire see E101/34/29 and E101/39/39.

[211] Michael Jones, *Ducal Brittany 1364–1399*, 1970, appendix B.

[212] *Froissart*, ed. Luce, viii, pp. 51–3, 133, 279; R. Memain, 'Les Misères de la Guerre en Bas Poitou au xive et xve siècles', *Bulletin de la Société des Antiquaires de l'Ouest*, 12, 1941, p. 652.

[213] E101/181/4 Pt. 2. no. 21; M. Barber, 'John Norbury: An Esquire of Henry IV', *EHR*, lxviii, 1953, pp. 66–76 gives little detail of his early career for which see Fowler, op. cit.

[214] *Archives Historiques du Département de la Gironde*, 12, 1870, pp. 328–41. Geoffrey of Frodsham, St Macaire; Hugh Calveley and John Griffyn, La Reole; John Legh, Montsegur; John Savage, Salveterre. *Froissart*, ed. Luce, viii, pp. 113, 133, 147, David Hulgreve, Niort; Hugh Browe, Derval.

[215] CRO, Leycester of Tabley MSS DLT/A11/85.

[216] An obvious example is provided by the resources of the court at Millau over which Wettenhall and Cradock presided, Artières, op. cit., p. 146 *et seq*.

[217] *Ibid*. (Hugh de Calveley said that he was a cousin of the seneschal.)

[218] Contamine, op. cit., pp. 381, 388–9.

[219] Artières, op. cit., p. 146.

[220] *Calendar of Papal Registers*, pp. 17–18, 20, 22.

[221] SC8/103 no. 5103.

[222] SC8/257 no. 12825; JRL, Bromley-Davenport Muniments II (3), Calveley Box 2/2.

[223] E101/39/9; Chester 25/8 m. 8, cited by Michael J. Bennett, *Community, Class and Careerism*, p. 184.

[224] Chester 29/72 m. 16.

[225] R. R. Davies, *Lordship and Society in the March of Wales*, 269 n. 55.

[226] E101/39/9 m. 1, m. 3; Chester 2/65 m. 1d.

[227] M. Sharp, *Contributions to a History of the Earldom of Chester, 1237–1399*, University of Manchester PhD, 1925, pp. 43–4 argues, however, that the government of Cheshire under the household of the Black Prince represented a slackening of the traditions of independence in the county.

[228] Froissart, *Chronicles*, ed. G. Brereton, 1968, pp. 377–8.

CHAPTER IV

THE MILITARY COMMUNITY

The conflict which we term the Hundred Years War had its origin in the feudal relationship of the kingdom of France and the cross-channel empires of English kings from the late eleventh century, and acquired a new impetus following Edward III's claim to the French throne in 1337.[1] Nevertheless, apart from the way in which the personal ambition of Plantagenet kings might masquerade as the public interest of the nation, there were other reasons why men fought.[2] Armies were raised in England and France by compulsion and by contract, and the relationship of the crown and its military servants, both noble and other, has as a result been much studied; but the nature of the military community and its interaction with the local and regional societies from which it was drawn has attracted far less attention.[3] In Cheshire I have sought to examine the role of compulsion in the exercise of lordship by the earl, and to relate the development of military service to the social and economic structure of the county. It seems unlikely that the peasant population had played a significant role in the military service of Cheshiremen after the Scottish campaigns of Edward I, and one cannot argue, in the way that Rodney Hilton has done for the west Midlands, that 'if employment, or the chance of squatting on some-body's waste, did not provide alternatives to starving in the village, the king's wars did.'[4] In the context of service in the Cheshire retinues in the fourteenth century, it was usual for men to maintain the equipment of both the man-at-arms and the horse archer, and membership of military society was therefore restricted to a comparatively narrow social *élite* which, I have suggested, is only intelligible in terms of the local gentry society from which it was drawn.

Warfare had quickly evolved its own diplomatic in which much of the detail of military organisation and, in particular, the raising of contractual armies may be observed. Such information as is contained in indentures of retinue, in muster rolls, and in the detail of military subcontracting clearly adds significantly to our knowledge of the operation of the military community, and in many instances provides the fundamental basis for further study.[5] That evidence, however, while emphasising the feudal and contractual element in military service, may ignore the bonds of personal and regional loyalty which underpinned the raising of retinues.[6] There is a clear distinction to be made, for example, between the evidence of the retinue roll of the Black Prince at Northampton in 1369, which it is argued represents a muster of the Prince's personal following and the military resources of his lordship in Cheshire, and that of a Provençal army at Aix-en-Provence in 1374 in which the soldiers are described with a precision normally confined to the valuation of horses.[7] Both were of course contractual armies, but whereas one represents an occasional professional and contractual force for which the Seneschal of Provence required precise and detailed information, the other reflects the success of the military lordship of the Black Prince over a period of years. Detailed study of the military community and recognition of the emergence of a new professional military class in the armies of the later fourteenth century depends, therefore, upon the use of the widest possible variety of documentation which will reveal the total experience of the soldier and not merely the details of military organisation.[8]

The retinue with which Sir Ralph Mobberley embarked on the Prince's service in September 1355 comprised the knight himself, an esquire and about thirty-two mounted archers. No muster roll survives, but the names of the greater part of the company can be recovered from documents dealing with the organisation of the campaign.[9] It is immediately apparent that this retinue was far removed from a muster of those impressed solely under the strength of the Prince's commission; rather it formed a loose association of men bound by a variety of relationships of mutual dependence and advantage. Most were recruited within ten miles of the Mobberley estate, and many were already members of the knight's following in the county. The inner core of that following, as one would imagine, comprised the members of Mobberley's kin, his dependents, tenants and neighbours, and it is that grouping which finds fullest expression in his military retinue.

Sir Ralph Mobberley had four sisters and died without male heir, although he had at least two illegitimate sons by Alice Rode, a spinster who held lands in her own right at Odd Rode on the Staffordshire border.[10] Nevertheless two kinsmen, Richard and Jenkin Mobberley, and the knight's nephew, John Leycester, who was made a joint heir under a will sealed in June 1355, do make an appearance in the retinue. The tenantry of the Mobberley estate, who were in that sense already

Table 5   The Retinue of Sir Ralph Mobberley, 1355

Henry of Acton	Richard Mobberley
William Appleton	Richard Page
John of Baguley	Robert Parkin
Roger of Boseden	William Peover
Adam Brown	Thomas of Rode
Frere	Roger of Rowley
William of Goostrey	William Smethwick
John Harper	Thomas Stathum
Robert of Lawton	Richard Taylor of Shipbrook
William of Lawton	Hugh Vernon
John Leycester	William Vernon
John Marbury	John Warburton
Hugh of Millington	William Warburton
Jenkin Mobberley	William White
John of Moreton	William Winnington

(Source: Duchy of Cornwall Office, *Journal* of John Henxteworth)

closely bound to Sir Ralph, do not figure greatly in the retinue, although Thomas Stathum had held three acres on the waste at Mobberley in 1337, and Adam Brown had received a twenty-three year lease on lands in the manor in 1350.[11] The service of the greater part of the retinue can be closely related to the operation of gentry society in which military service provides further examples of social cohesion. John and William Warburton were probably kinsmen of Sir Geoffrey Warburton, Hugh and William Vernon younger sons of the baron of Shipbrook, John Marbury the son of Hugh, lord of Marbury; and with them came their dependents, William Appleton, John Harper, Richard Taylor of Shipbrook, and William of Goostrey.[12] In addition, Sir Ralph Mobberley's links with Alice Rode and his own landholding at Holly in Somerford Booths and Odd Rode in the south of the county attracted the service of men in these areas: Thomas Rode, William and Robert Lawton, and John Moreton.[13] These were Mobberley's neighbours and peers who were already accustomed to acting together in a variety of roles, as charter witnesses, as sureties for each other at the county court, and often in the formation of marriage ties: minor gentry who took service with Mobberley as a result of this position in local society.

By far the most important member of the retinue was Thomas Stathum, who had himself been retained by the Prince but served in Gascony as Mobberley's lieutenant with his own retinue of four archers.[14] He may have been related to a Ralph Stathum who had

been active during the Crécy campaign and presumably originated from
Stathum in Lymm, but by the 1340s he held lands in Mobberley and
was retained by its lord.[15] During the campaign of 1359, however, he
had entered more fully into the Prince's service as a yeoman of the
household and leader of archers in the chamber. Even so he retained
links with Mobberley, acting as executor of his will with John Leycester
in 1360. Earlier, and almost certainly through Sir Ralph's patronage,
he had acquired the marriage of Mobberley's kinswoman, Isabella
Davenport, with the manors of Poynton and Stockport.[16] At the same
time he was much employed in the Prince's administration of the lordship of Denbigh, during the minority of the earl of March, and was
granted the profits of the office of constable of its castle. In 1365, as lord
of Stockport, he received letters of protection for service in the Principality of Aquitaine.[17] Scant though the evidence relating to his career
is, it provides a model of the opportunities for advancement through
military service, and demonstrates clearly that the network of mutual
dependence which is revealed in these sources was not exclusive. Men
might, and often did, seek the patronage of several lords, with the effect
that at many points the gentry affinities which comprised county society
merged imperceptibly into each other.

In war, however, a captain assumed important powers over the
membership of his retinue. Initially he was responsible for their recruitment, and for the issue of letters of protection which granted security
to their lands and immunity from legal prosecutions.[18] After their
general acceptance in Cheshire courts during the Crécy campaign, such
letters had enhanced the attractiveness of military service, alongside the
now traditional issue of pardons for crime.[19] Amongst those who had
embarked with Mobberley in 1355, both William Vernon and John
Marbury had cases suspended *sine die*, and William Lawton, Robert
Lawton and John Moreton had only recently been indicted in a case
concerning the wardship and marriage of Joan Byron.[20] These three
did in fact desert soon after the return to Bordeaux in December, and
their behaviour suggests that it was not uncommon for men to seek
service solely on account of the legal protection which such letters
afforded, and on occasion to attempt to obtain them fraudulently.[21]
Thereafter it was usual for letters of protection enrolled at Chester to
be invalid until the archer had embarked and if he returned from the
expedition without licence.[22] The granting of such licences and their
validation in letters patent, either of the crown or the earl, may have
originated in the household of the Prince at this date as a response to
the problems of desertion on earlier campaigns. They too remained the

responsibility of the captain and assumed a limited role in the patronage he was able to exercise within the retinue.[23] More important was the control over pay which the system of army finance allowed. In Gascony John Henxteworth had made interim payments of wages to captains or their attorneys at regular intervals during the period between the two *chevauchées* of 1355 and 1356, although in some instances final settlement was not made for several years.[24] In general, however, wages were not paid until the end of campaigns, often at the English port of disembarkation, in order to maintain cohesion and continuity in the retinue during its period of service.[25]

The payment of wages formed only a single element in the rewards of military service, amongst which booty and ransoms were often conceived of as vital to the success of individual retinues. Robert Bowden, for example, received a gift of money despite 'being left behind during the Prince's first ride through Gascony, having been wounded in a quarrel'.[26] In the aftermath of the campaign there are a number of references to the settlement of disputes over prisoners and to the sale of booty in the Cheshire retinues, but it remains impossible to quantify the impressions of individual profit contained in such examples.[27] Far more numerous were the many recorded instances of comital largesse on the Prince's return to England in 1357, occasionally as the result of personal petitions to him, but more commonly after the intercession of individual captains. Six archers in Mobberley's retinue received gifts of timber and pasture, pardons, or the grant of minor offices: to William Appleton as vendor of felons' goods in the county, to Roger Bosden as parker of Peckforton, and to Hugh Millington as catchpole of Middlewich.[28] As H. J. Hewitt has rightly observed, these are 'offices of no great eminence but desirable to men who expect to live their lives near their homes'.[29] The service of the Cheshire retinues in Gascony marked the success of the Prince's military lordship, not the widespread commitment of county society to the conduct of war.

Clearly there were those, like Mobberley and Stathum, who now saw military service as an alternative career; but we ought not, therefore, to expect any significant degree of continuity in the membership of the retinue of 1359. That of 1355 may indeed have been an expression of the local society from which it was drawn, an association of tenants and neighbours accustomed to acting together in a variety of roles; but, as we have suggested, such associations were not exclusive and often the relationship of mutual advantage and dependence on which they were based was of limited and temporary value. Sir Ralph Mobberley was again retained by the Prince with two esquires in August 1359, although unfortunately we know little of the retinue which he had assembled before his death at the siege of Rheims.[30] Thomas Stathum, as we have already noted, was now serving as the leader of archers in the Prince's chamber; and three others, William Winnington, Roger Rowley, and William Peover, had joined the retinues of Sir John Wingfield and Sir Bartholomew Burgherssh. Hugh Vernon, Richard Taylor of Shipbrook and William Goostrey did indeed serve again, but were soon incapacitated by illness and returned to England.[31] Of the remainder, and of those who now took service for the first time, we remain largely ignorant.

It should perhaps be noted at this juncture that military service was a career in which the advantages of war were often balanced by undoubted perils. Amongst the acts of comital largesse were grants to archers who had lost horses during the campaign, to Dafydd ap Bleddyn Fychan, whose house had been burnt, to William Stewhall who had been ransomed in the Périgord, and to Alice, the widow of John Taylor of Whatcroft, whose husband had been killed. It used to be argued that ransoms, better armour and the comparative rarity of pitched battles minimised the casualty rates in medieval armies, at least among the knightly class.[32] Nevertheless, the prospects of death or mutilation were real enough, as the examples of Sir Ralph Mobberley and a fellow Cheshire captain, Sir William Golborne, at the siege of Rheims, or Thomas Wettenhall in the defence of the Rouergue, illustrate.[33] John Carrington later recalled that his grandfather, Sir William Carrington, had been scalded in the face at the battle of Sluis in 1340, although he was retained by the Prince throughout the later Gascon campaigns.[34] A firm indication of the frequency of injuries is provided by the evidence of the Provençal army in 1374, of whom 25 per cent bore facial and manual scars. The burial pits of those killed at the battle of Wisby in Sweden (1361) also speak eloquently of the risks implicit in medieval warfare where, according to one recent estimate, the defeated armies often lost between 20 and 50 per cent of their strength.[35]

Initially, of course, the costs of equipment may have acted as an equally strong deterrent to service, particularly amongst the minor gentry. At the end of a long military career in 1404, Robert Winnington's possessions included four swords, one of Bordeaux and another called 'Bryggemask', several baselards and daggers, a longbow and arrows, a shield, a bascinet and three horses.[36] It could be argued that these items represent the customary accoutrements of knights in an undoubtedly violent society, but for those who sought employment in war these were costly investments. William and Thomas Hulgreve claimed in a petition to the Prince that it had cost their father £5 to equip them as archers in Aquitaine in 1367, and much later Hugh Venables claimed to have mortgaged his lands in order to equip himself as a man-at-arms in the service of Henry IV.[37]

In many cases, however, a major consideration was the inevitably disabling effect which military service had on a knight's position in local society during his absence. The appointment of attorneys and the issue of letters of protection were important safeguards, but they could not defend a soldier against assaults and unlawful acts against his lands and family. On occasion these were acts of violence which disturbed the peace of the county, as in 1341 when Peter Ardern and a large following attacked the manor-house of Sir John Ardern during his absence in Scotland, but more often than not they were cases of a purely local and personal significance.[38] In 1379, for example, whilst Robert Henbury was serving in the retinue of Sir Hugh Calveley, his wife was raped by a clerk named Richard Elton; in 1387 Sir Hugh Browe's manor-house at Christleton was robbed of clothes and silver objects during his absence with the Earl of Arundel; and in 1389 Richard Colt attempted to defraud Thomas Bartington's widow of money which her husband had sent from Spain prior to his death.[39] Some of the cases are relatively trivial assaults, but others demonstrate the real and damaging perils which faced those committed to military service. In an indictment before the county court in 1378 the jurors reported that after Ralph Legh had departed for Gascony in May 1371 his lands at Deslayheath had been unlawfully occupied by William Hichessone, who also took his wife as a concubine. Such was Hichessone's violent reputation, claimed the jurors, that Legh had been afraid to return home for six years.[40]

Long absence in France did not only expose the lands and family of the soldier to danger: it impaired his role in the affairs of local society. Thus, in December 1373 it was necessary for a group of knights and esquires, most of whom had recently served in France, to answer a summons on behalf of Roger Toft, who was then in Anjou with John of Gaunt, doing so 'as a work of charity for the preservation of the estate of the said Roger'.[41] Other soldiers might not be as fortunate; on his return from Gaunt's long Spanish campaign in January 1389, John Holford with his servants, tenants, and, one suspects, the residue of his military retinue, assaulted the manor of Lostock Gralam to prevent royal officials granting seisin to John Starkey.[42] Even the longest campaigns were, however, of limited duration compared to the garrison service of other knights whose prolonged absences magnified the problem of protecting their landed status and political influence at home. Sir

William Mainwaring had departed for Gascony in 1371 and, by his own account, did not return to England for over twenty years before attempting to recover his rights in the manor of Baddiley.[43] The sporadic campaigns of the English nobility might often be of a single season's duration, but increasingly in the 1370s and 1380s a career in war involved long service in the garrisons of Gascony, Brittany, Normany and Calais; and, if for no other reason than this, such service attracted those without status in local society, or at least those prepared to abandon it to the care of attorneys.

The long illness of the Prince during the last six years of his life (1370–6) had inevitably mitigated the compulsory element of lordship in the military service of Cheshiremen, and allows a fuller recognition of the new professional military class which, we have argued, came into being during the years of the Principality of Aquitaine. It remains difficult to distinguish the varieties of individual experience in war, for clearly the Cheshire squirearchy as a whole still conceived of itself as a martial class and paraded its claim to that status in the collective memory of occasional service recorded in the evidence of the Scrope-Grosvenor case. Nevertheless, amongst the witnesses in that court were the members of a group who had devoted themselves to warfare and formed a distinct community. Ours is perhaps not a distinction which contemporaries would readily have recognised, for in the context of the later fourteenth century the soldier was merely one of a number of careerists whose experience had served to disturb the territorial patterns of political leadership in the county.[44] The independence of military society is not to be doubted, however, and was perceived by those who shared in its actions. Thus John Fairchild, disputing the right to a prisoner taken at Poitiers, would claim a jury of 'twelve yeomen who were there'.[45] These, of all people, were his peers.

After the Prince's final return to England early in 1371 the royal exchequer renewed its commitment to the maintenance of permanent military forces in France, and during the 1370s financial subsidies once again reached the levels which had been found so burdensome in the years before the treaty of Brétigny.[46] Thus, in the garrisons of Gascony, Brittany, and Calais we may follow the careers of a small but significant group of Cheshire men for whom these years would be no less important than the period of the 'great expeditions'. Indeed, for a time these men occupied a pivotal role in the organisation of war, either as garrison captains in the administration of English lordship in France, or perhaps more significantly as military subcontractors in the recruitment of the noble retinues.

A few of the captains had originally served in the Prince's retinues at Poitiers and in the principality of Aquitaine, but even amongst those who could later claim only to have served 'in the garrisons and companies in France, and never on the great expeditions', the greatest opportunities were located in those areas where Cheshiremen had first found service with the Black Prince. In time, however, as the demands of the war in Richard II's reign declined, their concerns moved briefly to Ireland, the Welsh March and the Scottish border, only to return to France during the years of Lancastrian achievement under Henry V. A few men might indeed follow the entire circuit. John Savage had first served in the retinue of Thomas Wettenhall in the Rouergue before appearing again, first as a garrison captain in the Gascon March, and later as captain of Dieppe in 1417 and Calais in 1418.[47] In a limited sense his career illustrates the essential unity of military society in the years between the Principality of Aquitaine and the Lancastrian land settlement in Normandy. Equally, however, there was frequent contact with other captains, and in several cases with other conflicts in Italy and the Empire, which served to broaden and diversify the experience of the Cheshire soldiery. As a result the careers of these men had obviously ceased to be intelligible solely in terms of the pressures of Cheshire society, although many continued to maintain close contacts with the region alongside the investments which they had made elsewhere. In addition to those who sought to establish themselves in other counties, and indeed in Normandy and Gascony, on the profits of war, and of whom we so often lose sight in the records, there were others who hesitated before severing all connection with Cheshire.

In studying their careers, however, it remains difficult to dispel the assumptions of decadence which have characterised discussion of the war in the 1370s, and with the death of Edward III, as Kenneth Fowler has observed, 'the era of Crécy and Poitiers came to an end'.[48] And yet without doubt the character of the war of the English occupation had already changed profoundly during the years of the Prince's lordship in Aquitaine. Thus the long service of men like John Jodrell and Sir Hugh Browe not only illustrates the development of a new professional military class, but also reveals something of the social and economic pressure which often led men to look for some more permanent role in the regions over which they had fought. The character and scale of this involvement may have failed at many points to match that of the later land settlement in Normandy with its traffic in land and titles, but this was partly a consequence of the early decay of the Prince's lordship, and more importantly because of the allegiance of the Gascon nobility whose continued loyalty inhibited such a policy of dispossession as would mark the Norman experience.[49] The boundary, in the detail of military organisation, between the *chevauchée* of the fourteenth century and the colonising impulse of the fifteenth, has hitherto been too readily drawn, and as the records of the French archives are more fully explored, the number of recorded instances of early settlement grows.

Many of these men owed their advancement to the influence of the Prince's lordship, either in the form of royal grants or in the gift of marriages amongst the Gascon nobility. It would be misleading, however, to relate the ambition of many soldiers too closely to the ebb and flow of the war and to the fortunes of the English king, for in several cases settlement was first contemplated in defiance of apparent military and political realities. Sir William Mainwaring came to Gascony for the first time only during the collapse of 1369, but served there continuously until his death in 1399. At the same time Thomas Carrington, returning to England as a result of ill-health, lodged his younger son in the household of John, lord Neville of Raby, then in Gascony. John Carrington similarly did not return to England until he was twenty-six years old, and only then, we are told, as a result of his brother's early demise.[50] Clearly the decline of English military fortunes did reduce the opportunities for settlement, and in this context we have already met the unfortunate 'Jean Joudrell de Peytowe' whose lands had been jeopardised in the reconquest of the duke of Anjou. Nevertheless, although we know most about the commitment of English soldiers from the details of their dispossession, it was possible for men to retain title to their lands beyond the military collapse.[51] Jodrell's contemporary, John Stratton, having married Isabel Saint-Symphorien in 1358, continued to enjoy her lands in the lordship of Landiras until his own death in 1397.[52] Even in Poitou the Flintshire knight, Gregory Sais, who had held the lordship of Gençay by grant from the Prince and Mortemer in right of his wife, Ragonde Bechet, had striven to retain his lands. As late as 1375 Bertrand du Guesclin had undertaken to maintain Ragonde's lands and possessions, and it was not until a year or two later, and only then after a protracted lawsuit, that she gave up her title and joined her husband on his English and Welsh lands.[53] It is difficult to judge whether these examples represent deliberate attempts at permanent settlement, or whether, as in the case of Sir Hugh Calveley's many lands and titles, they simply added to the resources for short-term profits available to the military class. At this stage, therefore, it would be unwise to posit the existence of a cross-Channel relationship of anything more than passing military expediency. In all respects, however, these incidents marked the opportunities to be found during military service in the 1370s and 1380s which serve to separate the experience of the follower in the service of his lord from that of the professional soldier.

That experience might, as we have said, assume a variety of forms in the somewhat ragged and confused campaigns of the period leading to the reconquest of much of the former Principality of Aquitaine by Louis I, Duke of Anjou, and du Guesclin. In the duchy of Guyenne, although the greater number of garrisons had remained in the hands of Gascon lords, a number of the more vital fortresses had been committed to the keeping of English knights. Amongst these a group of Cheshiremen were to be found holding a strategic line of garrisons along the Garonne: at Caumont-sur-Garonne, La Réole, Monsegur, Saint Macaire and Sauveterre-de-Guyenne. Later, as the focus of military activity shifted northwards to the Dordogne, that same group assumed responsibility for the defence of Saint Foy-la-Grande, Libourne and the *pays* de Bordeaux. Most were by this stage captains of some stature in the English administration, and in 1377 John Norbury and William Mainwaring could each muster thirty men-at-arms in their retinues, while at Bergerac Thomas Venables held fifty men-at-arms in his service.[54] Neither indeed were their actions in those conflicts insignificant, and at least one Cheshire man, Thomas Halton, is celebrated in the town chronicle of Bazas for his defence of Monsegur and Sauveterre.[55] Those with less experience found themselves in the retinues of the seneschal, Sir Thomas Felton, and Sir Hugh Calveley, in attempts to support the beleaguered garrisons within the duchy.[56] Outside Guyenne the surviving English companies, notably those under Sir David Hulgreve at Niort and Sir Gregory Sais at Gençay, continued their resistance to the reconquest of Poitou and Saintonge until the siege of Chizé in 1373 when many, including Hulgreve himself and perhaps also John Jodrell, were captured and ransomed. Hulgreve had in fact only narrowly escaped a similar fate at Moncontour in the previous year when he was granted safe conduct to Poitiers by Louis II, Duke of Bourbon.[57] The situation was repeated in Brittany where the Montfortians found themselves limited to a small number of garrisons including that at Derval held by the Cheshire knight, Sir Hugh Browe.[58] In the campaigns of 1377 and 1378 the Seneschal of Aquitaine was captured, and Bordeaux itself threatened.[59] In the space of a decade Charles V had overturned the terms of the treaty of Brétigny, but by 1380 the *chevauchée* of Thomas of Woodstock confirmed that the war was not yet at an end, although for the remainder of the century both kings would move uncertainly towards a reconciliation and the hope of a final peace. It remains to be seen whether Richard II would indeed, as Philippe de Mézières had suggested, become the serf of those of his subjects who rejected peace; but it is clear that the commitment of Cheshiremen to military service had outlived the lordship of the Black Prince on which it had been founded, and that the membership of a new professional military class took its place in the garrisons and companies who would continue the war.[60]

The career details of many remain obscure, but that of John Norbury stands as a convenient example. Having served initially as a *routier* in the Breton march in the 1360s and later as captain of Libourne, he moved to Brest as lieutenant to Sir Thomas Percy when the strategic importance of the garrison there was renewed following the second treaty of Guérande in 1381. In that office he was accused of levying 8,000 francs in excess of the usual *appatis*, but served again between 1389 and 1397 as lieutenant to John Holland, Earl of Huntingdon. During the same period he was able to join the 1385 expedition to Portugal, and in 1390 he was retained by Henry of Bolingbroke, on the first campaign in Prussia. That connection and his valuable service during the deposition of Richard II brought Norbury closer still to Bolingbroke; and in the first years of the fifteenth century he was first captain of Guînes and later treasurer of the exchequer and one of the king's permanent councillors.[61]

The collapse of English lordship in much of France had in fact greatly reduced the number of garrison appointments, and Sir Gregory Sais, Norbury's predecessor at Brest under Sir Hugh Calveley, mixed his foreign service there and at Calais with periods as captain of Pembroke and Berwick.[62] At least one garrison, that at Fronsac, which had been retained by the English after the treachery of Guilhem-Sanche de Pommiers in 1377, enjoyed a tradition of Cheshire captains. Sir Richard Cradock, whose career had begun in the defence of the Rouergue, was lodged there between 1383 and 1389, while his father, Sir David Cradock, acted as mayor of Bordeaux.[63] Sir Richard Aston who held the castle from 1395 to 1402, in fact refused to surrender it to the Earl of Rutland, to whom it had been granted in 1401, despite the terms of his indenture and a royal writ, although the dispute was eventually resolved and Aston moved first to Denbigh and later to Calais where he was lieutenant and captain from 1404 until 1408.[64] His own lieutenant at Fronsac in these years, to whom the keeping of the garrison had devolved, was Jenkin Grosvenor, another Cheshire squire whose own kinsman, John Grosvenor, was also there as constable under the Northumberland knight, Sir Thomas Swynburn, between 1408 and

1412.[65] For almost thirty years, therefore, the inhabitants of the castle and vicomté of Fronsac had felt the lordship, not of their Gascon lord, but of Cheshire gentry. Under such circumstances it is far from surprising that a merchant of the neighbouring town of Libourne, also frequently in the hands of Cheshire captains, should speak of the 'love and honour which he bore to the city of Chester' and chose to bequeath a fragment of the cross in a gold shrine to one of its churches.[66] Military service during this period did in fact bring men into close contact with a cosmopolitan world drawn from the soldiery of several European nations whose continued loyalty supported the cause of the English crown.[67] John Norbury had for instance retained the company of Boniface of Provona, an Italian mercenary, in 1402; and John Grosvenor would later serve alongside Henry van Emeric, a Flemish knight, in the garrison of Fronsac.[68] Like the Bascot de Mauleon, a Gascon routier whose experiences are so vividly reported by Froissart, such men moved freely within a world in which the energy and direction of political authority had collapsed. On many occasions it may simply have been the shared profession of arms and the lure of booty which had brought a company together.[69] John Carrington describes his experiences in Italy, where he and Robert Ardern had enlisted in the company of Alberigo de Barbiano in the service of Gian Galeazzo Visconti, Duke of Milan. There were, he said, 'many more Englishmen and Gascones, and eke other strange nations that thether comen woren in hope of sallerye'.[70] It is apparent, however, that many found in warfare the whole range of social and economic relationships. Thus it remains difficult to explain the earlier presence in Italy of Sir Thomas Swynburn, amongst a party of German and Bohemian knights embarking on pilgrimage to the Holy land, in terms other than of a fellowship of arms.[71] A long and severe training in the bearing of arms, and the duration and distance of service away from the English local communities, had ensured the emergence of a professional military class which did not, however, entirely replace the conventional relationship of lord and follower. It has been argued that the nobility strengthened their pre-eminent role as leaders in war, although the noble retinue now resembled less the local and regional following of its lord than a kaledioscope of personal and contractual elements formed beyond the locality. Adopting a role as subcontractors, the new class of professional soldier dominated the organisation of the noble retinue and on occasion, as on the crusade of Bishop Despenser in Flanders in 1383, was entirely capable of replacing it.

Nevertheless, for a time it had seemed that John of Gaunt might adopt a role in the organisation of war akin to that of the Black Prince. However, although the duke had retained amongst Cheshire knights at Bordeaux in 1371 and continued to do so after his *chevauchée* from Calais in 1373, his retinues seldom offered the same consistency of employment, nor were they ever the single focus of loyalty that his elder brother's had been. In the absence of the Prince's lordship and during the minority of Richard II, Gaunt, as the county's next largest secular landowner, assumed a leading role in the recruitment of Cheshiremen in those retinues which continued to reflect closely the forces and demands which shaped local society.[72] Amongst the new class of professional soldier, however, the Duke of Lancaster as Lord of Halton provided only one, albeit a favoured, source of employment. In the 1370s and 1380s knights such as Sir Hugh Browe, Sir Richard Cradock, Sir David Hulgreve, and Sir William Mainwaring found their way into the retinues of the Earls of March, Arundel and Buckingham with equal frequency. Of the captains of the period, the best-documented and most studied career remains that of Sir Hugh Calveley.[73]

Calveley was already a soldier of some renown whose experience reached back almost to the Crécy campaign, and from the beginning of 1373 he was again almost continuously employed in the war under a number of captains. We see him then on Gaunt's *chevauchée* from Calais to Bordeaux, and in the same year he was retained by the Seneschal of Aquitaine to undertake the safe-keeping of the countryside which separated the hard-pressed and vulnerable garrisons in Gascony.[74] Later he served for long periods as captain of Calais and Brest and, in 1379, was with Sir John Arundel on that knight's ill-fated expedition to Brittany.[75] In 1380 he joined Thomas of Woodstock's expedition with a retinue of 200 men-at-arms and 200 archers and later played a decisive role in the leadership of Despenser's crusade.[76] Thereafter, the scale of his involvement in the war declined; and he seems to have retired to England in 1385, although at the time of his death in 1393 he was still actively recruiting in Cheshire.[77]

In time Calveley has perhaps achieved the greater fame, but the pattern of his career is in some degree matched by other Cheshire knights who belong to the same circle of professional captains. In a brief four-year period between 1373 and 1377 there was a group of Cheshire soldiers serving successively in the retinues of four separate leaders (Sir Thomas Felton and the Earls of March, Arundel, and Buckingham).[78] That same variety of employment is illustrated by the career of Sir Richard Cradock, who had served initially in the garrisons of the principality under his father, Sir David Cradock. In the 1380s he had held the garrison at Fronsac and served with his own company, first with John, Lord Neville, in Gascony, and later with Bishop Despenser in Flanders and the Earl of Arundel at Sluis.[79] Few noble captains could now make more than a passing claim to the military service of the greater part of their retinues. What had occurred, at least in the county of Cheshire, was a fundamental shift in the organisation of war. In the 1350s and to a lesser extent the 1360s the lordship of the Black Prince had determined the nature and scale of military service in the county. The development of contractual forms had placed the responsibility for recruitment with local gentry affinities, but exercised little influence over the final shape of the Prince's retinues. Under these circumstances the decline of the Prince's involvement in the war during his last years and the long minority of Richard II had allowed Cheshire knights to move freely within a community of arms which ranged over Europe from Italy to Ireland. Indeed, during the last quarter of the fourteenth century there can have been few armies raised which did not include at least one Cheshire company within their ranks.

Relatively few of the military subcontracts which underpinned the recruitment of such armies now survive, and as a result we are often ignorant of the detailed role of this new class of professional soldier. A recently discovered group of twenty-four related subcontracts sealed by Sir Hugh Hastings before Thomas of Woodstock's expedition in 1380 has revealed a complex internal organisation of which no clue appears in Hastings' own retinue roll later presented to the exchequer. A similar pattern is revealed in a smaller group of seven subcontracts sealed by the Northumberland knight, Sir John Strother, in 1374.[80] On an earlier campaign the Lincolnshire knight, John, Lord Welles, had simply announced that he had been retained to serve in France and invited his 'dear companion and loyal friend', John Healing, whose company he greatly desired, to visit him to discuss the terms of his own service.[81] The evidence of Hastings's subcontracts confirms that the core of the retinue was still composed of the knight's servants and permanent retainers, although the sealing of the majority of the contracts in London and the apparent lack of connection between Hastings and these men does suggest a purely professional military relationships within the rest of the company. At least one of the subcontractors, Jenkin Nowell, is reported to have been 'a professional soldier and military enterpriser'. Likewise, Strother's recruits appear to have been raised from a pool of 'unemployed military manpower that gravitated towards London'.[82]

On the whole, the retinues of Cheshire captains, although they soon acquired the same cosmopolitan air, still preserved a strong local and regional character. On the basis of surname evidence alone, it seems likely that at least 25 per cent of the retinues of both Sir David Hulgreve and Sir Hugh Calveley in 1380 had been recruited in Cheshire, either by the knights themselves, or more probably through a series of local subcontractors.[83] A number of knights who may have fulfilled that role were again retained on the bishop of Norwich's crusade in Flanders, and at least one subcontract, between Thomas Danyers and Thomas Beeston, is still extant.[84] Calveley's retinue had also included a small group of Londoners from Farringdon and Ludgate wards, and Hulgreve's retinue a company from Weardale in County Durham. The presence of these smaller companies within the larger retinues does suggest that many of the exchequer retinue rolls might be profitably studied in the light of the evidence relating to that of Sir Hugh Hastings and Sir John Strother. Sir Thomas Felton had, for instance, accounted to the Constable of Bordeaux for a retinue of nine knights, fifty esquires and sixty archers as Seneschal of Aquitaine in 1374.[85] Clearly he had subcontracted with a number of soldiers to provide that company, one of whom, John Leycester of Tabley, later accounted before Felton's own auditors on his return to Southampton with a retinue of three esquires and eight archers.[86] A second group of related subcontracts also survives for Thomas of Woodstock's proposed Irish expedition in 1392, when a group of fifty-five knights and esquires were retained to provide the service of 409 soldiers. John Mascy of Puddington then undertook to raise the second largest company of ten men-at-arms and forty archers, but the majority of contracts were for the service of an esquire and a small number of soldiers. Hugh Mascy, Ralph Ardern and John Burton were each retained to provide the service of a single archer.[87] These were not the duke's permanent retainers, nor his tenants and neighbours, but simply those men with whom he had entered into a passing military relationship. The contractual army had reached its fullest stage of development, and it was within a network of individual contractual bonds that the English crown was able to continue its claim to the throne of France.

John Leycester's own small company of 1374, although recruited entirely in the locality, nevertheless conforms to the pattern of the larger hybrid retinues. Of his three esquires, Jenkin Mobberley was undoubtedly the kinsman of Sir Ralph Mobberley, with whom Leycester had served in Gascony between 1355 ans 1357.[88] Another, John Mascy of Tatton, was a neighbouring landowner with whom Leycester had acted frequently as a charter witness.[89] Of the archers only John Peacock can tentatively be identified as a tenant, and indeed it seems likely that the remainder of the company had little further contact after their disembarkation.[90] Few appear in a near contemporary rental of the Leycester estate or in the remaining charters of the family. Apart from that inner core of dependents, even the smallest retinues may have been relatively short-lived associations. In fact we know very little about many of the Cheshire companies of this period outside a handful of surviving retinue rolls. There is none extant for Leycester's near neighbour at Over Peover, Sir William Mainwaring, who had by his own account served continuously in Gascony over a period of twenty years.[91] In 1393 he was about to embark with John of Gaunt and made detailed provision for the dispersal of his lands and wealth in the event of his death. Could we but recognise them amongst the beneficiaries of the will, we might identify several of that same inner core of dependents and familiars who had accompanied the knight on his campaigns.[92] A certain 'Gylymot' who stood to receive £10 was almost certainly the 'Gylymot le Gascune' who was later granted land at Stoneley near Nantwich.[93] John Snelson, the bailiff of Peover, may also have accompanied his lord, but we learn of his military career only in a gift of Richard II which recognised his later service at the battle of Radcot Bridge.[94] It is often fairly simple to recover the details of individual service, but quite another problem to explain the dynamic of military society at this level.

Among Mainwaring's bequests had been one of £10 to John Leycester, his kinsman, tenant, neighbour and fellow soldier. His appearance and the variety of relationships which he enjoyed with Mainwaring does raise a basic question regarding the nature of military society. To what extent did the experience of warfare add a new dimension to the framework of Cheshire society? Families which could count professional soldiers in their number did intermarry and frequently entered into a variety of relationships with each other; but, given the nature of the available evidence, it is often quite difficult to demonstrate that relationships which emerge only in the records of land tenure may in fact have originated in a shared experience of warfare. Occasionally the evidence is simple and direct: a group of soldiers answering a summons to protect the lands of an absent companion; another group pausing in Bristol to witness a charter of one of their number; and a knight receiving part-settlement of a marriage agreement from a member of his company in the garrison at Fronsac.[95] Amongst men who shared a common position in Cheshire society war provided a means of continuing and elaborating that role; but there were other relationships which carried men beyond the confines of their own local society and indeed beyond their own class.

At the close of a long and ultimately profitable military career Sir David Hulgreve had died in London in 1405 and directed that his body should rest either in Saint Bartholomew's Hospital or in the Franciscan church at Newgate. Jean de Chateaumorand, the companion and biographer of Louis II, Duke of Bourbon, later remembered Sir David as one of the greatest and most vainglorious of the English captains in Thomas of Woodstock's retinue in 1380.[96] In his will he had left six marks to pay for a mass priest for a year for himself and his wife, his mother and father, two surviving kinsmen, and Sir Gregory Sais. In addition the income from the sale of the manor of Preston-on-Wye in Herefordshire was to be used to found a perpetual chantry for himself and Sais wherever his body finally lay.[97] The two knights had earlier shared in the unsuccessful defence of Poitou in the early 1370s where Hulgreve had been captured at Chizé and ransomed by du Guesclin, and Sais had lost his title to the castle and lordship of Gençay, although the precise nature of the relationship commemorated in Hulgreve's will is not explained.[98] Both Sais and Hulgreve had for a long time also been closely involved with the captain of another of the Poitevin garrisons at Lusignan in a much more demonstrable fashion. John Cresswell was retained by Charles II, king of Navarre in 1366, and it is in Spain during the Black Prince's campaign that he is first clearly associated with Hulgreve.[99] Two years later the two men shared the leadership of one of the companies in the service of John IV, Duke of Brittany, and throughout the campaigns in Poitou Froissart habitually brackets them together.[100] The relationship between Hulgreve and Cresswell, and perhaps also that between Hulgreve and Sais, was undoubtedly one of brotherhood-in-arms, an arrangement entered into at all levels of military society which has unfortunately left little mark in the record evidence. It is important here, not because it gave legal basis to financially profitable partnerships in war, but because it remains the particular creation of military society: an expression, less of contractual obligations than of '*la vie "a pot commun" entre les gens de guerre*'.[101] In a community in which family alliances and regional solidarities could play only a limited role, brotherhood-in-arms, alongside a broadly understood body of laws of war, represented an attempt to create bonds of loyalty and necessity appropriate to a new social milieu.

Much of the evidence is doubtless equivocal, but nonetheless it seems reasonable to infer, from the record of shared garrison appointments

for instance, that many Cheshire soldiers had entered into such relationships. In the 1370s John Legh and William More held the castle at
Monsegur, Thomas Venables and Andrew Handax that at Bergerac,
whilst William Mainwaring and Philipot Ellis shared the leadership of
a retinue within the *pays* de Bordeaux.[102] On occasion these arrangements between soldiers may have been of a temporary and entirely
circumstantial nature, as for instance in 1380 when Richard Cradock
seems to have added his own company to that of Sir John Sandes in order
to muster a retinue of 100 men-at-arms and 100 archers under the
leadership of John, Lord Neville, in Gascony.[103] At other times and for
the majority of our subjects, they clearly represent one of the few points
at which it is possible to approach the detail of personal loyalties in the
surviving record material. It is, for instance, almost certainly a relationship of brotherhood-in-arms that is described in some detail in the
unusual early fifteenth-century autobiography of John Carrington.[104]
In 1400 he and another Cheshireman, Robert Ardern of Alvanley,
shared in the abortive attempt to raise the western counties in support
of Richard II and, after fleeing together to Paris, eventually took service
with other English and Gascon soldiers under Gian Galeazzo Visconti.
At the battle of Brescia in 1401 the two men shared in the ransom of
a Dutch squire, and later, following Ardern's death crossing the Alps,
Carrington lived for several years in Brabant on the shared profits of
their campaigns which Ardern had bequeathed to his companion.

Relationships formed entirely in war might often adopt the language
and many of the characteristic features of the kinship group, and indeed
it is interesting to note how brotherhood-in-arms was rapidly assimilated
by the operation of both kinship and landed society in the locality. After
his return to England, Sir David Hulgreve added to his recently acquired lands in Herefordshire by marrying Helen Bertram, the heir to
the castle and lordship of Bothal in Northumberland.[105] He was now
not only John Cresswell's brother-in-arms but also his near neighbour,
for Cresswell itself lay only a few miles from Bothal. That the arms of
a Cheshire knight, unknown from record evidence relating to his own
native county, should ultimately feature in the glass of a Northumberland parish church was therefore almost entirely the result of the actions
of the military community to which Hulgreve owed his position as a
member of landed society in that county. These men might come
together in adversity, out of simple friendship and the shared experience
of war, or out of economic necessity and the lure of profit; but such
relationships, once formed, often enjoyed the validity and vitality of
those created by the pressures and demands of local society.

At the time of his death, Hulgreve held land in four counties and in his will had made bequests amounting to £100. The obscurity of his origins, when compared with the final level of his success in regional society, clearly raises important questions about the recruitment of the military community and the degree of social mobility which occurred as a direct result of warfare. On the basis of the testimony of the Scope-Grosvenor witnesses, it is apparent that the leadership of landed society in Cheshire continued its participation in war during the final quarter of the fourteenth century. The occasions of that service, however, had been widespread musters of the earl's lordship which found service, first in Gascony in 1369, and again in Scotland in 1385. Few men had more than a passing experience of the war in France between those dates, and indeed the typical Cheshire knight was often the lord of a few manors which he managed directly and could ill-afford to leave for the duration of military campaigns. Inevitably the membership of that community of arms which we have argued had an existence during this period attracted those who, if not without prospect, were then certainly without immediate responsibility in local society. In a sense, therefore, it may be slightly misleading to speak of an essentially landless military community, although equally many of its members found only a somewhat truncated role in county society as a consequence of their military careers.

The prosopographical material is far from complete, but that which does survive may be seen to qualify, rather than undermine, the general validity of this hypothesis. John Norbury, Sir David Hulgreve, Sir Hugh Calveley, John Jodrell, and even Sir John Stanley, who in the 1380s moved from the garrison at Cherbourg to the lieutenancy of Ireland, are all to be counted amongst those who were either virtually landless or else the younger sons of minor gentry families.[106] Other soldiers such as Sir William Mainwaring and John Carrington, although both were later leading members of county society, played no active part in county governance and affairs during the years of their military campaigns. Carrington returned to England only after the death of his elder brother without male heir, a man of whom he observed, 'he levide ever more at whome one his livelihode and heritage'.[107] Mainwaring himself apparently sealed no charter in England between the early 1360s and his eventual return in the 1390s, a period during which his mother, who outlived him, retained her dower portion of the Peover estate.[108] Some knights did undoubtedly count themselves amongst the landed families of the county: Sir David Cradock held land in Nantwich, John Leycester at Tabley, and Sir Richard Aston at Aston near Runcorn.

But of the men whose names become familiar at even the most cursory reading of the records of the county court at Chester, there is little sign in the campaigns of the 1370s and 1380s.[109] A knight who served in France could not pursue the aggressively litigious role that so occupied the life of the late medieval gentry, and indeed much of the evidence speaks of the almost inevitable separation of roles between the active soldier and the member of county society.

A case in point is provided by the Maisterson family of Nantwich. Thomas Maisterson senior had pursued a military career in the years after the battle of Nájera in the retinues of John of Gaunt and Henry of Bolingbroke. Retained for life by Gaunt in 1371, he accompanied the duke on his remaining campaigns before leading the Lancastrian party in Cheshire during the reign of Richard II.[110] After the battle of Agincourt his younger son, Thomas, went to France as an officer in the English administration of Normandy, acquired lands in Rouen and the Pays de Caux, and was later married to a Frenchwoman, the Dame d'Aurichier, before his death shortly after 1428.[111] Of the son's military career, his descendant and the family biographer, Laurance Maisterson, was totally ignorant, although he had before him the family deed collection containing ample record of the father's military career in the years to 1399.[112] Thomas Maisterson junior's departure for France in 1419 was therefore a total and, in the event, final separation from his lineage in Cheshire. It was also, one suspects, an experience which was far from unique amongst the military community.

For many knights, however, the separation was broken by retirement to England in the 1380s, an event which often heralded the beginning of a renewed activity in the land-market and in the courts. On his return Sir William Mainwaring sought to recover his rights in the manor of Baddiley, of which he claimed to have been disseised during the time of his service in Gascony.[113] Calveley, Hulgreve, and Norbury all appear in earnest in the land-market at the same time, although in the main their activities were now concentrated outside Cheshire. Amongst his many purchases Calveley did acquire the manor of Eccleston in the county, but Norbury bought lands close to London in Hertfordshire, and Hulgreve invested in Herefordshire and Northumberland, suggesting thereby that men who had made good in the war were reluctant or unable to re-enter the local society from which they had sprung.[114] In their own communities they feared that, like the German brigand Crokart, whose cautionary tale is told by Froissart, their newly-found wealth would fail to impress lords they had once known.[115] Nevertheless, they were now men with wealth to invest, and indeed, on occasion,

they found themselves competing with one another for lucrative wardships of minors; a distinct community which now sought an active role
in English local society.[116] Of the high degree of social and political
success which often fell to such members of the military community,
there can be little doubt. In 1401 Sir John Stanley, Sir Hugh Browe,
Sir David Hulgreve, and John Norbury were among the knights and
esquires summoned by Henry IV for the second of his great councils,
each representing his adopted county.[117] Norbury's epitaph in the
Greyfriars' church in London described him in terms redolent of his
new status: '*valens armiger strenuus ac probus John Norbury quondam magnus
thesaurarius regni Angliae ...*'[118] At the same time Sir John Stanley, who
had forty years earlier avoided legal sanctions only through military
service after leading his elder brother's campaign of violence and murder
in the Wirral, could see his own arms amongst those of the political community in the newly-built cloister walks of Canterbury cathedral.[119]
The achievement of such careerists can come as little surprise to the
historian of the later middle ages, but amongst the avenues of recruitment whereby the composition of the *élite* groups of medieval society
underwent change, it is interesting to note that war provided one of the
most important and direct.[120]

Soldiers were by the very nature of the war in France transformed
into secular administrators, and in this role they prospered as the
privileged servants of the crown and nobility. In the time of the Black
Prince, Sir John Delves and Sir John Chandos had been the most
notable soldier/administrators of their day, but the pattern of their
careers can be matched throughout the military community, from the
knight who held the castle and lordship of Fronsac to his contemporary
who held the lieutenancy of Ireland. What is perhaps more important
is that experience gained in the garrisons of provincial France was often
held to be of value in England, providing a route along which many in
the military community were recruited into the ranks of English political
society proper.

Amongst those whose careers we have followed, four may stand as
convenient models: Sir David Cradock, John Norbury, Sir John Stanley
and Sir Richard Aston. Following the English withdrawal from the
Rouergue, where he had been lieutenant under Sir Thomas Wettenhall,
Sir David Cradock returned to England to play a leading role in the
administration of Wales, first as justiciar of North Wales and briefly
as justiciar of both North and South Wales.[121] In 1382 he returned to
Gascony for the last time and, for four years, held office as mayor of
Bordeaux.[122] John Norbury, who in the 1390s had been retained by

Henry of Bolingbroke in Prussia, was among the first to attach himself to Henry's cause at Leominster in 1399 and, even four weeks before Henry's accession to the throne, was appointed as treasurer of the Exchequer in his first appointments to the civil service.[123] For the next six years he was among the king's permanent councillors and, as a result of his early career in the Breton garrisons, acted as intermediary with Joan, Duchess of Brittany, soon to become Henry's queen.[124] Sir John Stanley after a meteoric rise in the following of Robert de Vere, Earl of Oxford, acted as justiciar of Ireland, as warden of the east March on the Scottish border, and as justice of Chester.[125] In the last years of Richard II's reign he became controller of the king's household, but then, like John Norbury, succeeded easily in reconciling himself to the new regime, serving thereafter in the household of Henry, Prince of Wales.[126] The social prestige which was often attached to such offices is equally apparent in the later career of Sir Richard Aston as lieutenant at Calais under Sir Thomas Beaufort, Henry IV's half-brother. His career in the garrison there is amply documented in a series of letters and petitions, and in 1405 his defence of the castle at Marck was to pass into the Brut chronicle; and, beyond his military duties, Aston retained an oversight of the complex and often laborious negotiations concerning commercial treaties with Flanders.[127] His surviving correspondence with Margaret de Mâle, Duchess of Burgundy, and with the council in England, suggests that he could speak on level terms with the European nobility.[128] Similar catalogues of official appointments provide convincing evidence that a proven military and administrative worth were qualities which commanded a high respect from both the crown and the nobility: foundations on which many were able to build a spectacular social and political success.

Detailed confirmation of such a career is provided by Sir John Stanley, born the younger son of a minor Cheshire knight, who died as justice of Ireland and lord of Man, and whose great-grandson was created Earl of Derby. Stanley had served in Gascony, probably from the early 1370s, although it was in Ireland that he was to make his mark in the dual role of soldier and administrator, serving as justiciar for no less than four separate periods between 1386 and his death in office at Ardee in 1414.[129] His early career belongs to the period of the defence of English lordship in Aquitaine, although like many of his contemporaries he makes only a fitful appearance in official documents. In 1377 a pardon for the murder of Thomas of Clotton spoke in conventional terms of past and future service in Gascony, and was issued on condition that he took service with Sir Thomas Trivet, at whose request the king had acted.[130] A sixteenth-century poem on his life written by Thomas Stanley, bishop of Sodor and Man (d. 1570), which elsewhere is plainly derived from Froissart's narrative, may preserve some part of the family tradition of his career when it associates him with the otherwise unremarkable campaign of Robert Knolles in 1372 on which Trivet also served.[131] Later in 1385 he was retained by Thomas Holland, Earl of Kent, in the garrison at Cherbourg, and was appointed as de Vere's lieutenant in Ireland in the following year.[132] The basis of his preferment is far from clear: either military experience and reputation, or perhaps more likely, a connection with the king's chamber knight, Sir Thomas Trivet.

In several respects Ireland ought perhaps to have been the perfect arena in which to deploy the talents of the military community. For much of the fourteenth century, as the Dublin council itself once observed, it seemed to be 'in continua guerra'. Furthermore, the frontier character of Irish lordship and the inevitable localisation of effective military and political power would have been instantly familiar to men who had learnt their craft in the defence of English lordship in France.[133] Nevertheless, Stanley's experience of Irish government remained unique, and the experiment of his appointment was not repeated amongst his peers. In total he served in Ireland for some six years; as justice in 1386 and 1387, again from 1389 to 1391 and from 1399 to 1401, and finally in 1413 and 1414. In the interval he had also joined Richard II on both his Irish campaigns. Assessments of his military and administrative achievement have varied widely, although if the venom of the Irish chroniclers and those who petitioned against his extortions is any guide, his rule was brutally efficient. In 1413 the Connacht annalist noted that 'John Stanley came to Ireland to destroy the Gaels of Ireland. He was a man who granted no protection to cleric or layman or to the poets of Ireland, for he plundered every one of its clerics and men of skill in every art on whom he laid hands, and exposed them to cold and beggary.' In the following year his death at Ardee in Louth was claimed as a poet's miracle for the rhymer Niall O'Higgin.[134] Later writers, relying on the terms of a commission in 1391, have found his conduct of Irish government to be unsatisfactory and incompetent.[135] Whatever the justice of criticisms levelled at his administration in 1391, and it should perhaps be remembered that he was appointed to the office twice more. It is clear that the debate has obscured Stanley's real contribution in precisely those areas which had been his original recommendation.

In early March 1386 Stanley had been appointed to arrest shipping for Robert de Vere's retinue, and on 20 March he was retained for one year as his lieutenant. There is some question as to whether de Vere ever intended to embark for Ireland, and certainly by April letters of protection issued to members of the justice's retinue spoke of 'John Stanley supplying the place of Robert de Vere'.[136] Stanley himself had scarcely begun the laborious work of organising a major military campaign against the Irish when he was recalled to England, doubtless as a result of the growing unpopularity of the court in general, and of the Earl of Oxford in particular.[137] In the aftermath of the battle of Radcot Bridge (December 1387) the Bishop of Meath was ordered to remove all de Vere's appointees and to destroy all symbols of his rule in Ireland, although Stanley appears to have escaped the venom of the Appellants.[138] In the same year he was appointed as warden of the east March on the Scottish border and received gifts from Henry of Bolingbrooke, then Earl of Derby.[139] On 1 August 1389 he was appointed as justice of Ireland in his own right, serving for three years with a retinue of five knights, 94 esquires, 300 mounted archers and 100 foot archers at an annual fee of 8,000 marks.[140]

The structure of the retinue followed the patterns which we have observed amongst those of the military community in France, with their readily identifiable kinship groups and local affinities. The inner core of dependents was composed of Stanley's own kinsmen and a small group of neighbouring knights and esquires, many of whom would continue to serve in his later campaigns. Thus John Audlem, who served as escheator in 1389, returned as treasurer in 1400, together with Nicholas Orrell and Gilbert Halsall.[141] Like his predecessor, Sir Ralph Ufford, Stanley employed the retinue to secure himself an independent military base, and by judicious use of rewards and grants sought to extend that independence into the political life of the lordship.[142] Almost inevitably such actions fuelled complaints regarding the conduct of Irish government, and early in 1391 the bishop of Ossory was empowered to enquire into Stanley's handling of the ransom of Niall O'Neill, into the size of his retinue and his employment of the Irish revenues. No record of the enquiries is now extant, although it is known that the retinue was found to be deficient in numbers at musters taken at Naas in May 1391. A few months later he was replaced as justice by the bishop of Meath, although no further action was taken against him.[143]

If Stanley was indeed guilty of peculation on a more than customary scale, there is little record of it in the grants and rewards made to members of his affinity, and even the shortfall in his retinue is perhaps less damning than has been suggested. In the original musters held at Dublin the bishop of Meath had observed that the hundred foot archers were of little use in Irish warfare and suggested that the justice be allowed to recruit extra men as the occasion demanded. Stanley did in fact employ large numbers of local hobelars and armed foot in a successful campaign against the grain stores of the Irish between May and July 1390.[144] Tactics learned on this campaign were later employed to great effect on Richard II's first expedition in 1394, in which Stanley was to play a leading military and diplomatic role.[145] Both serve to establish his reputation as an effective military captain and undermine the scant adverse detail which survives from the commission of 1391. In the interval no English successor had been appointed as justice, and it appears likely that the reasons for his dismissal are to be sought in the problems which the crown itself faced in governing Ireland. Stanley's attractiveness as a soldier/administrator continued undiminished, and in common with many of his contemporaries he was to occupy a leading role in the increasingly violent politics of Richard's reign.

War may be seen as a complementary and often alternative career to that of the knight in local society and as a means of social advancement, but to what extent did such concerns determine the actions of those who served in war? We have already argued that compulsion and even the operation of county society were now less important in the organisation of military recruitment. For a significant number of men military service was a matter of individual choice, and not a response to economic necessity, or to the pressure of social and political structure. The individual's perception of the advantages to be gained in war is therefore vital to an understanding of the emergence of the military community. The debate as to the costs of the Hundred Years War would here be out of place.[146] What is important is the question of motivation and the study of individual fortune amongst those whose membership of military society we have recognised.

Throughout our period it seems likely that risks were on the whole commensurate with opportunities; the latter attracted those with most to gain, the former deterred those with most to lose. In general it appears that both profit and risk were greatest during the years between 1360 and 1400. The payment of wages was often in arrears and, as a result, was seldom a critical determinant in the attractiveness of war-service. In an interesting series of petitions from the Calais garrison whose wages were two years in arrears, Sir Richard Aston reminded the king and the council in 1404 of 'the perils, and also the remedies which might be conceived', and urged them to expedite payment so that the garrison might not 'work for the maintenance of our lives and simple estates in a dishonest manner'.[147] Annuities, though clearly of a different order, were themselves often payable at set locations which did not always accord with a knight's later movements. In 1380 Thomas Halton appointed attorneys in Southwark to collect an annuity of 100 shillings at the Ombrière in Bordeaux, but Sir David Hulgreve let a similar grant from the Black Prince lapse whilst his service in France prevented collection in England.[148] There can be little doubt that irregular sources of income were seen as providing the major sources of wealth. The payment of wages may doubtless have provided ample opportunity for embezzlement by captains, but it was only when other advantages were missing, as at Calais in 1404, that they assumed a real importance in the fortunes of the ordinary soldier.[149]

Indentures make frequent reference to these irregular incidents of war in the form of ransoms, booty and *appatis*, and clearly suggest that great importance was attached to them by the respective parties. John Carrington was able, albeit modestly and often in monastic guest houses, to live for two years on the profit of a single ransom taken at the battle of Brescia in 1401.[150] Similar incidents of a like character are poorly documented in the surviving Cheshire evidence, and indeed much of our knowledge of the success of the military community comes, paradoxically, from the detail of their own ransoms. After his capture at the castle of Marck in 1405 Sir Richard Aston had petitioned Henry IV for 500 marks towards his ransom of 1,000 marks.[151] Losses of that order must, one supposes, have been balanced by the prospect, if not the reality, of similar gains. The experience of the Bascot de Mauléon, as recounted by Froissart, may again be typical: 'Sometimes I have been so thoroughly down that I hadn't even a horse to ride, and at other times fairly rich, as luck came and went'.[152] The same succession of fortune and loss can be observed in the career of Sir Richard Cradock. In 1379 he and a brother-in-arms, John Sandes, were able to lend the king nearly 4,000 pounds. Five years later he was captured on the bishop of Norwich's crusade in Flanders, and his father, Sir David Cradock, was obliged to arrange payment of 300 marks by the abbey of Sainte Croix in Bordeaux in part settlement of the ransom. In 1390 he petitioned Richard II after the loss of the *Katharine of Ipswich* at the mouth of the Thames, the ship having contained 'wines, iron and other merchandise, and certain coffers of jewels and other things, the apparatus of the said Richard'.[153]

Some of the wealth which they accumulated can be seen in the rebuilding of churches to which they were drawn by conventional piety, and in which they often proclaimed the extent of their advancement in war. John Carrington added a new lady chapel to the church at Rivenhall in Essex, Sir David Hulgreve the south chapel at Bothal, and Sir Hugh Calveley financed an extensive rebuilding at Bunbury to house the secular college which he had founded in 1387.[154] Nevertheless, Nantwich has some claim to be regarded as the most impressive of the Cheshire 'war churches', not least as a result of its splendid chancel, remodelled between 1391 and 1405.[155] A mutilated tomb, clearly a late-fourteenth-century date and bearing the arms of the Cradock family, now occupies a prominent position in the south transept. It would seem feasible to associate either Sir David or Sir Richard Cradock with the exactly contemporary rebuilding of the church in which it rests. Likewise, perhaps, we may associate the chancel in the church at nearby Audley (Staffordshire) with the tomb of Sir John Delves which originally rested in its centre. Little secular building can now be associated with the members of the military community, except perhaps the unusual tower house at Doddington which Sir John Delves received licence to crenellate in 1365.[156] There are the tombs of course, mostly no longer in the proprietorial positions that their occupants would wish, and doubtless paid for, but expressive nonetheless of the impact of military society in the locality. Those of John Norbury and Sir David Hulgreve in London were destroyed, but those of Sir Hugh Calveley at Bunbury, Sir David Cradock at Nantwich, Sir Thomas Wettenhall at Montlaur, Sir John Delves at Audley, and Sir William Mainwaring at Acton still survive.[157]

It is really only in wills that we begin to discover something of these men as individuals, although the small number of surviving examples hardly constitutes a representative sample.[158] The administrative role undertaken by Stanley, Norbury and Aston suggests a widespread degree of literacy which is supported by the mention of books in bequests. Robert Winnington possessed a psalter, Sir David Hulgreve a missal, and Roger Jodrell a psalter, a porthouse or portable breviary and a copy of a scientific work known as 'Sidrac'. Sir Richard Cradock may have been a minor poet.[159] John Carrington's autobiography, so we are told by its fifteenth-century copyist, survived in an autograph manuscript.[160] None of the wills, however, appears to be in the hand of the testator.

In all examples the ties of family and locality are apparent in the detail of bequests to the extended kinship group and, in some cases, to friends and neighbours. Sir William Mainwaring and Roger Jodrell both expressed a wish to be buried in their own parish churches at Acton and

Taxal, doubtless revealing a proprietary attitude; but both Sir David Hulgreve and Robert Winnington chose burial in London, the former in Saint Bartholomew's hospital and the latter in a chapel of St Martin-le-Grand. Both Sir William Mainwaring and Sir David Hulgreve dispensed charity among the poor and sick on their lands, but in all cases it appears likely that the major motive was a discriminatory interest in the safety of the testator's soul.

Most of the wills illustrate aspects of a piety conventional amongst the later medieval gentry. For instance, with the exception of a small gift to the local Cistercian house at Combermere, most bequests were directed to the newer orders, especially the friars. Much earlier, another member of the military community, Thomas Stathum, had endowed the Carmelite convent in Chester where the friars undertook to confer on him the title of founder.[161] All of the testators paid for masses to be said for their souls: Sir William Mainwaring for masses at Acton, Peover and Siddington. But only Sir David Hulgreve endowed a permanent chantry. Hulgreve's will conforms closely to the pattern we might expect of the professional soldier, pricked by conscience and apprehensive about purgatory. Apart from the permanent chantry which he endowed from the sale of Preston-on-Wye in Herefordshire, other large sums were to be distributed among the deaf, leprous and other poor, among the clergy of Ludgate, Newgate and Fleet wards, and amongst nine clerics who were to say masses for up to two years. Perhaps significantly, Hulgreve was also the only knight to exhibit a close knowledge of the liturgy, specifying that the daily collect '*Deus ordine nostre redemptionis*' be used in his masses. The will of Robert Winnington, on the other hand, after requesting prayers at the church at St Nicholas in Macclesfield and the payment of debts, is almost exclusively concerned with the dispersal of the knight's military equipment amongst his kinsmen and companions. There is scant evidence that military service had created a community with anything more than conventional religious and social attitudes.

During the last quarter of the fourteenth century a significant number of men had gained a great deal from war. Ultimately, much of the wealth and social standing of knights like Sir John Stanley had derived from their actions as members of the English political community, although their success there was in turn often a direct result of the exercise of military skills elsewhere. For Thomas Stanley, the sixteenth-century biographer of John Stanley, it was clear that these men had won 'advancement by warr', and in a sense this was a concept that the military community itself might have shared.[162] Certainly, when John

Carrington, deprived of his status and identity in the political traumas of Richard II's deposition, had settled in Essex and acquired through marriage and patronage a landed share in the community, he recounted his pedigree, his claim to ancient and noble status, to his wife. It was a pedigree referring to his own military exploits and those of his lineage.[168]

NOTES

[1] J. Le Patourel, 'The Origins of the War' in *The Hundred Years War*, ed. K. Fowler, 1971, pp. 28–50.

[2] B. C. Keeney, 'Military Service and the Development of Nationalism in England, 1272–1327', *Speculum*, xxii, 1947, pp. 534–49; G. L. Harriss, *King, Parliament and Public Finance in Medieval England to 1369*, 1975, pp. 509–7.

[3] Fundamental starting points are Pierre-Clement Timbal, *La Guerre de Cent Ans Vue À Travers Les Registres Du Parlement 1337–1369*, 1961; Philippe Contamine, *Guerre, État Et Société à la fin du Moyen Age*, 1972; H. J. Hewitt, *The Organization of War under Edward III*, 1966. The best recent work in English has concentrated on warfare as a single element in the experience of local and regional society, see R. R. Davies, *Lordship and Society in the March of Wales 1282–1400*, 1978, pp. 67–85; Robin Frame, 'Power and Society in Ireland 1272–1377', *Past and Present*, 76, 1977, pp. 3–33.

[4] See above pp. 42–3; R. H. Hilton, *A Medieval Society*, 1966, p. 166.

[5] A. Goodman, 'The Military Subcontracts of Sir Hugh Hastings, 1380', *EHR*, xcv, 1980, pp. 114–20; Simon Walker, 'Profit and Loss in the Hundred Years War: the Subcontracts of Sir John Strother, 1374', *BIHR*, lviii, 1985, pp. 100–6.

[6] See for example M. H. Keen, 'Brotherhood in Arms', *History*, xlvii, 1962, pp. 1–17.

[7] Michel Hébert, 'L'Armée Provençale en 1374', *Annales du Midi*, 91, 1979, pp. 5–27. The principal physical characteristics of individual soldiers are described in great detail.

[8] See above pp. 26–32. On the emergence of a new professional military class in the armies of the French king, see Contamine, op. cit., pp. 542–6.

[9] See Table 5.

[10] G. Ormerod, *The History of the County Palatine and City of Chester*, 3 vols, ed. T. Helsby, 2nd edition, 1882, II, p. 412; CRO, Baker-Wilbraham Deeds A/A/B 40–2.

[11] BL Additional Roll 74,131; BL Harley MS 2074 f. 223.

[12] The Warburtons were lords of Appleton, *Arley Charters*, ed. W. Beamont, 1866, p. 24; William Vernon held land at Goostrey, *BPR* III, p. 207; John Marbury appears with Mobberley in a charter of July 1355, CRO, Leycester Warren MSS, DLT/A14/13a,b.

[13] BL Additional Charter 72,533; CRO, Baker-Wilbraham Deeds A/A/G5.

[14] *BPR* III, p. 200; Duchy of Cornwall Office, *Journal of John Henxteworth*, m. 10d, John of Baguley, Robert Parkin, William White, and perhaps Roger of Boseden. Similar subgroupings in retinues were a common characteristic, see Goodman, op. cit., p. 117; Simon Walker, op. cit., pp. 100–6.

[15] *BPR* I, p. 50; KUL, Legh of Booths charter 36. His annuity was assigned for life to lands at Norshaw in Tatton in Mobberley's will, BL Additional Charter 72,415.

[16] *BPR* III, pp. 352, 357, 372; T. P. Highet, *The Early History of the Davenports of Davenport*, Chet. Soc., 3rd series, ix, 1960, p. 25.

[17] *BPR* III, pp. 383, 392, 405, 420, 463; C61/78 m. 5.

[18] A. L. Brown, 'The Authorization of Letters under the Great Seal', *BIHR*, xxxvii, 1964, pp. 30 – 1. See for example the petition of Sir Hugh Calveley on behalf of a member of his retinue, SC1/43/52.

[19] N. D. Hurnard, *The King's Pardon for Homicide before A. D. 1307*, 1969, p. 311 – 23.

[20] *BPR*, III, pp. 131, 178, 207, 213, 272, 455.

[21] The best-known example concerns the deceptions practised on two Portuguese envoys in London in 1384 by which a number of soldiers, including several Cheshiremen, obtained protections, see P. E. Russell, *The English Intervention in Spain and Portugal in the Time of Edward III and Richard II*, 1955, pp. 369 – 71. See also the record of an inquisition at Macclesfield in 1397 concerning a protection granted to Thomas son of Thomas Danyers for service at Berwick, *Calendar of Inquisitions Miscellaneous, 1377–1422*, p. 165.

[22] See for example Chester 29/72 m. 15.

[23] Chancery Warrants, C81/1722/26. Petition of Sir Hugh Calveley in favour of a member of his retinue. Three 'passes' were issued to Mobberley's retinue, two to his close kinsmen, Richard and Jenkin Mobberley, but a further seven archers deserted without licence, see above p. 112.

[24] H. J. Hewitt, *The Black Prince's Expedition of 1355 – 1357*, 1958, pp. 81 – 4.

[25] See for example the final account of John Leycester at Southampton in 1374, CRO, Leycester Warren MSS DLT/A11/85. Two original receipts for wages paid to members of Richard Aston's retinue in Spain in 1386, dated at Aston near Runcorn, survive in BL Additional Charters 51,120 – 1.

[26] *BPR*, III, p. 371.

[27] *BPR*, III, pp. 252, 254, 258. A curious incident in Knutsford Booths park, after the return to England, in which John Leycester took a coat and surcoat from John Baguley and carried it to Mobberley's home, may perhaps have been a dispute over booty, Chester 25/8 m. 6.

[28] *BPR*, III, pp. 238 – 40.

[29] Hewitt, op. cit., p. 163.

[30] *BPR*, III, p. 356.

[31] *BPR*, III, pp. 371 – 2.

[32] *BPR*, III, pp. 259, 265, 337. On this point see Maurice Keen, *Chivalry* (1984), 220 – 4 and Philippe Contamine, *War in the Middle Ages* (1984), pp. 255 – 9.

[33] Golborne's inquisition post mortem is dated in December 1359 while he was serving with the Prince at Rheims, see *BPR*, III, pp. 356, 371; Chester 3/3 (2).

[34] W. A. Copinger, *History and Records of the Smith-Carrington Family*, 1907, p. 37; *BPR*, III, pp. 200, 356.

[35] Hébert, op. cit., p. 23; B. Thordeman, *Armour from the Battle of Wisby, 1361*, I, 1939, pp. 149 – 97; Philippe Contamine, loc. cit.

[36] PCC, Probate 11/2a. f. 57.

[37] Chester 29/72 m. 16; SC1/56/87.

[38] Chester 1/1 part 5 (27) and see above pp. 116–17.

[39] Chester 25/8 m. 7, m. 23; Duchy of Lancaster Court Rolls, DL30/2/34 m. 2.

[40] Chester 25/8 m. 2. Hichessone's reputation was apparently justified for soon after the original indictment he had assaulted the jurors in their homes; *ibid.*, m. 5d, m. 6.

[41] W. A. Copinger, op. cit., pp. 38–9.

[42] CRO, Cholmondeley of Cholmondeley Deeds, DCH/H/12; Chester 25/8 m. 32d; *CCR, 1388–1392*, pp. 287, 308.

[43] SC8/126/6262; Chester 3/17 (7).

[44] A point made forcibly in M. J. Bennett, 'Sources and problems of social mobility: Cheshire in the later Middle Ages', *THLC*, 128, 1979, pp. 59–95.

[45] *BPR*, III, p. 258.

[46] K. Fowler, *Les finances et la discipline dans les armées Anglaises en France au xive siècle*; G. L. Harriss, *King, Parliament and Public Finance in Medieval England to 1369*, 1975, pp. 329–32.

[47] H. Bousquet, 'Comptes consulaires de la cité et du bourg de Rodez', *Archives Historiques du Rouergue*, xvii, 1943, p. 412; Michael J. Bennett, *Community, Class and Careerism. Cheshire and Lancashire Society in the Age of Sir Gawain and the Green Knight*, 1983, p. 172.

[48] Kenneth Fowler, *The Age of Plantagenet and Valois*, 1967, p. 70.

[49] See above p. 133; C. T. Allmand, 'The Lancastrian Land Settlement in Normandy, 1417–50', *Econ. H. R.*, 2nd Series, xxi, 1968, pp. 461–2.

[50] W. A. Copinger, op. cit., p. 73.

[51] See for example Paul Guerin, 'Recueil des documents concernant le Poitou contenus dans les registres de la chancellerie de France', iv, 1369–76, *Archives Historiques du Poitou*, xix, 1888, pp. 129, 166–9.

[52] Margaret Wade Labarge, *Gascony, England's First Colony 1204–1453*, 1980, p. 178.

[53] A. D. Carr, 'A Welsh Knight in the Hundred Years War: Sir Gregory Sais', *Transactions of the Honourable Society of Cymmrodorion*, 1977, pp. 47–8.

[54] *Comptes du connétable de Bordeaux*, Archives Historiques du Département de la Gironde, xii, 1870, pp. 328–41; E101/181/1 nos 16, 18, 24; E101/181/4 nos 16, 17, 21.

[55] *Chronique de Bazas*, Archives Historiques du Département de la Gironde, xv, 1874, p. 48.

[56] CRO, Leycester of Tabley MSS DLT/A11/85.

[57] Carr, op. cit., p. 46; *Chroniques de J. Froissart*, ed. Siméon Luce, viii, 1878, pp. 51–3, 133, 279.

[58] Michael Jones, *Ducal Brittany 1364–1399*, 1970, pp. 74–5; *Froissart*, ed. Luce, viii, 1878, pp. 133, 147.

[59] E101/181/1 nos 50, 66, 70–1.

[60] J. J. N. Palmer, *England, France and Christendom 1377–99*, 1972, *passim*; Philippe de Mézières, *Letter to King Richard II*, ed. G. W. Coopland, 1975, pp. 51–3, 124–7.

[61] K. Fowler, *Les Finance de la Discipline dans les Armées anglaises en France au xive siècle*, p. 70; M. Barber, 'John Norbury; An Esquire of Henry IV's', *EHR*, lxviii, 1953, pp. 66–76.

[62] Carr, op. cit., pp. 48–50.

[63] J. Sherborne, 'Indentured Retinues and English Expeditions to France', *EHR*, lxxix, 1964, p. 739.

[64] M. G. A. Vale, *English Gascony 1399–1453*, 1970, p. 44; BL Additional Charters 51,120, 51,131. F. Devon, *Issues of the Exchequer*, Record Commission, 1837, p. 290; E101/43/9; E101/404/24 m. 4, m. 9; J. L. Kirby, 'Calais sous les Anglais 1399–1413', *Revue du Nord*, 1955, p. 24.

[65] *Royal and Historical Letters during the Reign of Henry IV*, ed. F. C. Hingeston, Rolls Series, 1860, i, p. 451; E101/185/6.

[66] J. Hemingway, *History of the City of Chester*, 1831, i, pp. 138–9.

[67] J. Sherborne, op. cit., pp. 727–9.

[68] BL Additional Charter 5830; E101/185/6.

[69] Froissart, *Chronicles*, ed. G. Brereton, 1978, pp. 280–94.

[70] W. A. Copinger, op. cit., p. 74.

[71] 'Voyage en Terre-Sainte d'un Maire de Bordeaux au xive siècle', *Archives de L'Orient Latin publié par la Société de L'Orient Latin*, ii, 1884, pp. 378–88.

[72] *John of Gaunt's Register, 1372–6*, ed. S. Armitage-Smith, Camden Society, 3rd Series, xx, 1911, pp. 778–9; see above pp. 72–4.

[73] Most of the published records are described in G. A. Snead, *The Careers of Four Fourteenth Century Military Commanders serving Edward III and Richard II*, University of Kent MA, 1968, 59 *et. seq.*

[74] BL Additional MS 37494 m. 2d, m. 38d; *Comptes du Connétable de Bordeaux*, p. 332; J. Sherborne, op. cit., p. 728.

[75] Michael Jones, op. cit., pp. 148–54.

[76] E101/39/9 m. 3; R. Coulborn, *The Economic and Political Preliminaries of the Crusade of Henry Despenser, Bishop of Norwich in 1383*, University of London PhD, 1931, p. 231.

[77] Chester 2/65 m. 1d.

[78] CRO, Leycester of Tabley MS DLT/A11/85 (John Leycester); *Foedera, Conventiones, etc.*, ed. T. Rymer (Record Commission), III, part ii, 1013 (Hugh Browe, Thomas Carrington, William Mainwaring): E101/36/32 m. 2 (Hugh Browe).

[79] E101/38/27; *Archives Historiques du Département de la Gironde*, xiii, 1871, p. 99; E101/40/33 m. 1, m. 14.

[80] A. Goodman, 'The Military Subcontracts of Sir Hugh Hastings, 1380', *EHR*, xcv, 1980, pp. 114–20; E101/39/9 m. 4; Simon Walker, 'Profit and Loss in the Hundred Years War: the Subcontracts of Sir John Strother, 1374', *BIHR*, lviii, 1985, pp. 100–6.

[81] *Original Letters Illustrative of English History*, ed. H. Ellis, 1846, i, p. 45.

[82] Goodman, op. cit., p. 117; Simon Walker, op. cit., p. 104.

[83] E101/39/9 m. 1, m. 3.

[84] M. J. Bennett, *Sources and Problems*, p. 71.

[85] E101/179/14.

[86] CRO, Leycester of Tabley MSS DLT/A11/85.

[87] E101/74/1; BL Additional Roll 40859A. The latter is briefly described in K. B. McFarlane, *The Nobility of Later Medieval England*, 1973, p. 26.

[88] See above p. 119.

[89] CRO, DLT/A1/2; *ibid.*, A16/14; *ibid.*, A26/24.

[90] Peacock is a common local surname; a Richard Peacock held land in a rental of 1362, CRO, Leycester of Tabley MSS, DLT/B82 m.1d.

[91] See above pp. 155 – 6.

[92] JRL Mainwaring of Peover Charters 171, 173.

[93] *Ibid.*, 182.

[94] *Ibid.*, 184; Chester 1/1 part 2. no. 46; SC6/774/6 m.1d, cited in R. R. Davies, 'Richard II and the Principality of Chester, 1397–99', *The Reign of Richard II*, ed. F. R. H. Du Boulay and Caroline M. Barron, 1971, p. 261.

[95] See above p. 155; BL Additional Charters 5113, 51,131.

[96] J. Cabaret d'Orville, *La Chronique du bon duc Loys de Bourbon*, ed. A. M. Chazaud, Société de l'Histoire de France, 1876, p. 168.

[97] PCC, Probate 11/2a. f. 69. Sais also figures in the will of another member of the military community, Sir John Delves, see Sir Delves L. Broughton, *Records of an Old Cheshire Family. A History of the Lords of the Manors of Delves near Uttoxeter in the County of Stafford and Doddington in the County of Chester*, 1908, pp. 16 – 19.

[98] See above pp. 155, 158, 163.

[99] *John of Gaunt's Register, 1372 – 6*, ed. S. Armitage-Smith, 1911, I, p. 42; *Comptes du Connétable de Bordeaux*, p. 330; *Documents des Archives de la Chambre des Comptes de Navarre, 1196 – 1384*, ed. J. A. Brutails, 1890, pp. 145 – 51; *Oeuvres de Froissart*, ed. K. de Lettenhove, xvii, 1872, pp. 426.

[100] M. Jones, *Ducal Brittany, 1364 – 1399*, 1970, p. 216; Froissart, ed. Lettenhove, xvii, pp. 88 – 90, 149, 151, 168, 210, 226.

[101] M. Keen, 'Brotherhood in Arms', *History*, 47, 1962, pp. 1 – 17; K. B. McFarlane, 'A Business Partnership in War and Administration, 1421 – 45', *EHR*, lxxviii, 1963, pp. 290 – 308; P. Contamine, *Guerre, État et Société à la fin du Moyen Age*, 1972, pp. 483 – 4.

[102] E101/179/8; E101/179/15; E101/181/5.

[103] E101/38/27.

[104] W. A. Copinger, *History and Records of the Smith-Carington Family*, 1907, pp. 72 – 6, cited in M. J. Bennett, *Sources and Problems*, p. 71. The manuscript was only printed in part by Copinger from a transcript made by the Historical Manuscripts Commission in 1871. It was then amongst the Nevill of Holt charters, now deposited at Leicestershire Record Office, but was missing when the Commission acquired the collection in 1877 and remains untraced. J. H. Round's reservations about the authenticity of this document appear in 'The Great Carington Imposture', in *Peerage and Pedigree*, ii, 1910, pp. 134 – 257.

[105] Roland Bibby, *Bothal Observed: A Survey of a Northumbrian Castle, Village and Church*, 1973, pp. 35 – 9, 279.

[106] M. Barber, *John Norbury*, p. 66; BL Additional Chartes 49,951, 51,453; JRL Bromley-Davenport charters, Davenport of Calveley, Box 2/2; JRL, Jodrell deeds, 3a. A full account of Stanley's career appears in pp. 171 – 4.

[107] Copinger, op. cit., p. 73.

[108] JRL, Mainwaring of Peover charters; CRO, Leycester-Warren MSS, DLT/B2 f. 11 – 28.

[109] BL Harley MS 1967, f. 113d; BL Harley MS 506, f. 62d; BL Additional Charters 49,786 – 49,881. Leycester's estate is described above pp. 164 – 5.

[110] *John of Gaunt's Register, 1372 – 6*, ed. S. Armitage Smith, 1911, i, p. 292; *ibid.*, ii, pp. 12 – 13; Chester 2/64 m. 4d.

[111] C. T. Allmand, *Lancastrian Normandy 1414–1450. The History of a Medieval Occupation*, 1983, pp. 60, 80, 247.

[112] BL Harley MS 2119, f. 87–8, Laurance Maisterson, 'The Genealogy of the Antient and Warlike Family of the Maistresones', 1611.

[113] SC8/126 no. 6262.

[114] G. A. Snead, op. cit., pp. 78–80, West Suffolk Record Office, Bunbury MS E18/710/12.1; Barber, op. cit., pp. 68–9; PCC, Probate 11/2a. f. 69.

[115] Cited in *Society at War: The Experience of England and France during the Hundred Years War*, ed. C. T. Allmand, 1973, p. 89; Michael J. Bennett, *Community, Class and Careerism*, pp. 188–9.

[116] For competition between John, Lord Neville, Sir David Hulgreve and Sir Hugh Calveley, see *CPR, 1381–1385*, pp. 228, 241, 264, 324.

[117] *Proceedings and Ordinances of the Privy Council of England*, ed. N. H. Nicolas, I, 1834, p. 155.

[118] Barber, op. cit., p. 68.

[119] Thomas Willement, *Heraldic Notices of Canterbury Cathedral*, 1827, p. 125.

[120] M. J. Bennett, *Sources and Problems*, pp. 69–72, 82–3.

[121] R. A. Grifiths, *The Principality of Wales, The Structure and Personnel of Government: South Wales, 1277–1536*, 1972, p. 36.

[122] Eric Garton, *Nantwich: Saxon to Puritan*, 1972, p. 21.

[123] Barber, loc. cit., BL Additional Charter 5829.

[124] Barber, op. cit., pp. 68–70. His correspondence with the duchess is given in M. D. Legge, '*Anglo-Norman Letters and Petitions from All Souls MS 182*', Anglo-Norman Text Society, III, 1941, nos 353, 367.

[125] *Rotuli Scotiae*, ii, 96a; Chester 29/97 m. 18, m. 20. The development of his Irish service is discussed below, pp. 172–4.

[126] T. F. Tout, *Chapters in the Administrative History of Medieval England*, vi, 1930, p. 30; E101/404/24 m. 24.

[127] *The Brut or Chronicles of England*, ed. F. W. Brie, Early English Text Society, Original Series, cxxxiv, 1908, p. 550; Richard Vaughan, *John the Fearless*, 1966, pp. 19–24.

[128] Much of his correspondence is printed in *Royal and Historical Letters during the Reign of Henry IV*, i, pp. 214–27; 235–8; 284–93.

[129] J. Otway-Ruthven, *A History of Medieval Ireland*, 1968, pp. 321–47.

[130] Chester 2/51 m. 1. Stanley does not appear on the muster roll of Trivet's retinue at Plymouth taken a week after the pardon, although such records cannot be taken as final evidence of who did or did not serve on particular campaigns, E101/37/29 m. 1.

[131] J. O. Halliwell, *Palatine Anthology: A Collection of Ancient Poems and Ballads Relating to Lancashire and Cheshire*, 1850, pp. 208–16; E101/30/25.

[132] C76/69 m. 1; *CPR, 1385–1389*, pp. 114, 125; C47/10/24 m. 8.

[133] Robin Frame, 'Power and Society in Ireland 1272–1377', *Past and Present*, 76, 1977, pp. 17–18.

[134] *The Annals of Connacht*, ed. A. Martin Freeman, 1944, pp. 422–3; *Statutes and Ordinances and Acts of Parliament of Ireland*, ed. H. F. Berry, 1907, p. 569; *A Roll of the Proceedings of the King's Council in Ireland*, ed. J. Graves, Rolls Series, 1877, p. 94; Kenneth Nichols, *Gaelic and Gaelicised Ireland in the Middle Ages*, 1972, p. 82.

[135] Anthony Tuck, 'Anglo-Irish Relations 1382–1393', *Proceedings of the Royal Irish Academy*, 69, 1970, p. 27; J. F. Lydon, *Ireland in the Later Middle Ages*, 1973, p. 107.

[136] *CPR 1385–1389*, p. 125; C47/10/24 m. 8.

[137] A. Tuck, op. cit., pp. 25–6.

[138] Otway-Ruthven, op. cit., p. 321.

[139] *Rotuli Scotiae*, ii, 96a–b; J. H. Wylie, *History of England Under Henry IV*, 1884, ii, p. 289.

[140] *CPR, 1388–1392*, p. 91; E101/68/11.

[141] E101/247/1; E101/247/6; *Rotulorum Patentum Clausorum Hiberniae*, Irish Record Commission, 1828, p. 157.

[142] Robin Frame, 'The Justiciarship of Ralph Ufford: Warfare and Politics in Fourteenth Century Ireland', *Studia Hibernica*, 13, 1973, pp. 14–15; *CPR, 1388–1392*, pp. 275, 390; *CPR 1391–1396*, p. 387; *Rotulum Patentum Clausorum Hiberniae*, p. 146.

[143] *CPR, 1388–1392*, p. 405; E101/247/1; Tuck, op. cit., p. 27.

[144] E101/247/3.

[145] *CPR, 1391–1396*, pp. 448, 469; E101/402/20 m. 35d; E. Curtis, *Richard II in Ireland 1394–5 and the Submission of the Irish Chiefs*, 1927, pp. 64–5.

[146] A. R. Bridbury, 'The Hundred Years' War: Costs and Profits', in *Trade, Government and Economy in Pre-Industrial England*, ed. D. C. Coleman and A. H. John, 1977, pp. 80–95 contains full reference to the debate.

[147] *Royal and Historical Letters during the Reign of Henry IV*, i, pp. 145–8, 284–8.

[148] E30/1687; *CPR, 1377–1381*, p. 492.

[149] K. B. McFarlane, *The Nobility of Later Medieval England*, 1973, pp. 27–39, 126–8 remains the best survey of the incidents of war.

[150] Copinger, op. cit., p. 75.

[151] E28/20.

[152] Froissart, *Chronicles*, ed. G. Brereton, 1978, p. 288.

[153] *CPR, 1377–1381*, p. 385; *Archives Historiques du Département de la Gironde*, xiii, 1871, pp. 99–101, *CPR, 1388–1392*, p. 267.

[154] Copinger, op. cit., p. 76; Roland Bibby, *Bothal Observed: A Survey of a Northumbrian Castle, Village and Church*, 1973, pp. 262, 279; *CPR, 1385–1389*, p. 310.

[155] *Medieval and Early Renaissance Treasures in the North West*, Whitworth Art Gallery, 1976, pp. 84–7.

[156] *BPR*, III, p. 469; Sir Delves L. Broughton, *Records of an Old Cheshire Family*, pp. 16–19.

[157] JRL, Mainwaring of Peover Charters, 173 *Item lego una ymagine de alabaustro ad cooperiendum tumbam meam in ecclesia de Acton.*

[158] JRL, Mainwaring of Peover Charters, 173 (William Mainwaring 1394); PCC, Probate 11/2a f. 57 (Robert Winnington 1404), *ibid.*, f. 69 (David Hulgreve 1405); JRL, Jodrell deed 35 (Roger Jodrell 1423).

[159] U. T. Holmes, *A History of Old French Literature*, 1962, p. 242; Michael J. Bennett, *Community, Class and Careerism*, p. 234.

[160] Copinger, loc. cit.

[161] D. Jones, *The Church in Chester 1300–1540*, Chet. Soc., 3rd Series, vii, 1957, pp. 100–1.

[162] Halliwell, *Palatine Anthology*, p. 214.

[163] Copinger, op. cit., pp. 72–6.

CHAPTER V

THE CRISIS OF FACTION, 1385–1403

If the rule of the Black Prince had carried the concerns of Cheshiremen abroad, the reigns of Richard II and Henry IV were to bring them firmly home again. Between 1387 and 1403 the county would be witness to an intensity of military activity which, unmatched even at the height of Edward I's campaigns in Wales, would overshadow the recent experience of its military community in France. On no less than four separate occasions Cheshire would occupy a pivotal role in the factional warfare which was to re-appear in the reign of Richard II.[1] In 1387 Robert de Vere, Earl of Oxford, sought to use the justiciarship of Chester as a military base from which to mount the king's attack on the political opposition of the Lords Appellant. In December an army which had mustered at Flint and Pulford was routed at the battle of Radcot Bridge.[2] In 1393, according to the chronicler Walsingham, the county itself rose against the Dukes of Lancaster and Gloucester and the Earl of Derby who were reported to be seeking to destroy the liberties of Cheshire.[3] At the close of the reign the king himself recruited a guard of Cheshire troops, and then raised the county palatine to the status of a principality by parliamentary statute, although in the event the 'inner citadel … of Richard's kingdom' put up scant resistance to the army of Henry of Bolingbroke.[4] Later, moreover, the men of Cheshire gave support to the revolt of the Earls of Huntingdon, Kent, Salisbury and Rutland in 1400, and also to Sir Henry Percy in 1403 when, according to a later Waltham annalist, scarcely three knights and seven esquires were left in the whole country.[5] These outbreaks of civil war were not isolated incidents during which recruitment might disturb the peace of a few small estates but, if we accept the most conservative estimates of the chroniclers, large musters of local society, undertaken in a period when the county's traditional military responsibilities had seldom been higher. In 1385 and again in 1401 Cheshire was to provide large retinues for campaigns in Scotland, and throughout the early years of the fifteenth century the revolt of Owain Glyn Dŵr was to re-emphasise its role as a Marcher earldom. At no other time would organisation for war so dominate the life of Cheshire society. It is hardly surprising, therefore, that the county's inflated political and military authority as compared with the rest of England should have generated an extensive bibliography, much of which nonetheless suggests that these events are on the whole easily understood and explained. Richard II recruited there because, it is argued, like any other magnate, he sought to exploit his estates and the traditional loyalty of Cheshire for the king or his eldest son as earl. Recent events had moreover under- lined the latent militarism of local society which had been founded in the thirteenth century in campaigns against the Welsh. Robert de Vere's success in raising an army in the king's cause in 1387 demonstrated the strength of that loyalty, and in 1393 the county itself reaffirmed its commitment to the continuance of the war in France by rising against those magnates who threatened to deprive the king of his claim to its throne.[6] In Richard II's own search for personal loyalty and security against the threat of faction, it was therefore inevitable that he would be drawn to a county which appeared to guarantee both, and equally likely that those members of the nobility who remained dissatisfied with the political settlement under Henry IV would look to Cheshire where a militaristic society retained its affection for the memory of an open- handed prince.[7] This chapter seeks to chronicle the development of the county's role and its importance in the factional conflicts of the two kings' reigns, and to test the hypotheses on which this interpretation of events rests.

I. THE BATTLE OF RADCOT BRIDGE AND THE RISING OF 1393

There is little evidence of any degree of personal involvement between Richard II and the county of Chester during the early years of the reign, when many of the enduring political issues of the period were to emerge. The immediate occasion for the renewed relationship of the county and its earl may well have been the king's problems in mounting and financing his first military expedition to Scotland in 1385. Parliament had granted a subsidy of two fifteenths and tenths in December 1384 on condition that the king undertook a campaign in France.[8] When it became clear that Scotland posed the greater threat, the government, headed by Michael de la Pole, had resorted to a variety of financial expedients, including a levy of scutage, rather than compromise the terms of the parliamentary grant. The expedition nevertheless laid bare the king's financial embarrassment and provided further ammunition for the Commons' complaints in the parliament which met in Octobver 1385.[9] No doubt as part of the government's search for men and finance the county of Cheshire had been called upon to provide twenty-seven men-at-arms and twenty archers who were to be partly paid from the revenues of the earldom.[10]

These retinues represented the first muster of the lordship in the earl's name since the Black Prince's final campaign in Aquitaine in 1369. Indeed in the following year testimony from witnesses in the Scrope-Grosvenor case in the court of chivalry revealed an impressive continuity between these two campaigns. Of the fifteen knights who had seen Robert Grosvenor bear the arms *azure bend or* in Scotland in 1385, seven had also been with the Black Prince in Gascony in 1369.[11] As a result of the success of these musters the council had clearly determined to exploit fully the military resources of the king's lordship in Cheshire, and in the autumn of 1386 large numbers of troops were also raised in the county for the defence of the south coast during the French invasion scare.[12] Once again the government found it difficult to meet the wage bill for the army, and although the chamberlain of Chester paid wages for six days to 43 esquires and 818 archers under the lieutenant justice, Sir John Mascy of Puddington, it seems unlikely that they received any further payment.[13] On two occasions, however, the machinery of military recruitment and muster laid down by the household of the Black Prince had proved reliable. Thus, when in 1387 Richard II withdrew from London in protest at the parliamentary commission which was virtually empowered to take over the government of the country, it was perhaps inevitable that the king would visit his earldom in Cheshire for the first time. Having stayed for a day or two with Nicholas Audley at Heighley castle on the Staffordshire border, he moved to Chester and Malpas for five days in July.[14] No doubt as a result of this visit, Edmund, Duke of York, was replaced as justice of Chester by Robert de Vere, the king's favourite, as part of the preparations which Richard had begun to make at Shrewsbury and Nottingham to mobilise support against the parliamentary opposition.[15]

At this stage the king must still have hoped to gain support from the citizens of London and from other counties, although attempts to distribute in East Anglia money and, as a royal livery, golden crowns had already failed of their purpose.[16] The royal archers who had been recruited into the royal household prior to the Scottish campaign were drawn from fifteen counties, which suggests that Richard clearly felt little need then to depend exclusively on the service of his Cheshire men.[17] Nevertheless, as the general attitude of the country towards the court hardened, Cheshire was to find itself dangerously isolated in its support for the king. Feelings were doubtless exacerbated by the fact that de Vere's household, which was now lodged at Chester, was to be the scene of the earl's scandalous relationship with Agnes Lancecrona, a Bohemian woman in the queen's household.[18] It is not clear whether in fact de Vere did divorce his wife, Philippa de Coucy, or even if the Bohemian woman had been a willing partner, since William Stanley, a Cheshire esquire in the earl's following, was later accused of abducting her. The affair did, however, cause great offence and deepened the earl's unpopularity.[19]

In November and early December of that year (1387) both de Vere and the lieutenant justice, Sir Thomas Molyneux, began preparations in earnest to raise an army for the king in the county, addressing letters under the king's seal to the sheriff, and to the bailiffs and gentry in the hundreds.[20] Musters were to be held at Flint and Pulford during the first week in December, and the Kirkstall chronicle describes the force as moving south behind the royal standard from west Cheshire a week or two later.[21] Most of the preparations had, however, been watched from nearby Holt castle, which was garrisoned for the Earl of Arundel for six weeks at the height of the crisis by newly-armed and uniformed troops.[22] As a result the Lords Appellant were fully informed of de Vere's strength and movements during their own musters outside London, and were able to circulate letters explaining their actions across de Vere's likely route in the west Midlands.[23] Most of the chroniclers agree that the army which was to be routed by Gloucester, Arundel and Derby was in its essentials a Cheshire army, although it seems highly unlikely, given the traditional size of musters in the county, that it could have reached the widely quoted figure of 4,000 men without additional support.

The battle to which the small bridge across the Thames at Radcot gave its name was, it now appears, not a single decisive engagement but a series of skirmishes between de Vere's forces and those of the Lords Appellant over a wide area between Moreton-in-Marsh and the Thames.[24] According to the register of the bishop of Worcester, the earl had spent the night of 19 December at Chipping Campden on his way to join the king at Windsor, only to be blocked by Gloucester at Moreton-in-Marsh where a large section of his army promptly deserted.[25] Thereafter, the chroniclers differ somewhat in their accounts of events leading to de Vere's eventual escape across the Thames at Bablock Hythe. The 'Monk of Westminster' brings him to Witney where Sir Thomas Molyneux was killed by Sir Thomas Mortimer during a parley with the Earl of Arundel.[26] Both Mortimer and his servant, William Curtis, who were later charged with the murder by Richard II in 1397, had in fact served with Arundel on the earl's recent naval expedition. Mortimer was also chief steward of the estates of the Earl of March, then in the joint custody of Arundel and Gloucester.[27] On this basis it seems wise to admit the likelihood of a preliminary engagement on the Windrush at which de Vere's opponent was Arundel. Henry Knighton's chronicle on the other hand brings the earl directly to Radcot Bridge, which it describes as being held by the Earl of Derby, and places Molyneux's death there.[28] It is indeed in the siting of this incident, perhaps the most notable feature of the day, that the main chronicle accounts differ; elsewhere the outline of the campaign remains clear. Having divided their forces between the major crossings of the Thames and Windrush, and destroyed others, such as that at Lechlade and perhaps also Burford, the Appellants had succeeded in trapping de Vere, whose own intentions must always have been to avoid a pitched battle. Molyneux's death and the earl's own escape left the remainder of his following trapped in the marshes of Bampton-in-the-Bush where many were drowned or trampled to death, and those captured stripped of their arms and sent home.[29]

The fullest accounts, though not necessarily the most accurate, are those of Thomas Walsingham.[30] In the short or minor chronicle, written whilst he was Prior of Wymondham between 1394 and 1396, Walsingham does make some reference to an engagement on the Windrush, but was clearly not well informed about the battle as a whole. He later omitted this section from the revised version in the *Chronica Maiora* in favour of an account which closely follows Knighton. In the former de Vere appears almost as a courageous figure, quieting his men before the battle, whereas in the latter Walsingham relates how, out of cowardice, he had proposed to flee until restrained by the loyalty of Cheshire troops. The Dieulacres writer too drew attention to the steadfastness of the Cheshire men, explaining that it was absurd for any subject or slave to contemplate becoming a rebel against his lord, and quickly celebrating the divine justice which, it was claimed, had overtaken Gloucester, Warwick and Arundel in 1397.[31] The special loyalty of the county was indeed to be lavishly rewarded by Richard II when, in 1398, he retained widely among the minor Cheshire gentry, elevated the county to the status of a principality, and distributed a gift of 4,000 marks amongst those who had fought at Radcot Bridge.[32] Several of the chronicles had clearly fed on this official version for their accounts of the events of 1387, but although de Vere's following had undoubtedly been mainly a Cheshire one, there is some evidence that support for the king even there was far from total or unwavering.

A few individual grants to men who had served at Radcot Bridge are noted amongst the enrolments of the Chester exchequer, but the greatest part of the king's reward was apparently distributed through groups of local gentry appointed within the six hundreds in the county.[33] No explanation of the various amounts paid to the hundreds is given, although the relative sums do bear some relation to what is known of the ordinary taxation of the county. If Richard seems to have remained fairly ignorant as to exactly who had fought for him at Radcot Bridge, he was clearly more concerned to establish who had taken up arms against him. When parliament reassembled at Shrewsbury in January 1398 it quickly became apparent that the king would again refuse to issue a general pardon, and that those who had risen against him in 1387 would have to make individual petitions.[34] In the state of insecurity that resulted, it is perhaps hardly surprising that many were able to derive personal advantage. Robert Worsley later petitioned Henry IV that John Mascy of Tatton and Nicholas Worsley, both of whom were later among Richard's Cheshire retainers, had secured his imprisonment by falsely accusing him of having served with the Appellants.[35] Amongst those who were summoned before the king's council to pay fines for their pardons were at least eight Cheshire men, including Sir Hugh Browe and Sir John Calveley.[36]

In his account of de Vere's recruitment in Cheshire, Knighton reported that Molyneux, prior to his departure on campaign, had imprisoned the supporters of the Duke of Gloucester on a diet of bread and water. But little else is known of the degree of opposition to the king's cause, although de Vere's possessions in Chester castle were seized by Peter Legh after the battle. Hywel ap Tudur ap Ithel, under-sheriff of Flintshire, was also indicted for taking money from de Vere for troops who failed to muster.[37] Of those who took out pardons in 1398 perhaps the best known was Sir Hugh Browe, who during the 1370s had been a leading garrison captain in France. As with many of his contemporaries, his return to Cheshire ws marked by a period of activity on the land-market, in his case in the vicinity of Tushingham in the west of the county, where the Earl of Arundel was a near neighbour.[38] In March 1387 he raised a retinue amongst his neighbours in the earl's service on the naval expedition which led to the battle of Sluis. The presence also of Sir Richard Cradock, Sir John Haukeston and another neighbour, Sir John Calveley, in the earl's retinue, indicates the extent to which Arundel had become a figure in Cheshire society by this date.[39]

During Molyneux's and de Vere's preparations in the autumn of 1387, Arundel's constable at Holt was to make his own foray into the county at Shocklach and remained in contact with several Cheshire knights, one of whom, Sir William Legh, received letters from both Arundel and de Vere.[40] That both Browe and Calveley were later to receive pardons for their actions in support of the Appellants also suggests a degree of continuity between the earl's retinue in France and that which ultimately fought at Witney. Support for Richard II in Cheshire, although broad in its extent, was, it would now appear, far from universal.

Richard II was able, like his father, to raise the county in his service. The machinery which the Black Prince had established to furnish men for his campaigns in France had worked equally well to provide men for Scotland, for coastal defence, and even for factional battles. The military experience of many of the Cheshire gentry doubtless contributed to the efficiency of the system. Nevertheless, other concerns were beginning to disturb the operation of a single faction in county society, and in the role of the Earl of Arundel it is possible to discern the ways in which military service in *his* retinues had served to divert men from their loyalty to the king as Earl of Chester.

The campaign of Radcot Bridge had also demonstrated that the county was to occupy a central role in the factional politics of the reign. Within a week of the end of the Merciless Parliament in June 1388, Gloucester replaced de Vere as Justice of Chester, although Arundel had been a leading architect in the defeat of de Vere's Cheshire following and held estates bordering on the county.[41] He continued, however, to exert some influence particularly in west Cheshire. Sir Hugh Browe, who had been rewarded for his support of Arundel in 1387 with a life grant of the manors of Trafford and Dunham, accepted him as an arbitrator in a local dispute, and in March 1389 the earl was able to obtain a pardon for his constable at Holt, David Eyton, for an earlier assault at Shocklach.[42] Both Arundel and Gloucester recruited amongst the local gentry for their retinues, the former for his naval expedition in 1388, the latter for a proposed Irish campaign in 1392.[43] Arundel's recruitment for his campaigns since 1377 had been widespread among the leading families in the west of the county, and at Witney had clearly afforded a measure of social control which competed successfully against the king in his own lordship. Nevertheless, his ascendancy, as indeed that of the Duke of Gloucester, was to be shortlived, and in the early 1390s Richard II was able to recapture much of his independence and control of local society.

The failure of the Lords Appellant to consolidate the political supremacy which, as exemplified in the Merciless Parliament, had followed their military success allowed Richard to reassert his personal authority in May 1389. Almost immediately he sought to exploit the complaints of the Commons regarding finance, and livery and maintenance, and with John of Gaunt's support he was able to limit conciliar supervision of his activities.[44] The rapprochement between Gaunt and the king, which occurred after the duke's return from Spain in the autumn of 1389, was perhaps the most significant feature of the politics of the period. Gaunt's popularity had been at its lowest during the Peasants' Revolt, and in the early 1380s Richard's courtiers had pursued a calculated policy of opposition to him. The disputes of the court also reached into the locality, and in Cheshire itself, where Gaunt remained the largest landholder, an annuity for his quitclaim of the rights of the barony of Halton was allowed to fall into arrears of some £300 by 1389.[45] In the Westminster parliament in October 1385 he had complained unsuccessfully about the abduction of Isabel Lathom, heir to the Lancashire manors of Sir Thomas Lathom, by John Stanley, a Cheshire esquire who was later to be de Vere's lieutenant in Ireland.[46] Not long afterwards his rights in the manor of Barrow near Chester as lord of Halton were denied by Sir Thomas Molyneux in an inquisition held after the death of Sir Robert Swynnerton.[47] The removal of the king's friends in 1388, however, brought a new climate to relations between Richard and his uncle. The payment of Gaunt's annuity in respect of the barony of Halton was resumed soon after his return from Spain, part of the arrears being met by the English treasury; and when the duke petitioned the king concerning the manor of Barrow, the verdict of Molyneux's enquiry was reversed and payment of all receipts since Swynnerton's death made to his receiver, Sir Ralph de Ipres.[48] By 1391 Gaunt had recovered much of his local political standing, and in February of that year he secured the appointment of a former retainer, Thomas Maisterson, to the escheatorship in Cheshire.[49] Arundel, whose own position in Cheshire society rested on an insecure landed foundation, could only watch as much of the following which he had assiduously cultivated through his military patronage in the late 1380s disappeared with his own enforced idleness.

Richard's reconciliation with Gaunt had restored the duke to the leading role in Cheshire society which he had enjoyed under the Black Prince, but the king's courtship of parliament was to have a more profound effect upon his own authority in the county. In an effort to reduce the scale and frequency of direct taxation, Richard had endeavoured to exploit other sources of income and, although often without real success, the attempt would appear to have engendered an enduring resentment in Wales and London.[50] In June 1394 a crowd led by Hywel ap Tudur ap Ithel stamped on the exchequer records at the Flint county court and defiled them.[51] It was, however, in Cheshire that the most serious disturbances were to take place during 1393 and 1394.[52] Then, the county rose in arms against the Dukes of Lancaster and Gloucester and the Earl of Derby who, it was suspected, sought to deprive the king of his titles to the French throne and the Earldom of Chester of its liberties. Affixing their complaints to the doors of the parish churches, the rebels assembled in large numbers throughout the county and began to send letters to elicit support in neighbouring areas. According to Walsingham's account their intention was to kill the three lords and others in the king's party in the west Midlands who supported their cause.[53] The king and the council delayed their response until Gaunt and Gloucester had returned from the peace negotiations at Leulinghen to demonstrate their innocence, when Gaunt, who was immediately appointed as the king's first justice, moved first to Yorkshire, where a more localised outbreak of violence had occurred, and later to Cheshire, to restore order.

No record of Gaunt's hearings would appear to have survived, if indeed any were held in the formal sense, and we know little, from official records, of the background and progress of the rising. Thomas Walsingham argued that, 'because of their fickleness, the people of those parts are more ready and accustomed to doing such things; because of former wars and local disputes, they more readily resort to arms.'[54] Modern comment, too, points to the coincidence of the rising and the peace talks then in progress at Leulinghen, arguing that the prospects of a peace with France posed a threat to the continued employment of local men devoted to warfare, although it seems likely that Walsingham was himself referring to the Welsh campaigns of Edward I rather than to those of the Hundred Years War.[55] A more detailed knowledge of the county's reputation for militarism would suggest, however, that the rising of 1393 was a good deal more complex than recent accounts have indicated.

A group of thirty-two gentry had met at Chester in October 1389 to act for the community of Cheshire in voting a subsidy of 3,000 marks to the king in return for a charter confirming the liberties of the county.[56] Much of the record of the Cheshire courts at this date is in fact concerned with the collection of this subsidy, which appears to have provoked an unprecedented degree of opposition. Payment was to be made by the chamberlain and sheriff direct to the exchequer at

Westminster where it was accounted for as assigned *pro expensis hospicii*. It was clearly a part of the king's attempt to court the Commons in the matter of royal finance, by financing his household without resorting to parliamentary taxation.[57] Collection of the first thousand marks would appear to have proceeded quietly, but during 1391 further collection was met with continuous resistance. In February the sheriff, Sir John Mascy of Tatton, arrived at Mere with a schedule of obligations and distrained three mares valued at forty shillings which were then stolen.[58] In November he visited Malpas with an assessment agreed with the steward of John Sutton, lord of Malpas, but was thrown out of the village and chased by a crowd of sixty villagers as far as Chowley.[59] These two cases, which make an isolated appearance on the indictment rolls, were clearly part of a much larger protest, for in December the king ordered the justice to enquire as to those who had resisted the subsidy and risen against the sheriff, stealing what he had been able to collect at that stage.[60] Similar letters were also addressed to the chamberlain, the sheriff, and a group of twenty-five gentry, as the Duke of Gloucester, who was Justice of Chester, was still in London and his two lieutenants, Matthew Southworth and Richard, Lord Talbot, remained at Blakemere on the Shropshire border.[61] There was some further disorder early in 1392, when two baliffs were met by armed crowds outside Nantwich, but final collection of the subsidy would appear to have been completed in the early summer.[62]

Whilst these disturbances do not appear to have been unusually violent, their significance is heightened by the fact that they occurred at a time of increasing friction between a number of gentry affinities and of continuing petty assaults on the earl's officials. In December 1391 the lieutenant-sheriff, Henry Ravenscroft, was attacked by armed men at Middlewich as he attempted to make an arrest.[63] Earlier, in June, there had been riots among the Chester tailors which were put down by local gentry, although apart from this and an isolated case recorded on the court roll of Marbury in November 1392, when a villein was fined for uttering rebellious words to his lord, there is little evidence of any significant popular element in the disorders which appear to have affected Cheshire society during this period.[64] In October 1391, however, Sir John Mascy of Puddington, who had been lieutenant-justice under Robert de Vere, assembled a following of 100 men-at-arms and archers between Puddington and Chester and crossed the Dee to assault the earl of Salisbury's castle at Hawarden with scaling ladders.[65] Mascy would seem also to have been involved in a dispute with Sir Richard Aston, one of Gaunt's retainers, for the two knights enrolled recognizances of 1,000 pounds before Richard, Lord Talbot, to maintain the peace between them in 1392.[66] Aston's arrest had already been ordered when it was discovered that he had been raising a following in December 1391.[67] At the same time the Earl of Arundel may have petitioned the king concerning assaults which he claimed had been made against his officials and tenants in the lordship of Bromfield and Yale by the men of Cheshire.[68] The atmosphere of disorder clearly persisted, however, for the king was to issue commissions of the peace on three occasions during 1392, the last in August being directed to all seven hundreds in the county.[69] The underlying causes of these events are complex rather than simple, but their importance in any under-standing of the development of the rising in Cheshire in 1393 is clearly high.

In the accounts of the rising we are in fact able to identify only three of the leaders. Thomas Walsingham cites Nicholas Clifton as one.[70] A commission to a group of Cheshire gentry in October 1393 called for the arrest of Sir John Mascy of Tatton and Sir Thomas Talbot, and Gaunt and Gloucester pressed for Talbot's arrest and trial in the parliament of January 1394.[71] The exact progress of the rising remains equally obscure, but appears to have begun in the early months of 1393 when John Holland, Earl of Huntingdon, and Sir John Stanley were sent to Cheshire and Lancashire to express the king's displeasure and to prohibit further assemblies of troops on pain of forfeiture. They were also empowered to offer redress of grievances against the officials of the king and the Duke of Lancaster.[72] In May the king issued procla-mations in Lancashire, Cheshire, and five other Midland counties condemning the disturbances and denying that he had any intention of destroying the magnates of the realm.[73] These measures were in-effective, however, and Gaunt and Gloucester returned to England, having sealed a provisional treaty at Leulinghen on 16 June, and set about the suppression of disorder in the north. According to Walsingham's account, the Duke of Lancaster was able to restore order in Cheshire without violence, pardoning many of the rebels immediately and reserving others for the king's justice, although there seems still to have been activity in the county when the commissions were issued for the arrest of Mascy and Talbot in October. Many of the poorer soldiers (*pauperes*), who had grown impatient with the peace with France and had instigated the rising, were recruited into the retinue which Gaunt was raising for service in Aquitaine.[74] Indeed, in the aftermath of the rising it becomes clear that there was a political as well as social dimension to the revolt in Cheshire.

In the later stages of the revolt, we are told that the Earl of Arundel, having occupied Holt castle with a large force, had remained inactive while the county was in arms against the Duke of Lancaster.[75] After his own complaints about Gaunt's favourable treatment at court in the parliament of January 1394, Arundel was in fact accused of treachery by the duke, although the suggestion seemed incredible to Walsingham.[76] Sir Nicholas Clifton, the Lancashire knight, whom Walsingham had identified as a leader of the rising, did, however, serve in the earl's retinue in 1387 and 1388, although no more recent connection can be detected.[77] In April 1394 Arundel took out a pardon for all treasons or insurrections which he had committed with the commons, and for others committed at his instigation, but this failed to prevent his execution in 1397.[78] Richard's own involvement also seems likely, for the rising occurred within his earldom and implicated a number of men who were deeply involved in his service. As well as his somewhat equivocal role in its early months, Richard emerged as its major beneficiary, and furthermore refused to prosecute the rebels fully. Both Mascy and Talbot were in custody in London in January 1394, and Talbot made full confession to the Earl of Derby and John, Lord Lovell. Nevertheless, he was later allowed to escape and, in spite of Gaunt's efforts in this and later parliaments, the rebels were never brought to justice.[79] Mascy was released from the Tower in July 1394 and continued to draw his annuity at the Chester exchequer. Clifton served with the king in Ireland, and in 1396 he was retained for life as keeper of the castle and lordship of Bolsover.[80] Sir Thomas Talbot, who had been retained by the king only in September 1392, also continued in royal service and avoided all efforts by Gaunt to bring him to trial.[81]

The disorder attendant upon the collection of the subsidy in 1391–2 and in the rising of 1393 had also presented Richard with the opportunity to remove Gloucester as justice of Chester, and he was replaced by the Earl of Nottingham in March 1394, Sir William Bagot acting as the latter's lieutenant.[82] Sir John Stanley and the abbot of St Werburgh's had already served as justices *hac vice* between February and May 1394 and, although the Earl of Derby was granted a commission to arrest all persons causing insurrections in Cheshire and four other northern counties in March, only one case was heard at the county court.[83] As a response to the increasing impact of noble patronage during the 1370s and 1380s, Richard had in effect reasserted his personal authority in the Earldom of Chester, and the force of this renewed vigour is shown in an incident which occurred in July 1394 during the preparations for the king's expedition to Ireland. Sir Baldwin de Radyngton, the controller of the household, and Sir John Stanley were instructed to purvey victuals and transport for the royal household and apparently sailed from Denwall in the Wirral in late August to prepare for Richard's arrival in Ireland.[84] Whilst in Chester, however, Radyngton's retinue had occupied parts of St Werburgh's abbey and seized provisions from surrounding houses. Here a dispute occurred between Radyngton and the mayor of Chester, John Armourer, during which John Hoo, an esquire in the former's retinue, was killed. A week later, after several prisoners had been freed by the townspeople, Radyngton and Stanley, supported by the latter's retinue of Lancashire men-at-arms and archers, rode 'in manner of war within the county of Cheshire for five leagues from the city'.[85] Stanley's forcefulness on this occasions contrasts sharply with his apparent inability to control the rising in the previous year, and casts further suspicion on the king's role in those events.

The disturbances which had taken place in Cheshire since 1391 may have been led by members of the military community. Each of the three known leaders had had long experience in war, although Talbot and Clifton would appear to have had little previous connection with the county. Furthermore, there seems little reason to doubt Walsingham's analysis of the causes of the rising as they appeared to contemporaries. In July 1392 Richard II had cancelled Gloucester's appointment as lieutenant in Ireland after the duke had recruited widely in Cheshire, retaining, for example, Sir John Mascy of Puddington with thirty men-at-arms and archers.[86] Such actions and the knowledge that negotiations for peace with France were then in progress clearly added to the insecurity of many in Cheshire society. Nevertheless, these events cannot be seen as a protest against the king's peace policy from outside the political community. Cheshire's response to the political develop-ments and peace negotiations of the early 1390s was not in essence different from the rest of the country, whilst the violence of gentry affinities and local resistance to taxation had origins which were indepen-dent of developments in military service. In an era of falling incomes from land, competition for office brought with it an inevitable conflict between gentry affinities. In the Wirral, for instance, the activities of the Stanley family provide a clear example of the opportunities available to an aggressive local confederacy with control of the master forester-ship.[87] For the most part violence was tempered by the need for men to live with their neighbours, although since the 1380s competition had for the first time been submerged in a conflict of patronage between members of the nobility who had sought a role in county society.

The course of events in Cheshire was perhaps only a minor part of the search for territorial influence which characterised Richard's relations with the nobility, but the significance of a successful challenge to the king's faction in the one area which had mustered in his support in 1387 can have been lost on few observers. In his management of the disorders in Cheshire, Richard had acted as an opportunist and achieved a limited success against Arundel, Gloucester and Gaunt. In the months following the suppression of the rising, however, he made little further effort to conciliate the population of his earldom.

The expedition which Richard II led to Ireland in the summer of 1394 revealed a growing dependence on the resources of his household and a number of close friends amongst the nobility. Gaunt had already left to take possession of the duchy of Aquitaine, and both Warwick and Arundel stood aloof from the campaign in Ireland. Few Cheshire men of any importance, except Sir Richard Cradock and the clerk of the privy seal, John Macclesfield, who were already members of the royal household, found service with the king.[88] John of Gaunt does appear to have continued his close association with the gentry of the lordship of Halton, retaining a number of men in addition to those he had ostensibly collected during the Cheshire rising. Sir William Mainwaring's will of September 1393 was made in London prior to his return to Gascony, presumably with Gaunt. But elsewhere there were few new opportunities for military service.[89] William Scolehall did succeed in taking advantage of the visit to England of Archambaud de Grailly, captal de Buch, to find service in Gascony in 1394, but his example was not widely followed.[90] If the rising of 1393 had been engineered by those who feared the prospects of an Anglo-French peace, no immediate solution had been offered; indeed, Richard had continued to pursue a vigorous peace policy which, in 1396, would culminate in his marriage to Charles VI's daughter, Isabel, and the signing of a twenty-eight-year truce.[91] In the early 1390s the men of Cheshire had found little comfort in the lordship of their earl.

II. THE CHESHIRE RETINUE OF RICHARD II

Criticism of the royal household, which surfaced again in the parliament of January 1397, provoked a hostile response from the king, who declared that the Commons had given 'great offence'. At the same time his relationship with Gloucester and Arundel had deteriorated further in the face of their criticism of the Anglo-French peace, and in February both lords refused to attend the council. An atmosphere of insecurity, which reproduced the tensions of the 1380s, may have persuaded the king to strike first against his opponents.[92] In July Gloucester was arrested at Pleshy and sent to Calais, where he was apparently murdered by servants of the Earl of Nottingham.[93] Arundel and Warwick, who were arrested at the same time, were held in London to await trial before parliament. Three days after the arrests, the king addressed writs to the sheriff of Cheshire, Sir Robert Legh, calling to him to raise 2,000 archers for royal service and to muster them at Kingston-upon-Thames on 15 September. A proclamation was also issued prohibiting any archer from taking service with other lords until the musters had been completed.[94] From Kingston the retinue rode with the king to London, where a temporary timber hall had been erected at Westminster to accommodate the trial of the three leading Lords Appellant of 1388. According to Adam of Usk, the open-sided building was surrounded by archers raised in Cheshire who stood with bows drawn.[95] A London chronicle records that the retinue rioted in Friday Street in the city that night, and Thomas Walsingham observed that the king out of fear had summoned 'to the protection of his body many malefactors from the county of Cheshire', who were, moreover, not 'gentlemen but countrymen, cobblers and other tradesmen'.[96] Richard II had used his Cheshire lands and the men recruited there to overawe parliament and to support the political settlement which he advanced there. The organisation of the incursion followed closely that of 1387, although on this occasion recruitment had been in the hands of a Cheshire knight whilst the justice and his lieutenant were both absent at Calais. The speed and the success of the musters were themselves remarkable, for if the estimates of the chronicles and Walsingham's observations are to be believed, Sir Robert Legh had drawn into service many who must have had a limited experience of warfare. Not surprisingly he was immediately rewarded with an annuity of forty pounds.[97] If, however, the initial recruitment of this force was opportunist, the king quickly determined to create a more permanent Cheshire retinue within the royal household. Between September 1397 and July 1398 Richard retained a total of 750 men in his service at a cost of £514 a year. The organisation of this force, and its social and geographical composition have recently been the subject of detailed study.[98]

A core of 311 archers was arranged into seven squadrons or watches under the leadership of John Legh, Richard Cholmondeley, Ralph Davenport, Adam Bostock, John Donne, Thomas Beeston, and Thomas Holford. These watches were the king's personal bodyguard in daily rotation and accompanied him wherever he went.[99] John

Trefaur, bishop of Saint Asaph and later the chamberlain of Chester, recalled how the king visited Becket's shrine at Canterbury in 1399, and had 'with him a retinue with a great multitude of Cheshire men who watched over him by day and night'.[100] Richard's apparent reliance on the guard and their close familiarity with him appalled contemporaries, one of whom observed in retrospect that, 'This was a wondir world, ho so well lokyd, That gromes overe grewe so many grette maistris'.[101] Earlier the Kenilworth chronicle reported how the king's Cheshire guard addressed him boldly in their own dialect; 'Dycun, slep sicury quile we wake, and dreed nouzt quile we lyve seftow: for zif thow haddest weddet Perkyn dauzter of Lye thow mun well halde a love day with any man in Chester shire in ffaith.'[102] Walsingham too drew attention to their familiarity with the king and records that they undertook to defend him, not only against the whole of England, but against the whole world.[103] All the chronicles, however, dwelt on the oppressions and misdeeds which, they alleged, had been perpetrated by the retinue during the last two years of the reign. In a satirical vein the author of *Mum and the Sothsegger* claimed that he had sat for seven nights but been unable to complete a catalogue of their wrongdoing which had gone unpunished by the king. According to Walsingham they accompanied the king, flogging, wounding and killing, giving nothing in return for their food, and raping women and wives.[104] Successful maintenance always goes undetected of course, and in many respects the reputation of the Cheshire guard is perhaps sufficiently damning, but there are hints of their alleged crimes in the official records. In the early months of 1399, for instance, Richard and Thomas Willaboy, archers in the squadrons of John Legh and Thomas Beeston, are reported to have kidnapped and ransomed Thomas Rudyng after imprisoning him in the church of Saint Margaret at Westminister for a week.[105] The *gravamina* presented during the parliament of 1399 drew attention to the misdeeds of the 'esquiers maistres del wache de Chestreshire', and called for the repayment of the vast sums of money which had been paid to them.[106] They were, wrote Adam of Usk, the chief cause of the king's ruin.[107]

In addition to this itinerant bodyguard, a further 101 archers were retained for life and described as *extra vigilias*, and another 195 archers retained during pleasure. During periods of emergency, therefore, the guard could be virtually doubled in size to provide a formidable military retinue by itself. Nevertheless, the king had also retained ten knights and ninety-seven esquires at a variety of fees, whose role was clearly to act as a link between the crown and the military resources of Cheshire society.[108] The organisation of this Cheshire retinue can perhaps best be seen during the king's second campaign in Ireland in 1399. In February Richard addressed commissions to raise archers directly to groups of gentry in the Cheshire hundreds, the majority of whom were his retainers; and a force of ten knights, 110 men-at-arms, and 900 archers were paid for their service in Ireland between May and August. Five of the seven squadron leaders were also paid for 100 archers who acted as the king's personal bodyguard during the campaign.[109] The retinue was in fact the largest which had been raised in Cheshire during the fourteenth century, and clearly emphasises both the extent of the king's military dependence, and the significance of the period in the development of military service in the county.

At the same time as the Cheshire retinue was recruited, Richard had also elevated the county to the status of a principality by parliamentary statute, to which the county of Flint and Arundel's forfeited estates in the northern March of Wales and Shropshire were annexed. It was (to borrow Professor Davies' phrase) 'the crowning manifestation of Richard's "immense friendship and affection" for Cheshire': a friendship and affection, moreover, which was to flood local society with the resources of royal favour in the form of grants of office, pardons and rewards.[110] Cheshire men petitioned to leave their garrisons on the Scottish border to join his guard and to receive his fees.[111] John Snelson, an ageing member of the military community, sensitive to this climate of open-handed lordship, petitioned and received a reward for his service in the retinues of the Black Prince and at Radcot Bridge where he had been wounded.[112] In the following year the king himself recognised the loyalty which the county had shown in 1387, and granted the sum of 4,000 marks to be distributed amongst those who had fought at Radcot Bridge.[113]

Richard II's apparent infatuation with the county of Chester has prompted a good deal of recent comment, although most observers have stressed the traditional links between the crown and the earldom, and the county's martial reputation. J. L. Gillespie thought that the king had entered the 'retaining game' only in response to the threat of baronial faction, whilst Rees Davies stressed the importance of the political geography of the north-west and the memory of recent events in his explanation of the king's relationship with Cheshire.[114] There can be little doubt, however, that above all a search for personal loyalty and security against the threat of faction had marked the rapid growth of the royal household after 1397, and the development of the king's friendship for his new principality. Richard's Cheshire retinue did not follow the customary pattern of recruitment, for each man now held an individual contract with the king, a fact which no doubt explains much of the overbearing attitude of the bodyguard. In September 1398 Robert Parys, chamberlain of the former Arundel estates, accounted for some £436, received from over 500 members of the retinue in return for a letter patent of the grant of their annuity.[115] Whether recruitment was direct or through leaders, ties of association and obligation were not immediately dissolved by an individual contract with the king, although there is some evidence that Richard was here attempting to fix loyalty at every level of his retinue, and thus to interrupt those ties of association and obligation which weakened loyalty to him. Amongst the watches of the bodyguard there is some hint of the local affinities which had characterised retinues in France, with their bonds of kinship and locality: that of Richard Cholmondeley included at least three kinsmen and a number of near neighbours, five of whom had previously acted as charter witnesses on his behalf.[116] Nevertheless, the primary initiative in the organisation of the watches appears to have rested with Richard himself.[117] Kinsmen and neighbours were to be found serving in separate companies, whose leaders seldom appear to have acted as sureties or as patronage brokers. These men wore the king's livery and pocketed his fees; and in his absence they swore loyalty to him and undertook to report any rising against him.[118]

The same obsessive concern for security is apparent in the appointment of officials in the principality, granting power and authority to members of the retinue and the king's household, who would control regional society through a single faction more exclusive than any in recent Cheshire history. The Duke of Aumâle, the Earl of Salisbury and the Duke of Lancaster were granted the three honorific posts of chamberlain, steward, and constable of the new principality, whilst Hugh Legh, a Cheshire retainer, was appointed as its escheator.[119] Elsewhere, the constituent parts of the principality retained their own local bureaucracy, and the administrative unity of Richard's new creation was perhaps more imagined than real. In terms of personnel, however, the authority of the retinue was widely recognised. In the former Arundel lands there had been a complete purge of the earl's officials, who were replaced by members of the household and the Cheshire retinue. In Cheshire, too, members of the king's retinue were advanced to posts of authority in the earldom.[120] It was, moreover, a process which continued after the confiscation of Henry of Bolingbroke's duchy of Lancaster, for little more than three days after John of Gaunt's death in February 1399 Thomas Holford, one of the leaders of the king's bodyguard, had taken possession of Halton castle and was appointed as steward in place of Sir Richard Aston.[121] The end to any challenge to the king's authority within the principality had also embraced the ring of castles surrounding it, most of which were now held by members of the retinue.[122] It was in such circumstances that Richard left the security of his 'inner citadel' for Ireland in May 1399.

During the last two years of his reign Richard II had created within the limits of the principality of Chester a resource of loyalty and military support with which he sought to overawe any opponent. In part the process may have begun with the appointment of his close friends to positions of authority in Wales and the March, but it reached completion in the special affection which he expressed towards the men of Cheshire.[123] It is likely, as Michael Bennett has suggested, that here the king had found 'a more vibrant cultural tradition and a more congenial literary scene', in addition to the fact that the men of Cheshire, as recent events had demonstrated, possessed that quality of loyalty which the king now so actively sought.[124] In part this was the result of the tenurial structure of the county, with its relative paucity of noble landholding; in part the effect of the recent decline in military opportunity. The growth of royal patronage in Cheshire was, however, sudden and shortlived, an exercise in the politics of exclusion which resulted in the estrangement of the political community in the rest of England. Gifts, rewards and pardons, and the grant of minor offices and sinecures, many of them outside Cheshire, were showered on the membership of the retinue, who thereby monopolised access to the patronage of the prince of Chester.[125] The wealth which Richard II had lavished on his principality attracted the ill-will of those from whom it had been extorted, and in 1399 the county once again found itself perilously isolated in its support for the king.

Richard's principality could guarantee his personal security but not that of his realm and, stripped of its military strength for the campaign in Ireland, it could offer little resistance to Henry of Bolingbroke's campaign. Chester castle itself was garrisoned with perhaps thirty men-at-arms and archers, and even Holt, the repository of the king's treasure, had no more than 100 men-at-arms and archers.[126] As news of Bolingbroke's advance from Bristol reached Cheshire, William Egerton was ordered to garrison Heleigh castle in Staffordshire with as many men as were necessary; but soldiers in garrisons could not prevent the collapse of Richard's cause, and on 5 August Sir Robert Legh, the sheriff of Cheshire, travelled to Shrewsbury to negotiate with Bolingbroke for the submission of the city and castle of Chester. Four days later the Lancastrian duke entered the city to a welcome from the

monks of St Werburgh and the other clergy of the city; on 12 August
Peter Legh, a leading member of the Cheshire retinue, was captured
in the disguise of a monk and executed by Bolingbroke, who ordered
that his head should be fixed to the east gate of the city.[127] The 'inner
citadel' of Richard's kingdom had indeed fallen without a fight, and
for twelve days before the surrender of the king at Flint Bolingbroke's
army was stationed at Chester castle, pillaging the city and its surrounding countryside.[128]

A large measure of Bolingbroke's success was undoubtedly due to
the speed with which he attracted support during his campaign, not least
from his own estates.[129] At Gloucester he had been joined by an army
raised among his tenants in Cantrefselyf, Brecon and Llywel, and even
in Cheshire his servants and tenants were mustered by Gaunt's former
retainer, Thomas Maisterson.[130] Richard's patronage of his retinue
was no substitute for 'good lordship', and in 1399 the Earl of Salisbury,
returning from Ireland, could find little support for the king in Wales,
or indeed anywhere outside the earldom of Cheshire. The French writer,
Jean Creton, found evidence of treachery and cowardice even here, and
described Richard's melancholy entry into the capital of his principality
in these terms:'... the duke entered the city of Chester to whom the
common people paid great reverence, praising our lord and shouting
after their king as it were in mockery'.[131] Sir John Stanley, the controller of the king's household, had submitted to Henry at Chester, and
a few members of the retinue likewise found recognisances for their good
behaviour towards the Duke of Lancaster, but the collapse of Richard's
cause was really due to gross military incompetence and an absence of
political will, not to treachery.[132]

Bolingbroke left Chester on 20 August with Richard II, and travelled
south through Nantwich and Lichfield towards London.[133] According
to a subject of the Duke of Burgundy in the household of the Duke of
Exeter, the men of Cheshire made an attempt to rescue the king near
Lichfield. Walsingham too reports an attack on Bolingbroke, which he
claims was resisted by Sir Henry Percy.[134] The demonstration in
Richard's favour may in fact have taken place at Cholmondeston
outside Nantwich, where there is some record of an assault on Bolingbroke's retinue by members of the king's Cheshire retinue.[135] William
Swynburn, Percy's lieutenant as justice of Chester, was also paid shortly
afterwards for escorting a number of knights and esquires under arrest
from Chester to London.[136] Henry never faced the full strength of
Richard's Cheshire following, much of which had been dispersed in the
disaster of the king's journey through Wales, following his too long

delayed return from Ireland. Nevertheless, as the author of *Mum and the Sothsegger* observed, 'but yet they had hornes half a yere after'.[137]

In December 1399 the Earls of Huntingdon, Kent, Salisbury, and Rutland determined to capture Henry IV at Windsor and restore Richard to the throne. The plot was, however, soon betrayed to Henry by the Earl of Rutland and a servant of the Earl of Kent, Miles Hubbard, and the new king retreated to the security of London. The rebels meanwhile had gathered at Colnbrook near Windsor, where they debated their next course of action. Our source for that meeting, a Cheshire esquire in the retinue of the Earl of Salisbury, recorded that: 'Soe all night and eke the morowe there ware many letters enditen and many enquiers by yeomen sente into sunderye countereyes to rayes men for kinge Richarde'.[138] John and Adam Hesketh, two Lancashire men in the following of the Earl of Kent, were sent to Cheshire to inform the people that the Earls of Kent and Salisbury had put Henry to flight and forced him to retreat to the safety of the Tower of London. Richard's supporters were then called upon to muster at Shrewsbury on 14 January to force the restoration of the former king.[139] For two days the garrison at Chester castle, led by the constable, Sir William Venables of Kinderton, together with the sheriff, Sir John Mascy of Puddington, and the chamberlain, John Trefaur, resisted the rebels until, with the news of the collapse of the revolt of the earls, the rising ended as abruptly as it had begun.

John Carington's account of the meeting at Colnbrook makes it clear that no collaboration between the earls and Richard's former servants in Cheshire was mooted until the earls' own plans had gone badly awry with the escape of Henry IV from Windsor. The involvement of the Cheshire retinue in the events at Chester is, however, clear. On 22 May 1400 the king issued a general pardon to the county, from which 125 men were excepted. In the main these were men whose names had figured in Sir Henry Percy's inquiries into the rising, and who were now required to sue for individual pardons. Of the rebels forty-four can be identified as members of Richard II's retinue, including four of the leaders of his personal bodyguard: John Legh, John Donne, Thomas Beeston and Thomas Holford.[140] A fifth, Ralph Davenport, thought it prudent too to take out a pardon, as also did the former keeper of the king's wardrobe, John Macclesfield.[141] In the company of these men were their kinsmen, servants and neighbours. Sir Richard Winnington, a leader of the rising and a former annuitant, can be associated with Hugh Smyth, who is described as his servant, and with a kinsman, John Winnington, who had acted as a charter witness a few weeks before the rising.[142] Elsewhere, a large group of townsmen can be identified, either from their designation as tradesmen, or from their appearance in the city records. Thus, Thomas and William Banaster, both glovers, and Walter Goldsmith had all made recent appearances in the mayor's court.[143] The two main groups coincide with what is known of the events of the rising in its local aspect. On the first day a body of citizens wearing the livery of Richard II had made two unsuccessful attempts to seize the castle, and had taken down the head of Peter Legh from the east gate of the city. The following day, joined by the Heskeths and a larger number of Richard's former retinue, they marched from the city to raise support in the surrounding countryside. By this stage, however, news of the failure of the rising in the south had reached Cheshire, and the Cheshire force dispersed as quickly as it had formed.[144]

As a result of the rapid collapse of the rising in Chester, historians have tended to regard it as part of a larger but unrealised conspiracy amongst the Cheshire gentry in support of Richard II. In the first instance, however, the rebels had been opposed by a garrison of eight men-at-arms and thirty-five archers under the constable, Sir William Venables, and with the support of the sheriff, Sir John Mascy of Puddington, both of whom were later rewarded with annuities.[145] The response of Prince Henry of Monmouth, already invested with the earldom, was to issue commissions of the peace in the Cheshire hundreds and to the mayor and sheriffs of Chester, who were ordered to raise men within the city and to defend the walls as in time of war.[146] A general proclamation was issued before the opening of inquiries into the insurrection, which were initially organised by Cheshire officials themselves. Percy's own hearings in March 1400 made use of the same juries of local gentry who told much the same story.[147] The lack of urgency in the official response does suggest that the events were not seen as a serious threat to Henry's position. Support for the rising had been restricted to the leaders of Richard II's personal bodyguard and the tradesmen of Chester. Amongst the king's former knightly annuitants in Cheshire only Sir Richard Winnington had been implicated. In Chester itself, although the leader, Thomas Cotingham, had formerly been retained by Richard II *extra vigilia*, it is likely that much of the early momentum of the rising derived equally from the violence latent in an urban society, as from loyalty to the ex-king. The city had been witness to a number of violent demonstrations since 1390, and as late as May 1399 the Chester weavers had rioted during the festival of Corpus Christi.[148] In short, the Cheshire rising of 1400 illustrates the narrowness of support for Richard II after the deposition, and the extent to which, divorced from the flood of royal patronage, the leaders of his personal bodyguard were now unable to control the resources of local society.

III. THE BATTLE OF SHREWSBURY, 1403

Little more than three years after the abortive demonstrations in Richard's favour at Chester the county was to be deeply involved in the rising of Sir Henry Percy (Hotspur) against Henry IV, which ended at the battle of Shrewsbury. Contemporaries were unanimous that the greater part of Percy's army had been recruited in Cheshire, and that many had been persuaded to serve by proclamations that Richard II was alive and would lead his former supporters.[149] Unrequited loyalty would seem to be a poor recruiting agent, however, and the events of 1403 can only be adequately understood in the light of the relationship which had developed between the crown, Percy, and the county since 1399.

Bolingbroke's entry into Chester in August 1399 had inaugurated a widespread purge of the Cheshire administration. Nicholas Rygby, a member of the duke's retinue, immediately took over as constable of Chester castle, although he was later replaced by a Cheshire knight, Sir William Venables. On the same day the duke's retinue had entered the lordship of Halton and restored Sir Richard Aston as steward.[150] Later in August Sir Henry Percy replaced the late Sir William Lescrope as justice of Chester, and John Trefaur, bishop of Saint Asaph, assumed the office of chamberlain instead of Robert Parys, who had fled into Wales with the great seal of the principality. The purge of the major office-holders in the earldom was completed in November with the appointment of Sir John Mascy of Puddington as sheriff and of Richard Manley, formerly the lieutenant-steward of Halton, as escheator.[151] Elsewhere, Bolingbroke had clearly determined to deprive the members of the Cheshire retinue of those offices which they held as a result of previous royal patronage, and consequently there was a considerable change in demesne personnel in the first weeks of the new reign.[152] Initially, Henry had sought to advance and reward his own servants and supporters in Cheshire, but increasingly the direction of royal patronage, both in terms of demesne appointments, and the grant of annuities at the Chester exchequer, was turned towards outsiders who had achieved prominence in royal and princely service. Lancastrian policy was, it appears, aimed at assimilating the county more fully into the royal demesne.[153]

If Henry's policy towards the administration of Cheshire was far from conciliatory, he had nonetheless resisted demands for reparations from the county, which had been sought at the Westminster parliament in October 1399. Cheshire was, however, excepted from the king's order allowing legal redress to be sought against trespasses committed by his army during the campaign in 1399, and according to one London chronicle he acceded to a petition from the community of Shropshire by allowing Cheshire men to be cited in courts outside the county, 'nat withstandyng her liberte'.[154] Commissions of the peace had been issued in the Cheshire hundreds during August, and to these the king now added a proclamation against the assaults on neighbouring counties of which the community of Shropshire had complained.[155] There is, however, little evidence of any real challenge to the county's judicial liberties during this period, and in 1414 there were still cases outstanding on the roll of the Shropshire commission of the peace which had involved Cheshire men. A number of these cases affected former members of Richard II's bodyguard, and one, concerning an assault on the manor of Wem in July 1400, noted that the offenders had also risen against the king, presumably during the Chester rising.[156] It is possible, there-fore, that an increase in lawlessness had been related to a degree of political disaffection amongst Richard II's former supporters. At the same time a desire to quieten Cheshire society may have persuaded the king to issue writs at the end of June to the sheriff, Sir John Mascy of Puddington, ordering him to raise sixty men-at-arms and 500 archers for service in Scotland.[157]

Henry IV's promise to 'live of his own' forced him, paradoxically, to finance this first campaign in Scotland largely from loans, although even then it was successful only because the army remained in essence a muster of the king's retainers in the north of England and the Duchy of Lancaster.[158] The service of a number of Cheshire men from the lord-ship of Halton fitted closely into this pattern, and indeed on a number of occasions later in the reign the king would issue a personal summons there.[159] Elsewhere in the county, Mascy's retinue had been raised with the support of leading gentry, although as sheriff his appointment con-tinued a recent departure from custom[160] A full retinue roll was to be deposited at the Chester exchequer along with the names of those archers who had resisted service. In response to a parliamentary demand that Richard's Cheshire guard be required to repay the large sum of money which had been granted to them, Henry had stated that they would be made to serve him for a time, and it is conceivable that service on this Scottish campaign could have been represented as that commitment.[161]

Table 6   The Cheshire retinue in Scotland, 1400

Nomina militum et armigerorum comitatus Cestrie qui gubernationem et ductum quingentorum sagittariorum comitatus predicti habuerunt versus partes Scotiae mensis Julii anno regni regis Henrici quarti post conquestum primo, videlicet:

In hundredo de Macclesfield
Robert de Legh chivaler
Ralph de Davenport   24 sagitt'
William de Assheton
Reginald del Dounes
John filius Hugh de Arderne
Robert de Davenport   34 sagitt'
John de Honford de Honford
Nicholas de Davenport
William de Venables de   24 sagitt'
Bolyn
Laurence de Fytoun
Thomas de Worth   6 sagitt'

La some 100 sagitt'

In hundredo de Bucklowe
John de Mascy de Tatton 24 sagitt'
Thomas de Mascy filius eius
William de Legh   25 sagitt'
John Savage
Peter de Dutton   12 sagitt'
John de Holford   12 sagitt'
Robert de Toft
Ralph de Legh   8 sagitt'
John Doumville de Lyme

Thomas Danyers   12 sagitt'
George de Caryngton
Hugh de Legh   10 sagitt'
Robert de Asheton
La some 103 sagitt'

In hundredo de Northwico
Richard de Venables   20 sagitt'
chivaler
William de Brerton
Thomas le Grosvenor   16 sagitt'
Ranulph le Maynwaring
Adam le Bostock   16 sagitt'
John de Whelok
William de Holt junior   8 sagitt'
John Hardyng de Twemlow

La some 60 sagitt'

In hundredo de Broxon
Richard de Colmondelegh 20 sagitt'

John Brid   10 sagitt'
Ralph de Eggerton
John de Eton   10 sagitt'
William le Belewe loco
David de Bostok eo
quod infirma est
William de Mulneton   10 sagitt'
junior
John del Lee
David de Eggerton   10 sagitt'
La some 60 sagitt'

In hundredo Wici Malbanki
Richard de Vernon   20 sagitt'

Richard Masy del Hogh 10 sagitt'
Thomas le Maistressone
Thomas le Vernon   10 sagitt'
John de Kyngeslegh
Roger de Mascy per se et 10 sagitt'
William de Crue de Sonde
Peter de Mynshull   10 sagitt'
Nicholas de Bulkylegh
La some 60 archiers

In hundredo de Edesbury
Richard de Wynynton   20 sagitt'
chivaler
John de Wynynton filius eius
Richard de Bromley   15 sagitt'
William le Rotour
Thomas de Beeston   15 sagitt'
Roger Bruyn
Hugh de Dutton   15 sagitt'
William de Venables de
Troghford
La some 65 sagitt'

Table 6   continued

In hundredo de Wyrehal

John de Pulle chivaler	20 sagitt'
Jacob de Pulle filius eius	
John de Whitemore	10 sagitt'
Gilbert Clegge	6 sagitt'
John de Tildeslegh	4 sagitt'
John de Meols	
La some 40 archiers	

(Source: E101/42/29)

Five of the seven leaders of Richard II's bodyguard were indeed recruited for the expedition, although of these only Richard Cholmondeley, who had not been implicated in the conspiracy against Henry IV in January 1400, appeared as the leader of a company. Excluded from the patronage of the crown, these men now had little influence outside the immediate locality, and Henry had clearly preferred the leadership of landed society in the hundreds for the recruitment of his retinue.[162] Many of these Cheshire knights had been in receipt of fees and annuities from Richard II, but few played a significant role in the seven squadrons of his guard, and in no real sense could the retinue which was now paid for twenty days' service in Scotland be regarded as identical with that which accompanied Richard II on his journeys. In another sense, however, Henry's brief campaign, whilst it achieved little of permanent value in Scotland, may perhaps be thought to have demonstrated the success of the new regime's lordship in Cheshire: a lordship which, moreover, was soon to develop against a background of renewed military activity in the Welsh March.

The rising of Owain Glyn Dŵr, which began in September 1400, was to impose a severe burden upon the new king's administration in Cheshire and North Wales, and also upon the border counties where military service had continued to be an obligation on land and was often performed personally.[163] In Cheshire, as elsewhere in the March, the financial and military resources of local society were for a decade to be directed increasingly towards Wales, although it now seems unlikely that this simple reassertion of the county's historic role can have been responsible for the disaffection which erupted in 1403. Indeed, it was not until after that date that Prince Henry began in earnest a policy designed to increase the contribution of his lordship in Cheshire to the campaigns in Wales.[164] The early years of Glyn Dŵr's rising created an atmosphere of disorder in Cheshire, perhaps less real than is suggested by petitions to the chamberlain of Chester, but in which the absence of an effective and personal lordship by the prince enabled Sir Henry Percy to build a military following. The politics of faction and exclusion, as Henry IV's recent treatment of the Cheshire administration had demonstrated, had not ceased with the deposition of Richard II.

Although it was not until his appointment as lieutenant in the March that Prince Henry sought to increase demesne revenues in order to meet the expenses of his campaign in Wales, the resources of the earldom were already heavily committed. In an ordinance of March 1403 the king's council envisaged that the chamberlain of Chester would assume financial responsibility only for the defence of the castles in Flint and Rhuddlan, although in practice John Trefaur had for some years been making regular payments to the constables of Caernarfon and Conwy, and occasional payments to the garrisons at Harlech, Denbigh and Beaumaris.[165] Purveyance of victuals for these garrisons, for the prince's army at Bala in 1401, and even for the justices' sessions in North Wales, also fell to the chamberlain, although clearly such charges could not be met indefinitely from the ordinary revenues of the earldom.[166] Much of the deficit was in fact met from the collection of a gift of 3,000 marks, granted to the prince by the communities of Chester and Flint in June 1401, although in the event little was collected in Flintshire and Halton, and in some cases lords received quittances in place of wages of war.[167]

The extent to which these financial and administrative demands, and the events of the Welsh rising itself, brought disruption to the life of the county is difficult to judge. Pulford, Dodleston, Kinnerton, Marlston, Eccleston, Lache, Eaton and Claverton were reportedly destroyed in August 1403 when Chester itself seemed threatened by Glyn Dŵr, but there is no record of devastation east of the river Dee.[168] Attempts to bring the trade between Cheshire and Flintshire under close supervision seems to have had little impact on the economic life of the city, and by 1403 the council complained that Anglo-Welsh trade in grain, horses and cattle had continued unabated.[169] In the reign of Edward I it had been the manpower demands of the crown which had had the greatest effect on the county, a circumstance which appears to have been repeated after 1400. In November of that year the portmoot court at Chester was suspended whilst the mayor and sheriffs organised the victualling of the Welsh garrisons.[170] At Halton the manorial court could muster only six jurors in May 1402, the remainder having been recruited to serve in Wales, and at Newbold Astbury the bailiff was unable to collect rents due to his own absence.[171]

The organisation of campaigns in Wales had, however, changed greatly with developments in warfare during the fourteenth century, and although the prince's council was to issue a number of general summonses to the gentry of the county, large scale musters of troops were not on the whole a successful element in the early response to Glyn Dŵr's rising.[172] In September 1400 and again in 1401 significant numbers of such troops were reported to have deserted the royal army, taking with them large quantities of livestock. The author of the Dieulacres chronicle found the fact important enough to include it in his brief account of the early years of the reign.[173] Later in May 1403 many of the Cheshire gentry failed to attend an assembly at which the council's proposals for another expedition in North Wales were to be presented.[174] More characteristic of the period were the forays mounted by garrison-troops who had been retained by the Justice of Chester, Sir Henry Percy. The organisation of the war in North Wales around a network of garrisons, supported by itinerant companies under the leadership of the justice, must have seemed remarkably familiar to men like Sir Hugh Browe and Sir Richard Aston whose own early experience had been in the defence of Gascony in the 1370s and 1380s.

Much of the activity may be followed in the accounts of the chamberlain of Chester and in the enrolments of the Chester exchequer where, for instance, we learn of Robert Mascy of Hale's resistance against Glyn Dŵr himself at Flint, and of John Pulle's voyage to Beaumaris in an armoured barge manned by ten men-at-arms, thirty archers and twenty rowers.[175] In the Dieulacres chronicle we are told that Conwy castle was taken by stealth in June 1401 whilst the constable, Sir John Mascy of Puddington, and the greater part of his company were attending a service at the parish church.[176] Perhaps the best source, however, is the financial account of Sir Richard Aston as constable of Denbigh between April 1402 and April 1403, much of which is devoted to routine matters but nevertheless reveals payments for the maintenance of the fabric and to the garrison of five men-at-arms and eleven archers. The appearance of rebels in the early months of 1403 and the burning of parts of the lordship provoked a hurried exchange of letters with the garrisons at Flint and Hawarden, with Thomas Percy, Earl of Worcester, at Chester, and with Sir Henry Percy at Berwick, and even with the prince's council at Hereford.[177] The immediate response of the council was to organise a new campaign in North Wales under the leadership of Thomas Percy, the account of the controller of the prince's household for which is still extant.[178] It is a fortunate survival which now allows us to follow much of the recruitment of Cheshire companies in the weeks before the battle of Shrewsbury on 21 July 1403.

Sir Henry Percy returned to Cheshire on 9 July 1403, '*cum parva comitiva, pacem simulans*'. Here he issued a proclamation calling for the muster of his supporters at Sandiway in Delamere forest, and announcing that they would be joined there by a great army led by Richard II and his own father, the Earl of Northumberland.[179] According to Walsingham, he recruited other men-at-arms and archers with the promise that Richard would appear at Chester castle.[180] Such rumours of the late king's survival were not uncommon, for twelve months earlier a John Lancaster had defrauded a number of men at Winnington, claiming that he had seen Richard II at Berwick: and in 1404 John Kingsley, who had joined Percy's revolt, continued to assert that Richard was alive and raising an army in Scotland.[181] In the eyes of contemporaries, such incidents explained the unusual success with which Sir Henry Percy was able to recruit in Cheshire. Walsingham in particular wrote of a substantial number of the late king's former retainers in Percy's following, although he also stressed the degree of support amongst the 'baronial' class in the county. The later Waltham annalist, reporting what had clearly become the popular view of the rising, observed that scarcely three knights and seven esquires were left in Cheshire.[182] That the rising of 1403 was in essence a Cheshire rising is clear too from the details of its suppression. A surprisingly high percentage of those whose forfeitures and pardons are recorded were indeed Cheshire men, and the city and county were later required to pay a fine of 3,300 marks for a general pardon from Henry IV.[183]

For the third time in the space of a generation the county had found itself on the losing side in a factional battle. Recent work on the progress of the rising in Cheshire has stressed the durability of support for Richard II, and pointed to the apparently close correlation between the origins of many of the known rebels and the actual route taken by Percy's force in July 1403.[184] There are three major sources which enable us to identify participants in the battle of Shrewsbury (21 July), of which perhaps the best known are the forfeitures and pardons entered on the patent rolls of the royal chancery and the court rolls of the county court at Chester.[185] The escheator, Richard Manley, also took inquisitions of the goods of thirty-four knights and esquires in the county between August and September.[186] By far the most comprehensive source, however, is contained in an indictment laid four days after the battle in which 514 Cheshire men were accused of abducting horses from the battlefield.[187] The indictment unfortunately gives no detail as to the companies in which these men had served, although in the circumstances one might safely assume that they had been with Percy.[188]

Knowing who took part in the battle is an important step towards answering the larger question as to why certain sections of Cheshire society cast in their lot with the Percies. The complex mesh of loyalties amongst the lesser gentry is, however, notoriously difficult to unravel, nowhere more so than in Cheshire where the absence of a sustained tenurial presence deprived the nobility of an effective social and economic lever in retaining the services of their followers in the county. A single source-reference cannot, therefore, always be regarded as conclusive evidence of an enduring association in a local society where connections with the nobility were commonly of a temporary nature. As an example, the alabaster effigy of Sir William Mainwaring in Acton church shows the knight wearing the livery collar of the house of Lancaster, although there is now no record of his having been retained by John of Gaunt beyond a single campaign in 1393. Were it not for a codicil to Mainwaring's will, written at Kidwelly in June 1399, which spoke of the knight's reverence for his lord, Richard II, we would have assumed a permanent Lancastrian connection which did not in fact exist. The tomb effigy at Acton was the responsibility of the knight's heir, John Mainwaring, who became sheriff in Chester in 1403 and was, it now appears, anxious to demonstrate the longevity of his family's loyalty to Henry IV's cause.[189] With that caution in mind, however, it is possible to draw several broad conclusions on the recruitment of the retinues at Shrewsbury which amplify those derived from a study of the military community in the reign of Richard II.

The extent to which Sir Henry Percy was able to draw support from Richard's former retinue is immediately apparent; indeed, in his proclamations he appealed only for that loyalty which had been directed to the former king. Six of the seven leaders of Richard's personal bodyguard are known to have been at Shrewsbury, together with other members of the retinue who had been pardoned after the rising of 1400. Many of those who joined Percy's following on its march from Sandiway to Prees in Shropshire, and who were responsible for burning the house of a prominent supporter of Henry IV at Nantwich, may have been persuaded by claims that Richard II was indeed alive.[190] The Dieulacres writer describes them as a 'great mass of the feeble-minded'.[191] More importantly, however, many of these men had been excluded from the resources of county society in the political settlement of 1400, and provided a ready source of opposition to Henry IV. In 1399, for instance, the Legh family had been important office holders in the Principality of Chester: John Legh of Booths served as a leader of the king's guard; Sir Hugh Legh as escheator; Sir Robert Legh as sheriff of the county; and Peter Legh as steward of Macclesfield. In 1403 none remained in office or in a position of influence in the administration of the county. Access to the resources of office had been vital in the success of the Legh affinity, which now looked to Sir Henry Percy to restore the losses sustained in the deposition of Richard II.

The rising of 1403 was, however, far from being a belated response to the events of the deposition mounted from within 'the inner citadel' of Richard's kingdom. Those charged with administration of the county under Prince Henry remained overwhelmingly loyal, and the king's retinue at Shrewsbury is known to have included the mayor of Chester, the attorney-general of the county, the Constable of Chester castle, and the prince's lieutenant in Cheshire and Flintshire.[192] The sheriff, Sir John Mascy of Puddington, who, with the justice, was the county's leading military official, was also amongst those killed on the king's side in the battle.[193] Furthermore, amongst the local gentry who periodically undertook a governmental role in the county, fewer than half of the commissioners of the peace appointed in 1400 and of the collectors of the subsidy of 1402 are known to have been involved in the rising.[194] Support for Sir Henry Percy in Cheshire was widespread but far from universal, and in general would seem to have included those who had been most closely associated with Richard II, and whose claims to comital favour were now of little standing.

Beyond the degree of response or reconciliation to the events of 1399, the participation of other local gentry was conditioned by a variety of more immediate causes. Tenurial pressure appears to have played a significant role on a number of estates, notably in the lordship of Halton and, contrariwise, on the Cheshire lands of Lord Lestraunge. Unfortunately the court rolls of Halton manor itself do not survive for 1403, but those at nearby Whitley record the deaths of a number of the king's tenants at Shrewsbury.[195] Sir Richard Aston, steward of Halton under Richard II, is also known to have fought on the king's side. The recruitment of tenants on the estates of Lord Lestraunge provides an interesting link with Glyn Dŵr's rising itself, for the steward, John Kynaston, is reported to have been present at the meeting at Glyn Dyfrdwy in 1400, and to have acted as a messenger between Sir Henry Percy and Glyn Dŵr in the weeks before the battle of Shrewsbury.[196] In the lordship of Ellesmere in Shropshire, he is reported to have summoned the tenants of Richard, lord Lestraunge, to join their lord at Myddle, and then forced them to join Sir Henry Percy under pain of decapitation.[197]

Kynaston also controlled a number of manors in Cheshire, including Dunham Massey, Kelsall, Moreton and Bidston, from which tenants are also known to have been recruited for service in the rebel cause.[198]

Elsewhere, the role of kinship and the operation of gentry affinities would seem to have had some importance. A number of rebels can for instance be identified as kinsmen and neighbours of the Legh family, amongst them Richard Bromley and William Legh of Baguley.[199] Arthur Davenport was related by marriage to another rebel, Sir John Calveley, and had served as an attorney for members of the family during their absence in France in 1379.[200] Detailed study reveals an impressive network of interdependence amongst many of those known to have participated in the rising, and demonstrates the vitality of local gentry society. Peter Warburton, who was not only a tenant of the lordship of Halton but had served in Bolingbroke's household in 1398, nevertheless preferred service with Percy, perhaps in company with his former guardian and neighbour, Sir John Mascy of Tatton.[201] Somewhat surprisingly, Sir John Calveley was another rebel, despite his grant of the manor of Stapleford in Leicestershire by Henry IV in December 1400. Walsingham records his death fighting on the king's side at Shrewsbury, but a keeper of his estate was appointed in 1404 'by reason of his forfeiture and outlawry'.[202] Such apparently peculiar allegiances were not uncommon, and cannot now be explained by reference to either Richard II's deposition and its aftermath, or the erstwhile allegiances of the local gentry.

It now seems clear that the Earl of Northumberland's hesitancy in joining his son's rebellion and the failure of the alliance with Glyn Dŵr enabled Henry IV to strike quickly at Sir Henry Percy whilst he was supported by a smaller and predominantly Cheshire army. The king was informed of the rising at Nottingham on 12 July, whilst on his way north to aid the Percies against the Scots, and immediately moved westwards towards the Welsh border. Here he was joined by the Prince of Wales who had been raising an army for a campaign in the March, and together they met Percy's force north of Shrewsbury on 21 July.[203] The battle was a hard-fought and bloody affair in which archers on both sides inflicted heavy casualties. According to the Dieulacres chronicler, thirty-six of the king's knights and eight of Percy's were killed, and the 1,847 dead were buried in a single pit on the battlefield.[204] The ramshackle army which was assembled at Sandiway seems hardly likely to have been capable of inflicting such heavy damage on the king's army, and indeed much of Percy's strength would appear to have been the result of defections from the prince's retinue in the March.

The controller of the Prince's household presented an account for a retinue of twenty knights, 454 esquires and 2,350 archers for the period between 17 April and 18 July 1403, and also made payments to a Cheshire company of some fifty-two knights, fifty-seven esquires and 753 archers who had been raised under the leadership of the steward of the prince's household, Sir John Stanley, for the relief of Harlech castle.[205] From the evidence of pardons and forfeitures, it is possible to identify a substantial part of Percy's army within John Spenser's account. Amongst the defections from the prince's retinue itself, the most important were those of the Earl of Worcester and Sir Hugh Browe. A few smaller companies under Sir Richard Aston, Sir John Mascy of Puddington, and Matthew Mere remained with the prince, but their loyalty was balanced by the widespread losses of men from the retinue which had served in the relief of Harlech castle. In all some eight knights, ninety-six esquires and 866 archers are known to have joined Percy's army. These men cannot have been persuaded by the extravagant claims made at Sandiway, Chester, and Prees Heath that Richard II was still alive; indeed, considerations of locality apart, it is likely that political judgement was paramount in decisions about loyalty.

The defections of Sir Hugh Browe, Sir William Stanley, and Sir John Pulle in particular seem difficult to relate to any fantasy of Richard's restoration or to dissatisfaction with the rule of Prince Henry's council. Browe had for a number of years been associated with the late Earl of Arundel and had fought against de Vere at Radcot Bridge, whilst Stanley, as a kinsman of the steward of the prince's household, clearly had access to the resources of comital and indeed royal patronage.[206] All three knights had, however, recently found service with Sir Henry Percy in the Welsh March, where his undoubted ability and willingness to meet the costs of the retinue out of his own pocket were in stark contrast to the cumbersome military and financial arrangements of the prince's council.[207] Stanley and Pulle were retained by Sir Henry Percy in May 1402 to relieve Beaumaris by sea, whilst Browe had accompanied him during the campaign which forced Glyn Dŵr to retreat in the summer of 1401.[208] The memory of these campaigns and of the Percies' recent victory over the Scots at Homildon Hill were clearly a powerful catalyst in attracting the service of members of the military community like Sir Hugh Browe and Sir John Mascy of Tatton, who had remained aloof from the events of Richard's 'tyranny'. It is only benefit of hindsight that allows us to imagine that contemporaries were not faced by a perplexing decision, and perhaps appropriate that great military ability and reputation should, at that moment, have played so decisive a role in turning men from their traditional loyalty to the Earl of Chester.

According to a tradition preserved in the Brut Chronicle, the king sent a messenger to Sir John Stanley on the battlefield to seek his advice on the treatment of Cheshire in the aftermath of the rising. Wounded in the throat by an arrow 'so as he myght speke rattelynge in the throte', the knight's response was both simple and direct: 'Brenne and sle'! Brenne and sle!'[209] Sir Richard Vernon, Baron of Shipbrook, and Sir Richard Venables, Baron of Kynderton, were indeed executed as the highest representatives of the social order in the county, and their heads fixed on the east gate of Chester castle.[210] One chronicler records some retribution conducted by Henry's disbanded army, but the official punishment, a fine of 3,000 marks on the county which was given to the prince for the maintenance of the castles of North Wales, and a fine of 300 marks imposed on the city of Chester, but remitted in favour of ships and victuals for the garrison at Beaumaris, was not unduly harsh.[211] Those who had been killed in the battle forfeited their estates, although mostly to the advantage of those Cheshire gentry who had remained loyal; the survivors, however, were soon readmitted to the earl's affinity through pardons.[212]

Thus the politics of faction and exclusion, which had begun during the minority of Richard II, were ended on the field at Shrewsbury. Almost immediately Prince Henry's own vigorous campaign in North Wales was to forge new links with the earldom which, once he had become king, were hardened by renewed campaigns in France, in which the men of Cheshire were again to play a significant part.[213]

NOTES

[1] Anthony Tuck, *Richard II and the English Nobility*, 1973, pp. 110–20, 165–9, 187–225.

[2] J. N. L. Myres, 'The Campaign of Radcot Bridge in December 1387', *EHR*, xlii, 1927, pp. 20–33; J. L. Gillespie, 'Thomas Mortimer and Thomas Molineux: Radcot Bridge and the Appeal of 1397', *Albion*, 1975, pp. 161–73.

[3] *Annales Ricardi Secundi et Henrici Quarti Regum Angliae* in J. de Trokelowe et Anon., *Chronica et Annales*, ed. H. T. Riley, Rolls Series 1866, pp. 159–61; J. G. Bellamy, 'The Northern Rebellions in the Later Years of Richard II', *BJRL*, xlvii, 1964–5, pp. 254–74.

[4] J. L. Gillespie, 'Richard II's Cheshire Archers', *THLC*, 125, 1975, pp. 1–39; *idem.*, *The Cheshire Archers of Richard II: A Royal Experiment in Bastard Feudalism*, University of Princeton PhD, 1972; R. R. Davies, 'Richard II and the Principality of Chester 1397–9', in F. R. H. du Boulay & Caroline M. Barron (eds), *The Reign of Richard II*, 1971, pp. 256–79.

[5] P. McNiven, 'The Cheshire Rising of 1400', *BJRL*, lii, 1970, pp. 375 – 96; *idem.*, 'The Men of Cheshire and the Rebellion of 1403', *THLC*, 129, 1980, pp. 1 – 29; Charles L. Kingsford, *English Historical Literature in the Fifteenth Century*, 1913, p. 350.

[6] Tuck, op. cit., pp. 116, 166, 180.

[7] P. McNiven, *The Men of Cheshire and the Rebellion of 1403*, p. 25.

[8] *Rotuli Parliamentorum*, III, p. 185.

[9] N. B. Lewis, 'The Last Medieval Summons of the English Feudal Levy, 13 June 1385', *EHR*, lxxiii, 1958, pp. 1 – 26; J. J. N. Palmer, 'The Last Summons of the Feudal Army in England', *EHR*, lxxxiii, 1968, pp. 771 – 5; *idem.* 'The Parliament of 1385 and the Constitutional Crisis of 1386', *Speculum*, xlvi, 1971, pp. 477 – 90; N. B. Lewis, 'The Feudal Summons of 1385', *EHR*, c, 1985, pp. 729 – 46.

[10] Lewis, *The Last Medieval Summons*, p. 20; SC6/772/20 (Account of the Chamberlain of Chester, September 1385 – September 1386), m. 2d.

[11] N. H. Nicolas, *The Scrope-Grosvenor Controversy*, I, 1832; see above, p. 129.

[12] J. J. N. Palmer, *England, France and Christendom, 1377 – 99*, 1972, pp. 67 – 85.

[13] SC6/772/20 m. 3d; Chester 2/57 m. 6d; CRO, Leycester-Warren MSS, DLT, Liber C f. 181; BL Stowe MS 440 f. 15, f. 16.

[14] Chester Record Office, Cotton of Combermere Deeds, CR72/6/1 (Account of the Manor of Newhall, November 1386 – November 1387), m. 3; Tuck, op. cit., Appendix, p. 227.

[15] Chester 2/59 m. 7.

[16] Tuck, op. cit., p. 111; *The Westminster Chronicle, 1381 – 1394*, L. C. Hector and Barbara F. Harvey (eds), 1982, p. 186.

[17] C47/2/49 no. 12; *CPR, 1385 – 1389*, p. 9; J. L. Gillespie, *The Cheshire Archers of Richard II: A Royal Experiment in Bastard Feudalism*, University of Princeton PhD, 1972, pp. 15, 33 – 99; *idem*, 'Richard II's Archers of the Crown', *Journal of British Studies*, xviii, 1979, pp. 14 – 29.

[18] SC6/773/2 (Account of the Chamberlain of Chester, September 1387 – September 1388); *Chronicle of Dieulacres Abbey, 1381 – 1403* in 'The Deposition of Richard II' ed. V. H. Galbraith & M. V. Clarke, *BJRL*, xiv, 1930, p. 107.

[19] *CPR, 1388 – 1392*, p. 20; Tuck, op. cit., p. 78.

[20] SC6/773/3 (Account of the clerk to the Chamberlain of Chester, September 1387 – September 1388), m. 1d.

[21] Chester 25/8 m. 36; *The Kirkstall Chronicle, 1355 – 1400*, ed. M. V. Clarke & N. Denholm-Young, *BJRL*, xv, 1931, p. 126.

[22] SC6/1234/5 (Account of the receiver of Holt, 1387 – 1388).

[23] R. G. Davies, 'Some Notes from the Register of Henry de Wakefield Bishop of Worcester on the Political Crisis of 1386 – 1388', *EHR*, lxxxvi, 1971, pp. 550, 556.

[24] J. N. L. Myres, 'The Campaign of Radcot Bridge in December 1387', *EHR*, xlii, 1927, pp. 20 – 33; A. Goodman, *The Loyal Conspiracy*, 1971, pp. 27 – 32, 129 – 30.

[25] R. G. Davies, loc. cit.

[26] *The Westminser Chronicle*, p. 222.

[27] E101/40/33; Chester 24/19 bundle 21 Richard II; BL Egerton Roll 8730.

220   WAR AND SOCIETY IN MEDIEVAL CHESHIRE

[28] *Chronicon Henrici Knighton*, ed. J.R. Lumby, Rolls Series, 1895, ii, pp. 251-2.

[29] *The Westminster Chronicle*, loc. cit.; *Knighton*, p. 254; *Dieulacres*, p. 168.

[30] *Chronicon Angliae auctore monacho quodam Sancti Albani*, ed. E.M. Thompson, Rolls Series, 1874, p. 385; Thomas Walsingham, *Historia Anglicana*, ed. H.T. Riley, Rolls Series, 1864, ii, pp. 167-8; V.H. Galbraith, 'Thomas Walsingham and the Saint Albans Chronicle, 1272-1422', *EHR*, xlvii, 1932, pp. 12-30.

[31] *Dieulacres*, loc. cit.

[32] R.R. Davies, loc. cit.; Chester 2/79 m.7d; Chester 2/73 m.6.

[33] E163/6/12.

[34] Caroline M. Barron, 'The Tyranny of Richard II', *BIHR*, xli, 1968, pp. 6-10.

[35] J.L. Gillespie, *Richard II's Cheshire Archers*, p. 25.

[36] C67/30 m.2., m.3. A pardon to Richard Weston appears as BL Additional charter 74,036.

[37] *Knighton*, 251; Chester 25/8 m.25, m.36; E101/631/13.

[38] CRO, Cholmondeley of Cholmondeley deeds, DCH/C/846-73.

[39] E101/36/32.

[40] A. Goodman, op. cit., p. 133; SC6/773/2 m.1d; SC6/1234/5.

[41] Chester 2/61 m.1; see above p. 74.

[42] A. Goodman, op. cit., pp. 113, 120-1.

[43] E101/41/5; BL Additional MS 40859A; E101/74/1.

[44] Tuck, op. cit., pp. 137-50.

[45] SC6/773/6 (Account of the Chamberlain of Chester, September 1389 – September 1390), m.1d.

[46] *Rotuli Parliamentorum*, iii, pp. 204-5.

[47] CRO, DCH/G/62.

[48] SC6/773/6 m.1d; Chester 29/92 m.17, m.29; SC8/888.

[49] Chester 2/63 m.3.

[50] Tuck, op. cit., pp. 144-5, 152.

[51] Chester 25/24 m.26. I am grateful to Professor R.R. Davies for this reference.

[52] J.G. Bellamy, 'The Northern Rebellions in the Later Years of Richard II's Reign, *BJRL*, xlvii, 1965, pp. 254-74.

[53] *Annales Ricardi Secundi*, pp. 159-60.

[54] *Annales Ricardi Secundi*, p. 159.

[55] Bellamy, op. cit., p. 272; Tuck, op. cit., pp. 165-6.

[56] Chester 2/62 m.2.

[57] T.F. Tout, *Chapters in the Administrative History of Medieval England*, iii, 1928, p. 482.

[58] Chester 25/8 m.30d. For resistance to the mise of 1416 see Michael J. Bennett, *Community, Class and Careerism. Lancashire and Cheshire Society in the Age of Sir Gawain and the Green Knight*, 1983, pp. 51-2.

[59] Chester 25/8 m.31d; Chester 2/64 m.8.

[60] Chester 2/64 m.2; *CPR, 1391-1396*, p. 77.

[61] Chester 2/64 m.1; SC6/773/9 (Clerk to the Chamberlain of Chester's account, September 1391 – September 1392).

[62] Chester 25/8 m.31d; Chester 2/64 m.8.

[63] Chester 25/8 m.31d.

[64] Chester 25/8 m.35; Shropshire Record Office, Bridgewater Estate, Box 68.

[65] SC8/125 no.6217 printed in *Calendar of Ancient Petitions relating to Wales*, ed. W. Rees, 1975, p.209, where it is wrongly dated as 1381; Chester 25/8 m.36d.

[66] Chester 2/64 m.3, m.8.

[67] Chester 24/17, 15 Richard II, bundle 3.

[68] SC8/88 no.4387.

[69] Chester 2/64 m.5d, m.8d.

[70] *Annales Ricardi Secundi*, p.166.

[71] Bellamy, op. cit., p.266; *Rotuli Parliamentorum*, iii, pp.316–7.

[72] C47/14/6 no.44.

[73] *Foedera, Conventiones, Litterae etc.*, ed. T. Rymer, Record Commission 1816–1869, vii, p.747.

[74] *Annales Ricardi Secundi*, p.161.

[75] *Historia Anglicana*, p.214; Margaret Aston, *Thomas Arundel*, 1967, p.154.

[76] *Rotuli Parliamentorum*, iii, pp.313–4; *Annales Ricardi Secundi*, p.162.

[77] E101/40/33; E101/41/5.

[78] Bellamy, op. cit., pp.266–9.

[79] *Rotuli Parliamentorum*, iii, pp.316–17; Tuck, op. cit., p.167. Talbot's annuity was cancelled by Henry IV but later renewed, E163/6/35; *CPR, 1399–1401*, p.486.

[80] E101/402/20 m.35d; *CCR, 1392–1396*, p.305; Bellamy, op. cit., pp.268–9.

[81] *CPR, 1388–1392*, p.377; Bellamy, op. cit., pp.273–4; Tuck, loc. cit.

[82] Chester 29/97 m.24.

[83] Chester 29/97 m.18, m.20; *CCR, 1392–1396*, p.433; Chester 25/8 m.40.

[84] J.F. Lydon, 'Richard II's Expeditions to Ireland', *Journal of the Royal Society of Antiquaries of Ireland*, xciii, 1963, p.136; SC6/774/3 (Account of the Chamberlain of Chester, September 1394 – September 1395), m.2d.

[85] *English Historical Documents*, iv, 1327–1485, ed. A.R. Myers, 1969, no.721; R.V.H. Burne, *The Monks of Chester*, 1962, pp.106–9; E101/402/20 m.31.

[86] K.B. McFarlane, *The Nobility of Later Medieval England*, 1973, p.26; E101/74/1.

[87] See above, pp.89–91.

[88] J.F. Lydon, op. cit., pp.141–2; E101/402/20 m.31–m.40d; E101/69/1. The suggestion by Lydon, loc. cit., that large numbers of Cheshire archers had also served is to be discarded.

[89] C61/104 m.5–m.7; BL Additional Charter, 51131; JRL, Mainwaring deeds 171–2.

[90] C61/104 m.3.

[91] J.J.N. Palmer, *England, France and Christendom, 1377–99*, 1972, pp.166–78.

[92] Tuck, op. cit., pp.181–4.

[93] Goodman, op. cit., pp.68–9. Nicholas Colfox, a Cheshire esquire who had been in the Earl's service since 1388, was later pardoned by Henry IV for his part in the murder; E101/41/5 m.2; SC8/254 no.12671; *CPR, 1401–1405*, p.381; M.D. Legge, *Anglo-Norman Letters*, Anglo-Norman Text Society, 3, 1941, p.446.

[94] Chester 2/70 m.7d.

[95] *Chronicon Adae de Usk*, ed. E. M. Thompson, 1904, p.11.

[96] Tuck, op. cit., p.187; *Annales Ricardi Secundi*, p.208; *Historia Anglicana*, p.224.

[97] *CPR, 1396–1399*, p.179.

[98] R.R. Davies, *Richard II and the Principality of Chester, 1397–9*, pp.256–79; J.L. Gillespie, *The Cheshire Archers of Richard II: A Royal Experiment in Bastard Feudalism*, University of Princeton PhD thesis, 1972, *passim*; *idem., Richard II's Cheshire Archers*, pp.1–39.

[99] Davies, op. cit., p.269; *Historia Anglicana*, p.224; Michael J. Bennett, *Community, Class and Careerism*, 42n.5 suggests that the squadrons may have evolved from musters within the seven Cheshire hundreds.

[100] *Eulogium Historiarum Sive Temporis*, ed. F.S. Haydon, Rolls Series 1863, iii, p.380.

[101] *Mum and the Sothsegger*, ed. M. Day, Early English Text Society, cxcix, 1936, p.24.

[102] Cited in J.L. Gillespie, *Richard II's Cheshire Archers*, p.32.

[103] *Annales Ricardi Secundi*, p.237.

[104] *Mum and the Sothsegger*, loc. cit.; *Annales Ricardi Secundi*, p.208.

[105] KB9/184/1 m.9. Other instances are cited in Davies, op. cit., p.270; J.L. Gillespie, *Richard II's Cheshire Archers*, p.24.

[106] *Rotuli Parliamentorum*, iii, p.439.

[107] *Adam of Usk*, p.23.

[108] E101/42/10; Davies, op. cit., p.269.

[109] Chester 2/73 m.2; E364/37 m.32; E403/562 m.10, m.16.

[110] Davies, op. cit., pp.256–60.

[111] Davies, op. cit., p.269; Chester Record Office, Earwaker MS, CR63/2/665 (petition of Hugh Ardern).

[112] SC6/774/6 (Account of the Chamberlain of Chester, September 1396 – September 1397), m.1d; Chester 1/1 part 2 no.46.

[113] See above pp.189–90.

[114] J.L. Gillespie, *Richard II's Cheshire Archers*, pp.1–8; Davies, op. cit., pp.259–60.

[115] SC6/1234/7 (Account of the Chamberlain of Bromfield and Yale, Chirkland and Oswestry April 1398 – September 1398), m.1d. See for example the letters patent granting annuities to John Beeston, BL Additional Charter 49,956; Robert Davenport, CRO, Davenport of Bramhall deeds, DDA/31/2, and Ralph Davenport, JRL, Bromley-Davenport deeds, II, 3, Davenport of Davenport, vi.

[116] E101/42/10 m.2; CRO, Cholmondeley of Cholmondeley deeds, DCH/A/103; DCH/A/110–11.

[117] J.L. Gillespie, *Richard II's Cheshire Archers*, p.22.

[118] *CCR, 1396–1399*, 505 (oath of Robert Legh), cited by Davies, op. cit., 276 n.94.

[119] Davies, op. cit., p.266; JRL Cornwall-Legh deeds, p.69 (appointment of Hugh Legh as escheator of the principality of Chester, October 1397). A similar, though far less comprehensive, effort to control local government can be seen in East Anglia, see Roger Virgoe, 'The Crown and Local Government: East Anglia under Richard II', *The Reign of Richard II*, pp.218–41.

[120] Davies, op. cit., pp. 262 – 3; J. L. Gillespie, *The Cheshire Archers of Richard II*, University of Princeton PhD, 1972, appendix C.

[121] DL30/3/41 m.1d, m.2.

[122] Davies, op. cit., pp. 262 – 3, 270; SC6/1234/7 m.12. In 1399 repairs were undertaken at Beeston, Flint, Rhuddlan and Shotwick, and the Audley castle at Heleigh in Staffordshire was garrisoned by William Egerton, SC6/774/10 (Account of the Chamberlain of Chester, September 1398 – August 1399), m.2d; Chester 2/73 m.1.

[123] Tuck, op. cit., pp. 180 – 1; K. B. McFarlane, *Lancastrian Kings and Lollard Knights*, 1972, pp. 188 – 9.

[124] Michael J. Bennett, 'Sir Gawain and the Green Knight and the Literary Achievement of the North-West Midlands: the Historical Background', *Journal of Medieval History*, 5, 1979, p. 80.

[125] J. L. Gillespie, loc. cit.; Davies, op. cit., p. 263; SC6/774/6 m.1d.

[126] SC6/774/10 m.2d; *Adam of Usk*, p. 28.

[127] Davies, op. cit., p. 276; *Historia Vitae et Regni Ricardi Secundi a monacho quodam de Evesham*, ed. T. Hearne, 1729, p. 154; R. V. H. Burne, op. cit., p. 115; *Adam of Usk*, p. 27; *Dieulacres*, p. 172.

[128] *Adam of Usk*, pp. 26 – 7; *Dieulacres*, pp. 171 – 2; SC6/774/10 m.2d.

[129] R. Somerville, *History of the Duchy of Lancaster*, i, 1953, pp. 136 – 7; Tuck, op. cit., pp. 214 – 15.

[130] R. R. Davies, *Lordship and Society in the March of Wales, 1282 – 1400*, 1978, p. 84 – 5; BL Harley MS 2119, f. 87d.

[131] Jean Creton, *Histoire du Roy d'Angleterre Richard etc.*, ed. J. Webb, Archaeologia, xx, 1824, p. 149.

[132] Tuck, loc. cit., J. W. Sherborne, 'Richard II's Return to Wales, July 1399', *Welsh History Review*, 7, 1974, p. 392; Dorothy Johnston, 'Richard II's Departure from Ireland, July 1399', *EHR*, xcvii, 1983, pp. 785 – 805.

[133] *Evesham*, p. 156.

[134] *Chronique de la Traison et Mort du Richard II*, ed. B. Williams, 1846, p. 55; J. J. N. Palmer, 'The Authorship, Date and Historical Value of the French Chronicles on the Lancastrian Revolution', *BJRL*, lxi, 1978 – 9, p. 163. *Annales Ricardi Secundi*, pp. 250 – 1.

[135] Chester 25/10 m.5. The leader, Adam Bordhewer, had been one of Richard's annuitants, E101/42/10 m.1.

[136] SC6/774/12 (Account of the Chamberlain of Chester, August 1399 – March 1400), m.1.

[137] *Mum and the Sothsegger*, p. 7.

[138] W. A. Copinger, *History and Records of the Smith-Carrington Family*, 1907, pp. 73 – 4. John Carrington and Robert Ardern were sent into Dorset and Wiltshire, and escaped to Brittany after the collapse of the revolt, see above, p. 167.

[139] Peter McNiven, 'The Cheshire Rising of 1400', *BJRL*, lii, 1970, pp. 375 – 96.

[140] *CPR, 1399 – 1401*, pp. 285 – 6; Chester 25/10 m.1 – m.4. A pardon granted to John Malpas survives as BL Additional Charter 74,038.

[141] T. P. Highet, *The Early History of the Davenports of Davenport*, Chet. Soc., New Series, ix, 1960, p. 30; BL Cotton MS Cleopatra D VI, f. 2.

[142] JRL, Arley Charters, box 27, 32.

[143] Chester 25/10 m.2; Chester Record Office, Mayor's Books, MB/1, f.4d, f.19d.

[144] McNiven, op. cit., pp.387–9.

[145] SC6/774/13 (Account of the Chamberlain of Chester, September 1400 – September 1401), m.3d; CRO, DVE/3/CII/1; DL42/15 f.82d.

[146] Chester 2/73 m.3, m.3v; Chester Record Office, The Black Book of the City of Chester, CHB/1 f.3.

[147] McNiven, loc. cit.

[148] See above, pp.194–5; Chester Record Office, MB/1 f.55d; R.H. Morris, Chester in the Plantagenet and Tudor Reigns, 1893, p.32.

[149] Dieulacres, p.177; Thomas Walsingham, Ypodigma Neustriae, ed. H.T. Riley, Rolls Series 1876, p.399; Peter McNiven, The Men of Cheshire and the Rebellion of 1403, p.1.

[150] Davies, Richard II and the Principality of Chester 1397–9, p.278; SC6/774/12, m.1; DL30/3/41 m.2.

[151] Chester 2/73 m.9; Chester 2/74 m.1, m.7.

[152] See for instance the appointment of Henry Ravenscroft as steward of Northwich, Eaton Hall near Chester, Eaton charter 389; and Thomas Wednesley as steward of Macclesfield, SC2/255/3 m.1. In general, see Anne E. Curry, 'Cheshire and the Royal Demesne, 1399–1422', Medieval Cheshire, ed. J.I. Kermode and C.B. Phillips, THLC, 128, 1979, pp.116–17.

[153] Curry, op. cit., pp.117–19, 129–30. Prince Henry had rewarded two archers in his retinue with grants of land after his return from Ireland, Chester 2/74 m.1d; JRL Rylands Charters, 1309, 1310.

[154] Rotuli Parliamentorum, iii, pp.433, 440; Chronicles of London, ed. C.L. Kingsford, 1905, p.66.

[155] Chester 2/74 m.3.

[156] E.C. Kimball, The Shropshire Peace Roll, 1400–1414, 1959, pp.52–3, 60, 82, 105–7.

[157] Chester 2/74 m.6.

[158] A.L. Brown, 'The English Campaign in Scotland in 1400', in British Government and Administration, ed. H. Hearder and H.R. Loyn, 1974, pp.48, 53.

[159] E101/43/3 m.2, m.3, m.5, m.6; DL42/16 f.75d, f.201.

[160] See above, p.199.

[161] Rotuli Parliamentorum, iii, p.439.

[162] E101/42/29; see Table 6.

[163] J.E. Lloyd, Owen Glendower: Owen Glyn Dŵr, 1931; R.R. Davies, Lordship and Society in the March of Wales, 1282–1400, pp.426–66; J.E. Messham, 'The County of Flint and the Rebellion of Owen Glyndŵr in the Records of the Earldom of Chester', Journal of the Flintshire Historical Society, xxiii, 1967–8, pp.1–34; see above, pp.35–6.

[164] Curry, op. cit., pp.121–7.

[165] Curry, loc. cit., SC6/774/14 (Account of the Chamberlain of Chester, September 1401 – September 1402), m.3d, m.4d; SC6/774/15 (Account of the Chamberlain of Chester, September 1402 – September 1403), m.2, m.3d, m.4d.

[166] SC6/774/13 (Account of the Chamberlain of Chester, September 1400 – September 1401), m.3d, m.4d; Calendar of Ancient Correspondence concerning Wales, ed. J. Goronwy Edwards, 1935, p.200.

[167] SC6/774/13 m.2; Messham, op. cit., pp. 3–6; SC6/775/3 (Account of the Chamberlain of Chester, September 1402 – September 1403), m.2.

[168] Messham, op. cit., pp. 9–15; SC6/775/4 (Account of the Chamberlain of Chester, September 1403 – September 1404), m.1.

[169] Messham, op. cit., pp. 4–8; Eaton Hall, Eaton charter 389.

[170] Chester Record Office, Mayor's Records, MR3/67 m.2d.

[171] DL/30/3/42 m.4d, m.5d; SC6/810/13 m.3.

[172] Chester 2/75 m.5.

[173] Chester 2/75 m.1; Chester 24/20; Chester 25/10 m.9, m.9d; Dieulacres, 176.

[174] Messham, op. cit., p. 8.

[175] Messham, op. cit., p. 2; SC6/774/15 m.3d.

[176] Dieulacres, p. 175.

[177] E101/43/9.

[178] E101/404/24.

[179] Dieulacres, p. 177.

[180] Annales Ricardi Secundi et Henrici Quarti, p. 363.

[181] Chester 25/10 m.10d, m.34.

[182] Historia Anglicana, p. 256; Annales Ricardi Secundi et Henrici Quarti, p. 366; C. L. Kingsford, English Historical Literature in the Fifteenth Century, 1913, p. 350.

[183] CPR, 1401–1405, p. 330; Chester Record Office, Corporation Charters, CH24.

[184] P. McNiven, The Men of Cheshire and the Rebellion of 1403, pp. 1–25.

[185] CPR, 1401–1405, pp. 238–66, 293, 330–1; Chester 29/107 m.7.

[186] Chester 3/21.

[187] Chester 25/10 m.16, m.16d.

[188] A Thomas Hoggekinson appears in the indictment and received a pardon for his rebellion at Shrewsbury in the company of William Stanley and John Pulle, CPR, 1401–1405, p. 253. The Dieulacres Chronicle does, however, note that a section of the east flank of the royal army fled with the carriage horses of their friends at an early stage of the battle, Dieulacres, p. 80.

[189] CRO, Leycester Warren MSS, DLT/B2 f. 28; Curry, op. cit., p. 118.

[190] Chester 2/75 m.15.

[191] Dieulacres, p. 178.

[192] McNiven, op. cit., p. 21.

[193] Annales Ricardi Secundi et Henrici Quarti, p. 369.

[194] McNiven, op. cit., p. 20.

[195] DL30/3/43 m.3.

[196] J. E. Lloyd, op. cit., p. 31; Messham, op. cit., pp. 10–11.

[197] CPR, 1401–1405, p. 253.

[198] CPR, 1399–1401, p. 424; CPR, 1401–1405, p. 253; CRO, Leycester Warren MSS, DLT/B2 f. 208.

[199] JRL Cornwall-Legh deeds, 63.

[200] JRL Bromley Davenport Muniments II (3), Calveley, box 2/2.

[201] DL28/1/10 f. 32. He was later pardoned at the request of the queen, Joan of Navarre, JRL, Arley Charters, box 6/1, 16.

[202] DL42/15 f.17d, f.185; Annales Ricardi Secundi et Henrici Quarti, p. 369.

[203] E. J. Priestly, The Battle of Shrewsbury 1403, 1979.

[204] Dieulacres, p. 180; Priestly, op. cit., pp. 14–16.

[205] E101/404/24 m.4–m.16; P. McNiven, 'The Scottish Policies of the Percies and the Strategy of the Rebellion of 1403', *BJRL*, lxii, 1979–80, pp. 520–1.

[206] He was later pardoned for his rebellion after the intercession of Sir John Stanley, Chester 29/107 m.7; *CPR, 1401–1405*, p. 253.

[207] *Issues of the Exchequer*, ed. F. Devon, 1837, p. 283.

[208] Chester 2/75 m.7d; *Proceedings and Ordinances of the Privy Council*, ed. N. H. Nicolas, 1834, i, pp. 152–3.

[209] *The Brut or the Chronicles of England*, ed. F. W. Brie, Early English Text Society, 1908, ii, p. 548.

[210] *Dieulacres*, p. 181.

[211] *CPR, 1401–1405*, p. 330; Chester Record Office, Corporation Charters CH/24.

[212] BL Cotton MS, Cleopatra D VI, *The Macclesfield Cartulary*, f. 5, grant of the lands of Sir Hugh Browe to John Mainwaring.

[213] J. T. Driver, *Cheshire in the Later Middle Ages*, 1971, pp. 10–22.

CONCLUSION

The events surrounding the battle of Shrewsbury in 1403 have seemed a fitting point to break off this survey of the military service of Cheshire men in the century following the Welsh wars of Edward I. In many respects the organisation of war in the county had passed through a period of profound change, the full effects of which had clearly been felt by the early years of the fifteenth century. At the heart of these changes was the development of the retinue, which by the middle of the fourteenth century had emerged as the main device by which any lord or knight might muster men in his service. In Cheshire the relationship between the military obligations of the earl's subjects and use of indentured retinues was established after the failure of the Black Prince's recruitment before the Crécy campaign. Thereafter, commissions of array were in effect little more than subcontracts between the justice or the sheriff and the retinues of the Cheshire gentry.

Throughout the period under discussion there was seldom any separation between the domestic affinity and the retinue in war; indeed the retinue was often the expression of the social and political status of its captain, and in practice men might serve on an expedition in France, in a factional battle, or simply in support of a local gentry affinity for the same reasons and under the same pressures. In feudal societies, the boundary between public and private warfare was ill-drawn, and perceptions of national and civil conflicts grew slowly. Military service, therefore, could clearly extend to a variety of occasions on which men might bear arms in the service of others. In Cheshire the operation of gentry affinities and the impact of faction on county society were probably just as important in the development of local military service than was the conflict in Europe.

Analysis of the dynamic of the retinue in war in Cheshire has produced a complex model in which elements of kinship, land and locality were variously balanced and modified by access to comital patronage and to the resources of office. A number of examples have provided valuable evidence on the origins of service in war on a regular basis, foremost of which were lack of land, influence, or responsibility in the locality. War, however, was far from being a panacea for the problems of the landless or the younger son in gentry society, and its opportunities were on the whole only commensurate with its risks. Other examples studied reveal a variety of quite unique forms which caution against too dogmatic a definition of the typical retinue.

It is clear that as a result of changes in military practice during the 1330s, in which the county played a leading role, military service was in Cheshire restricted to the ranks of gentry society. Within a comparatively narrow social milieu, the role of retinues and affinities, both in war and in the locality, assumed a greater importance, largely as a result of a developing competition for office and connections which characterised medieval society in an era of declining incomes from land. Amongst that section of local society which served regularly in war we have been able to identify the operation of a military community for whom war became important as a career. Such developments aside, however, war remained a commonplace element in the lives of the Cheshire gentry in the later middle ages, part indeed of the 'totality of human experience'.

SOURCES

This list includes manuscripts, books and articles mentioned in the text and in footnotes. The major manuscript sources are noted, and where no definition is given it may be assumed that the reference is to a collection of deeds, letters, or other miscellaneous material. Unless otherwise stated, the place of publication is London.

A. MANUSCRIPT SOURCES

i. Public Record Office

Chancery
C.47 Miscellanea
C.61 Gascon rolls
C.71 Scotch rolls
C.76 Treaty rolls
C.81 Warrants

Duchy of Lancaster
D.L.28 Accounts various
D.L.29 Ministers' accounts
D.L.30 Court rolls
D.L.42 Miscellaneous books

Exchequer
E.28 Treasury of receipt, Council and Privy Seal Records.
E.30 TR, diplomatic documents.
E.36 TR, books.
E.101 King's Remembrancer, accounts various.
E.163 KR, miscellanea of the Exchequer.
E.198 KR, documents relation to Serjeanties, knights' fees, etc.
E.372 Lord Treasurer's remembrancer, pipe rolls.
E.404 Exchequer of receipt, issue rolls.

Judicial Records
K.B.9   King's Bench, ancient indictments.
K.B.27 King's Bench, plea rolls.

Palatinate of Chester
Chester 1   Warrants
Chester 2   Enrolments
Chester 3   Inquisitions post mortem
Chester 17 Eyre rolls
Chester 19 Sheriff's tourns
Chester 23 Essoin rolls
Chester 24 Gaol files, writs etc.
Chester 25 Indictments
Chester 29 Plea rolls
Chester 33 Forest proceedings

Probate
Prob 11 Prerogative Court of Canterbury, wills

Special Collections
S.C.1   Ancient correspondence
S.C.6   Ministers' accounts
S.C.8   Ancient petitions
S.C.11   Rentals and surveys

ii. *British Library*

Additional charters
Additional manuscripts
  7,967 (Wardrobe Book, 1324–1326)
  1,7362 (Wardrobe Book, 1319–1322)
  36,764 (Rental of St Werburgh's Abbey, 1398)
  37,494 (Expenses of the war with France, 1372–1374)
  40,859A (Account of the Duke of Gloucester's treasurer of war, 1392)
Additional rolls
  74,131 (Rental of Mobberley, 1337)
Cotton Manuscripts
  Nero C VIII (Wardrobe Book, 1334–1337)
  Cleopatra C VI (The Macclesfield Cartulary)
Harleian Manuscripts
Stowe Manuscripts
  553 (Wardrobe Book, 1322–1323)

iii. *Duchy of Cornwall Office*

Journal of John Henxteworth

iv. *Cheshire Record Office*

Baker-Wilbraham deeds
Cholmondeley of Cholmondeley deeds
Crewe of Crewe deeds
Davenport of Bramhall deeds
Egerton of Tatton deeds
Leycester-Warren of Tabley manuscripts
Vernon deeds

v. *Chester Record Office*

City charters
Sheriff's records
Mayor's records
Cotton of Combermere collection
Earwaker Manuscripts
Mayor's records

vi. *Eaton Hall, Chester*

Eaton charters

vii. *John Rylands Library*

Arley charters
Bromley-Davenport collection
Cornwall-Legh deeds
Jodrell deeds
Langford-Brooke deeds
Mainwaring of Peover collection
Rylands charters

viii. *University of Keele*

Legh of Booths charters

ix. *Lancashire Record Office*

De Trafford of Trafford collection

x. *Shropshire Record Office*

Bridgewater collection
Powis Estate

xi. *West Suffolk Record Office*

Bunbury collection

B. PRINTED SOURCES

Accounts of the Chamberlain and other Officers of the County of Chester, 1301 – 1360, ed. R. Stewart-Brown, LCRS, lix, 1910.

Anglo-Norman Letters and Petitions from All Souls MS 182, ed. M.D. Legge, Anglo-Norman Text Society, iii, 1941.

Annales Cestrienses, ed. R.C. Christie, LCRS, xiv, 1897.

Annals of Connacht, ed. A. Martin Freeman, Dublin, 1944.

Annales Ricardi Secundi et Henrici Quarti Regum Angliae, ed. H.T. Riley, in *Johannis de Trokelowe, Chronica et Annales*, Rolls Series 1866.

Archives Historiques du Département de la Gironde, xiii, Bordeaux, 1871.

Artières, Jules, 'Documents sur la Ville de Millau', *Archives Historiques de Rouergue*, vii, Millau, 1930.

Arley Charters, ed. W. Beamont, 1866.

Bousquet, H., 'Comptes Consulaires de la Cité et du Bourg de Rodez', *Archives Historiques du Rouergue*, xvii, Millau, 1943.

Bruell, J.L.C., *An Edition of the Cartulary of John of Macclesfield*, University of London MA, 1969.

The Brut or Chronicles of England, ed. F.W. Brie, Early English Text Society, Original Series, cxxxiv, 1908.

Calendar of Ancient Correspondence Concerning Wales, ed. J.G. Edwards, Cardiff, 1935.

Calendar of Ancient Petitions relating to Wales, ed. W. Rees, Cardiff, 1975.

Calendar of Charter Rolls, 4 vols., 1908–16.

Calendar of Close Rolls.

Calendar of County Court, City Court and Eyre Rolls of Chester, 1259–1297, ed. R. Stewart-Brown, Chet. Soc., New Series, lxxxiv, 1925.

Calendar of Entries in the Papal Registers, W.H. Bliss & J.A. Twemlow (eds.) III, 1900.

Calendar of Fine Rolls.

Calendar of Inquisitions Miscellaneous, 1377–1422.

Calendar of Inquisitions Post Mortem.

Calendar of Patent Rolls.

Calendar of Recognizance Rolls of the Palatinate of Chester to the End of the Reign of Henry IV, Report of the Deputy Keeper of the Public Records, 36, Appendix II, 1875.

Chandos Herald, *La Vie du Prince Noir*, ed. D.B. Tyson, *Beiheft zur Zeitschrift für Romanische Philologie*, 147, Tübingen, 1975.

Chaplais, P., *Some Documents Regarding the Fulfilment and Interpretation of the Treaty of Brétigny, 1361–1369*, Camden Miscellany, xix, 1952.

The Chartulary or Register of Chester Abbey, ed. J. Tait, Chet. Soc., New Series, lxxix, 1920.

Chartulary of Dieulacres, ed. G. Wrottesley, SHC, New Series, ix, 1906.

Cheshire in the Pipe Rolls, 1158–1301, ed. R. Stewart-Brown, LCRS, xcii, 1938.

The Chronicle of Dieulacres Abbey, in M.V. Clarke & V.H. Galbraith (eds.) 'The Deposition of Richard II', *BJRL*, xiv, 1930, pp.125–81.

Chronicles of London, ed. C.L. Kingsford, 1905.

Chronicon Adae de Usk, ed. E.M. Thompson, 1904.

Chronicon Angliae auctore monacho quodam Sancti Albani, ed. E.M. Thompson, Rolls Series, 1874.

Chronicon Henrici Knighton, ed. J.R. Lumby, Rolls Series, 1895.

Chronique de la Traison et Mort du Richard II, ed. B. Wiliams, 1846.

Chroniques de Bazas, 1299–1355, Archives Historiques du Département de la Gironde xv, Bordeaux, 1874.

Chroniques de J. Froissart, ed. Siméon Luce, 14 vols, Société de l'Histoire de France, Paris, 1869–1967.

Comptes du Connétable de Bordeaux, Archives Historiques de la Département de la Gironde, 12, Bordeaux, 1870.

Creton, Jean, *Histoire du Roy d'Angleterre Richard etc*, ed. J. Webb, *Archaeologia*, xx, 1824.

Curtis, E., *Richard II in Ireland 1394–5 and the Submission of the Irish Chiefs*, Oxford 1927.

Delpit, M.J., *Collection Générale des Documents qui se trouvent en Angleterre*, Paris, 1847.

Documents des Archives de la Chambre des Comptes de Navarre 1196–1384, ed. J.A. Brutails, Paris, 1890.

Domesday Book, ed. A. Farley, 2 vols., 1783.

English Historical Documents iv, 1327–1485, ed. A.R. Myers, 1969.

Eulogium Historiarum sive Temporis, ed. F.S. Haydon, Rolls Series, 1863.

Foedera, Conventiones, Litterae etc., ed. T. Rymer. Revised edition by A. Clarke, F. Holbrooke and J. Coley, 4 vols in 7 parts, Record Commission, 1816–69.

Froissart, *Chronicles*, ed. G. Brereton, Harmondsworth, 1978.

Oeuvres de Froissart, ed. K. de Lettenhove, 25 vols, Brussels, 1867 – 77.

La Guerre de Cent Ans vue à travers les Registres du Parlement 1337 – 1367, ed. Pierre-Clément Timbal, Paris, 1961.

Guèrin, Paul, 'Receuil des documents concernant le Poitou contenus dans les registres de la chancellerie de France', iv, 1369 – 76, *Archives Historiques du Poitou*, xix, Poitiers, 1888.

Halliwell, J. O., *Palatine Anthology: A Collection of Ancient Poems and Ballads relating to Lancashire and Cheshire*, 1850.

Historia Vitae et Regni Ricardi Secundi a monacho quodam de Evesham, ed. T. Hearne, Oxford, 1729.

Index to Inquisitions, etc. – *Counties of Chester and Flint*, Report of the Deputy Keeper of the Public Records, 25, Appendix 3, 1864.

Issues of the Exchequer, ed. F. Devon, Record Commission, 1847.

John of Gaunt's Register, 1372 – 6, ed. S. Armitage-Smith, Camden Society 3rd Series, xx – xxi, 1911.

John of Gaunt's Register, 1379 – 83, ed. E. C. Lodge & R. Somerville, Camden Society, 3rd Series, lvi-vii, 1937.

Kimball, E. G., *The Shropshire Peace Rolls, 1400 – 1414*, Shrewsbury, 1959.

The Kirkstall Chronicle, 1355 – 1400, ed. M. V. Clarke & N. Denholm Young, *BJRL*, xv, 1931, pp. 100 – 37.

Ledger Book of Vale Royal Abbey, ed. J. Brownbill, LCRS, lxviii, 1914.

Liber Luciani de Laude Cestrie, ed. M. V. Taylor, LCRS, lxiv, 1912.

Liber Quotidianus Contrarotulatoris Garderobae, ed. J. Topham, Society of Antiquaries, 1797.

Le Livre des Hommages d'Aquitaine, ed. J. P. Trabut-Cussac, Bordeaux, 1959.

Magnum Registrum Album of Lichfield, ed. H. E. Savage, SHC, 3rd Series, 1925.

Philippe de Mézières, *Letter to King Richard II*, ed. G. W. Coopland, 1975.

Mum and the Sothsegger, ed. M. Day, Early English Text Society, cxcix 1936.

Adae Murimuth, Continuatio Chronicarum and *Robertus de Avesbury, De Gestis Mirabilibus Regis Edwardi Tertii*, ed. E. M. Thompson, Rolls Series, 1889.

Nicolas, N. H., *The Scrope Grosvenor Controversy*, 2 vols, 1832.

Original Letters Illustrative of English History, ed. H. Ellis, 1846.

Cabaret d'Orville, J., *La Chronique du Bon duc Loys de Bourbon*, ed. A – M Chazaud, Société de l'Histoire de France, Paris, 1876.

Parliamentary Writs and Writs of Military Summons, ed. F. Palgrave, Record Commission, 2 vols in 4, 1827 – 34.

Proceeding and Ordinances of the Privy Council of England, ed. N.H. Nicolas, 1834.

Register of Edward the Black Prince, ed. M.C.B. Dawes, 4 vols, 1930–33.

Registrum Vulgariter Nuncupatum 'The Record of Caernarvon', Record Commission, 1838.

A Roll of Proceedings of the King's Council in Ireland, ed. J. Graves, Rolls Series, 1877.

Rotuli Parliamentorum, 7 vols, Record Commission, 1783–1832.

Rotuli Scotiae, 2 vols, Record Commission, 1814–19.

Rotulorum Patentum Clausorum Hiberniae, Irish Record Commission, Dublin, 1828.

Royal and Historical Letters during the Reign of Henry IV, ed. F.C. Hingeston, Rolls Series, 1860.

Scotland in 1298: Documents relating to the Campaigns of Edward I in that year, ed. H. Gough, 1888.

Select Cases in the Court of the King's Bench under Edward I, ed. G.O. Sayles, Selden Society, 58, 1939.

Select Charters, ed. W. Stubbs, 9th edition revised H.W.C. Davies, Oxford, 1913.

Society at War: The Experience of England and France during the Hundred Years War, ed. C.T. Allmand, 1973.

Statutes and Ordinances and Acts of Parliament of Ireland, ed. H.F. Berry, Dublin 1907.

Two Estate Surveys of the Fitzalan Earls of Arundel, ed. M. Clough, Sussex Record Society, lxvii, 1969.

Voyage en Terre Sainte d'un Maire de Bordeaux au xive siècle, Archives de l'Orient Latin, publie par la Société de l'Orient Latin, ii, Paris 1884, pp.378–88.

Thomas Walsingham, *Historia Anglicana*, ed. H.T. Riley, Rolls Series, 1864.

Thomas Walsingham, *Ypodigma Neustriae*, ed. H.T. Riley, Rolls Series, 1876.

The Westminster Chronicle, 1381–1394, L.C. Hector and Barbara F. Harvey (eds), 1982.

Wrottesley, G., *Crécy and Calais*, 1898.

C. SECONDARY SOURCES

Alexander, J.W., 'New Evidence on the Palatinate of Chester', *EHR*, lxxxv, 1970, p.715–29.

Allmand, C. T., 'Lancastrian Land Settlement in Normandy, 1417 –
50', *Econ. H.R.*, 2nd Series, xxi, 1968, pp. 461 – 79.
——, *Lancastrian Normandy 1414 – 1450. The History of a Medieval Occu-
pation*, 1983.
Andreski, S., *Military Organization and Society*, 2nd edition, 1968.
Aspeden, T., *Historical Sketches of the House of Stanley*, Preston, 1877.
Aston, Margaret, *Thomas Arundel*, Oxford, 1967.
Barber, M., 'John Norbury: An Esquire of Henry IV', *EHR*, lxviii,
1953, pp. 66 – 76.
Barber, R., *Edward, Prince of Wales and Aquitaine*, 1978.
Barnie, J., *War in Medieval Society*, 1974.
Barraclough, G., *The Earldom and County Palatine of Chester*, 1953.
——, 'Some Charters of the Earls of Chester', in Patricia M. Barnes &
C. F. Slade (eds), *A Medieval Miscellany for Doris Mary Stenton*, Pipe
Roll Society, New Series, xxxvi, 1960, pp. 25 – 43.
Barron, Caroline M., 'The Tyranny of Richard II', *BIHR*, xli, 1968,
pp. 1 – 18.
Barrow, G. W. S., 'The Pattern of Lordship and Feudal Settlement in
Cumbria', *Journal of Medieval History*, 1, 1975, pp. 117 – 38.
Bean, J. M. W., *The Decline of English Feudalism*, 1215 – 1540, Manchester,
1968.
Bellamy, John, 'The Coterel Gang: An Anatomy of a Band of Four-
teenth Century Criminals', *EHR*, lxxix, 1964, pp. 698 – 717.
——, *Crime and Public Order in England in the Later Middle Ages*, 1973,
——, 'The Northern Rebellions in the Later Years of Richard II's
Reign', *BJRL*, xlvii, 1965, pp. 254 – 74.
Bennett, Michael, J., 'The Lancashire and Cheshire Clergy, 1379',
THLC, cxxiv, 1972, pp. 1 – 30.
——, 'A County Community: Social Cohesion amongst the Cheshire
Gentry 1400 – 25', *Northern History*, viii, 1973, pp. 24 – 44.
——, 'Sources and Problems of Social Mobility: Cheshire in the Later
Middle Ages', in *Medieval Cheshire*, THLC, 128, 1979, pp. 59 – 95.
——, 'Sir Gawain and the Green Knight and the Literary Achievement
of the North-West Midlands: the Historical Background', *Journal of
Medieval History*, 5, 1979, pp. 63 – 89.
——, *Community, Class and Careerism. Cheshire and Lancashire Society in the
Age of Sir Gawain and the Green Knight*, 1983.
Bibby, Roland, *Bothal Observed: A Survey of a Northumbrian Castle, Village
and Church*, Newcastle, 1973.
Booth, P. H. W., 'Taxation and Public Order: Cheshire in 1353',
Northern History, xii, 1976, pp. 16 – 31.

Booth, P. H. W., ' "Farming for Profit" in the Fourteenth Century: The Cheshire Estates of the Earldom of Chester', *Journal of the Chester Archaeological Society*, 62, 1980 for 1979, pp. 73 – 90.

——, *The Financial Administration of the Lordship and of the County of Cheshire, 1272 – 1377*, Chet. Soc., 3rd Series, xxviii, 1981.

——, & Dodd, J. Phillip, 'The Manor and Fields of Frodsham', in *Medieval Cheshire*, THLC, 128, 1979, pp. 25 – 57.

Brown, A. L., 'The Authorization of Letters under the Great Seal', *BIHR*, xxxvii, 1964, pp. 16 – 31.

——, 'The English Campaign in Scotland in 1400', in H. Hearder & H. R. Loyn (eds), *British Government and Administration*, Cardiff, 1974, pp. 40 – 54.

Brown, R. Allen, *The Normans and the Norman Conquest*, 1969.

——, H. M. Colvin & A. J. Taylor, *The History of the King's Works*, 1963.

Bridbury, A. R., 'The Hundred Years War: Costs and Profits', in D. C. Coleman & A. H. John (eds), *Trade, Government and Economy in Pre-Industrial England*, 1977, pp. 80 – 95.

Broughton, Sir Delves L., *Records of an Old Cheshire Family. A History of the Lords of the Manors of Delves near Uttoxeter in the County of Stafford and Doddington in the County of Chester*, 1908.

Burne, R. V. H., *The Monks of Chester*, 1962.

Capra, P. J., 'Les Bases Sociales du Pouvoir Anglo-Gascon au milieu du xive siècle', *Le Moyen Âge*, lxxxi, 1975, pp. 273 – 99, 447 – 73.

Carr, A. D. 'Welshmen and the Hundred Years War', *The Welsh History Review*, 4, 1968, pp. 21 – 46.

——, 'A Welsh Knight in the Hundred Years War: Sir Gregory Sais', *Transactions of the Honourable Society of Cymmrodorion*, 1977, pp. 40 – 53.

Clanchy, M. T., 'Law, Government and Society in Medieval England', *History*, 59, 1974, pp. 73 – 8.

Contamine, Philippe, *Guerre, État et Société à la fin du Moyen Age*, Paris, 1972.

——, *War in the Middle Ages*, 1984.

——, 'Les Compagnies d' Aventure en France Pendant la Guerre de Cent Ans', *Mélanges de l'École Française de Rome*, 87, 1975, pp. 365 – 96.

Copinger, W. A., *History and Records of the Smith Carrington Family*, 1907.

Cornwall, J., 'English Population in the Early Sixteenth Century', *Econ. H. R.*, xxiii, 1970, pp. 32 – 44.

Coulborn, R., *The Economic and Political Preliminaries of the Crusade of Henry Despenser Bishop of Norwich in 1383*, University of London PhD, 1931.

Coward, Barry, *The Stanleys, Lords Stanley and Earls of Derby 1385 – 1672:*

The Origins, Wealth and Power of a Landowning Family, Chet. Soc., 3rd Series, xxx, 1983.

Curry, Anne E., *The Demesne of the County Palatine of Chester in the Early Fifteenth Century*, University of Manchester MA, 1977.

——, 'Cheshire and the Royal Demesne, 1399–1422', in *Medieval Cheshire*, THLC, 128, 1979, pp. 113–38.

Darby, H. C., *Domesday England*, Cambridge, 1977.

——, *A New Historical Geography of England*, Cambridge, 1973.

Davies, R. G., 'Some Notes from the Register of Henry de Wakefield Bishop of Worcester on the Political Crisis of 1386–1388', EHR, lxxxvi, 1971, pp. 547–58.

Davies, R. R., 'Richard II and the Principality of Chester, 1397–99', in *The Reign of Richard II*, ed. F. R. H. du Boulay & Caroline M. Barron, 1971, pp. 256–79.

——, *Lordship and Society in the March of Wales, 1282–1400*, Oxford, 1978.

Dodgson, J. McN., *The Place-Names of Cheshire*, English Place-Name Society, xliv–xlviii, li, 1970–81.

Douch, R., *The Career, Lands and Family of William Montague Earl of Salisbury, 1301–1344*, University of London MA, 1950).

Draper, P., *House of Stanley*, Ormskirk, 1864.

Driver, J. T., *Cheshire in the Later Middle Ages*, Chester 1971.

Duby, G., *The Early Growth of the European Economy*, 1974.

Edwards, Sir J. Goronwy, *The Second Century of the English Parliament*, Oxford, 1979.

Evans, D. L., 'Some Notes on the History of the Principality of Wales in the Time of the Black Prince', *Transactions of the Honourable Society of Cymmrodorion*, 1925–6, pp. 25–100.

Fowler, K., 'Les Finances et la Discipline dans les Armées Anglaises en France au xive siècle', *Les Cahiers Vernonnais*, iv, 1964, pp. 55–84.

——, *The Age of Plantagenet and Valois*, 1967.

——, *The King's Lieutenant*, 1969.

Frame, Robin, 'The Justiciarship of Ralph Ufford: Warfare and Politics in Fourteenth Century Ireland', *Studia Hibernica*, 13, 1973, pp. 7–47.

——, 'Power and Society in Ireland 1272–1377', *Past and Present*, 76 1977, pp. 3–33.

Fryde, Natalie M., 'Welsh Troops in the Scottish Campaign of 1322', *Bulletin of the Board of Celtic Studies*, xxvi, 1975, pp. 82–9.

Galbraith, V. H., 'Thomas Walsingham and the Saint Albans Chronicle, 1272–1422', *EHR*, xlvii, 1932, pp. 12–30.

Garton, Eric, *Nantwich: Saxon to Puritan*, Nantwich, 1972.

Gerbet, M.C., 'Les Guerres et l'Accès à la Noblesse en Espagne de 1465 à 1592', *Mélanges de la Casa Velasquez*, viii, 1972, pp. 295–326.

Gillespie, J.L., *The Cheshire Archers of Richard II: A Royal Experiment in Bastard Feudalism*, University of Princeton PhD, 1972.

——, 'Richard II's Cheshire Archers', *THLC*, 125, 1975, pp. 1–39.

——, 'Thomas Mortimer and Thomas Molyneux: Radcot Bridge and the Appeal of 1397', *Albion*, 1975, pp. 161–73.

——, 'Richard II's Archers of the Crown', *Journal of British Studies*, xviii, 1979, pp. 14–29.

Goodman, A., *The Loyal Conspiracy*, 1971.

——, 'The Military Subcontracts of Sir Hugh Hastings, 1380', *EHR*, xcv, 1980, pp. 114–20.

——, 'Responses to Requests in Yorkshire for Military Service under Henry V', *Northern History*, xvii, 1981, pp. 240–52.

Griffiths, R.A., *The Principality of Wales, The Structure and Personnel of Government in South Wales, 1277–1536*, Cardiff, 1972.

Hardy, R., *Longbow: A Social and Military History*, 1976.

Harriss, G.L., *King, Parliament and Public Finance in Medieval England to 1369*, Oxford, 1975.

Hatcher, J., *Rural Economy and Society in the Duchy of Cornwall, 1300–1500*, 1970.

Heath, P., 'The Medieval Archdeaconry and Tudor Bishopric of Chester', *Journal of Ecclesiastical History*, xx, 1969, pp. 243–52.

Hébert, Michel, 'L'Armée Provençale en 1374', *Annales du Midi*, 91, 1979, pp. 5–27.

Hemingway, J., *History of the City of Chester*, Chester, 1831.

Hewitt, H.J., *Medieval Cheshire: An Economic and Social History of Cheshire in the Reigns of the Three Edwards*, Manchester, 1929.

——, *The Black Prince's Expedition, 1355–1357*, Manchester, 1958.

——, *The Organization of War under Edward III*, Manchester, 1966.

——, *Cheshire under the Three Edwards*, Chester, 1967.

Highet, T.P., *The Early History of the Davenports of Davenport*, Chet. Soc., 3rd series, ix, 1960.

Hilton, R.H., *The English Peasantry in the Later Middle Ages*, Oxford, 1975.

——, *A Medieval Society*, 1966.

Holmes, G.A., *The Estates of the Higher Nobility in XIV Century England*, Cambridge, 1957.

Holmes, U.T., *Old French Literature*, 1962.

Hudson, W., 'Norwich Militia in the Fourteenth Century', *Norfolk & Norwich Archaeological Society*, xiv, 1901, pp. 263–20.

Hurnard, N.D., *The King's Pardon for Homicide before A.D. 1307*, Oxford, 1969.

Husain, B.M.C., 'The Delamere Forest in Later Medieval Times', *THLC*, cvii, 1956, pp. 18–34.

——, *Cheshire under the Norman Earls*, Chester, 1972.

James, M., *Family, Lineage and Civil Society: A Study of Politics, Society and Mentality in the Durham Region, 1500–1640*, Oxford, 1974.

Johnston, Dorothy, 'Richard II's Departure from Ireland, July 1399', *EHR*, xcvii, 1983, pp. 785–805.

Jones, D., *The Church in Chester 1300–1540*, Chet. Soc., 3rd series, vii 1957.

Jones, Michael, *Ducal Brittany 1364–1399*, Oxford, 1970.

Kaeuper, Richard, 'Law, Government and Society: The Evidence of Special Commissions of Oyer and Terminer', *Speculum*, liv, 1979, pp. 734–84.

Keen, M.H., 'Brotherhood in Arms', *History*, xlvii, 1962, pp. 1–17.

——, *The Laws of War in the Later Middle Ages*, 1965.

——, *Chivalry*, 1984.

Keeney, B.C., 'Military Service and the Development of Nationalism in England, 1272–1327', *Speculum*, xxii, 1947, pp. 534–49.

Kingsford, C.L., *English Historical Literature in the Fifteenth Century*, Oxford, 1913.

Kelsey, Charles E., *Cheshire*, Oxford County Histories, 1911.

Kirby, J.L., 'Calais sous les Anglais, 1399–1413', *Revue du Nord*, 1955, pp. 19–30.

Knowles, D. & R. Neville Hadcock, *Medieval Religious Houses*, 1971.

Labarge, Margaret Wade, *Gascony, England's First Colony 1204–1453*, 1980.

Lewis, N.B., 'The Organisation of Indentured Retinues in Fourteenth Century England', *TRHS*, 4th Series, xxvii, 1944, pp. 29–39.

——, 'The Last Medieval Summons of the English Feudal Levy, 13th June 1385', *EHR*, lxxiii, 1958, pp. 1–26.

——, 'The Feudal Summons of 1385', *EHR*, c, 1985, pp. 729–46.

Lloyd, J.E., *Owen Glendower: Owen Glyn Dŵr*, Oxford, 1931.

Lydon, J.F., 'The Hobelar: An Irish Contribution to Medieval Warfare', *Irish Sword*, 2, 1954, p. 12–16.

——, 'Richard II's Expeditions to Ireland', *Journal of the Royal Society of Antiquaries of Ireland*, xciii, 1963, pp. 135–49.

——, *Ireland in the Later Middle Ages*, 1973.

McFarlane, K.B., 'Bastard Feudalism', *BIHR*, xx, 1943/5, pp. 161–80.

McFarlane, K. B., 'War, Economy and Social Change: England and the Hundred Years War', *Past and Present*, xxii, 1962, pp. 3–13.

——, 'A Business Partnership in War and Administration, 1421–45', *EHR*, lxxviii, 1963, pp. 290–308.

——, *Lancastrian Kings and Lollard Knights*, Oxford, 1972.

——, *The Nobility of Later Medieval England*, Oxford, 1973.

MacKay, A., *Spain in the Middle Ages*, 1977.

Maclagan, M., 'Genealogy and Heraldry in the 16th and 17th Centuries', in L. Fox (ed), *English Historical Scholarship in the 16th and 17th Centuries*, 1956.

McNiven, P., 'The Cheshire Rising of 1400', *BJRL*, lii, 1969–70, pp. 375–96.

——, 'The Men of Cheshire and the Rebellion of 1403', *THLC*, 129, 1980, pp. 1–29.

——, 'The Scottish Policies of the Percies and the Strategy of the Rebellion of 1403', *BJRL*, lxii, 1979–80, pp. 498–530.

Maddicott, J. R., *Thomas of Lancaster, 1307–22*, Oxford, 1970.

——, 'Thomas of Lancaster and Sir Robert Holland: A Study in Noble Patronage', *EHR*, cccxl, 1971, pp. 449–72.

——, 'The English Peasantry and the Demands of the Crown, 1294–1341', *Past and Present Supplement*, 1, 1975.

——, 'The County Community and the Making of Public Opinion in Fourteenth Century England', *TRHS*, 5th Series, xxviii, 1978, pp. 27–43.

Medieval and Early Renaissance Treasures in the North-West, Whitworth Art Gallery, Manchester, 1976.

Memain, R., 'Les Misères de la Guerre en Bas Poitou au xive siècle', *Bulletin de la Société des Antiquaires de l'Ouest*, 12, 1941.

Messham, J. E., 'The County of Flint and the Rebellion of Owen Glyndŵr in the Records of the Earldom of Chester', *Journal of the Flintshire Historical Society*, xxiii, 1967–8, pp. 1–34.

Miller, Edward, 'War, Taxation and the English Economy in the Late Thirteenth and Early Fourteenth Centuries', in J. M., Winter (ed), *War and Economic Development*, Cambridge, 1975, pp. 11–31.

Moor, C., *Knights of Edward I*, Harleian Society, lxxxii, 1930.

Morgan, Philip, 'Cheshire and the Defence of the Principality of Aquitaine', in *Medieval Cheshire*, THLC, 128, 1979, pp. 139–60.

Morrill, J. S., *Cheshire, 1630–1660: County Government and Society during the English Revolution*, Oxford, 1974.

Morris, J. E., *The Welsh Wars of Edward I*, Oxford, 1901.

Morris, J. E., 'Cumberland and Westmorland Military Levies in the Time of Edward I and Edward II', *Transactions of the Cumberland and Westmorland Architectural and Archaeological Society*, New Series, II, 1903, pp. 307 – 27.

——, 'Mounted Infantry in Medieval Warfare', *TRHS*, 3rd series, vii, 1914, pp. 77 – 102.

Morris, R. H., *Chester in the Plantagenet and Tudor Reigns*, Chester, 1893.

Myres, J. N. L., 'The Campaign of Radcot Bridge in December 1387', *EHR*, xlii, 1927, pp. 20 – 33.

Nichols, K., *Gaelic and Gaelicised Ireland in the Middle Ages*, Dublin, 1972.

Nicholson, R. *Edward III and the Scots*, Oxford, 1965.

Ormerod, G. *The History of the County Palatine and City of Chester*, 3 vols, ed. T. Helsby, 2nd edition, 1882.

Palmer, A. N. & Owen, E. *A History of Ancient Tenures of Land in Wales and the March*, 2nd edition, Wrexham, 1910.

Palmer, J. J. N., 'The Last Summons of the Feudal Army in England', *EHR*, lxxxiii, 1968, pp. 771 – 5.

——, 'The Parliament of 1385 and the Constitutional Crisis of 1386', *Speculum*, xlvi, 1971, pp. 477 – 90.

——, *England, France and Christendom, 1377 – 99*, 1972.

——, 'The Authorship, Date and Historical Value of the French Chronicles on the Lancastrian Revolution', *BJRL*, lxi, 1978 – 79, pp. 145 – 81, 398 – 421.

Patourel, Le J., 'The Origins of the War', in K. Fowler (ed), *The Hundred Years War* (1971), pp. 28 – 50.

Perroy, E., *The Hundred Years War*, 1951.

Pevsner, N. & Hubbard, E., *The Buildings of England: Cheshire*, Harmondsworth, 1971.

Pollard, A. J., *The Family of Talbot, Lords Talbot and Earls of Shrewsbury in the Fifteenth Century*, Bristol University PhD, 1968.

——, *John Talbot and the War in France, 1427 – 1453*, 1983.

Poole, R. L., *The Exchequer in the 12th Century*, Oxford, 1912.

Postan, M. M., 'Some Social Consequences of the Hundred Years War', *Econ. H.R.*, xii, 1942, pp. 1 – 12.

——, 'The Costs of the Hundred Years War', *Past and Present*, xxvii, 1964, pp. 34 – 53.

Powell, E. & Trevelyan, G. M., *The Peasants' Rising and the Lollards*, Cambridge, 1899.

Powicke, M., *Military Obligation in Medieval England*, Oxford, 1962.

Prestwich, M., *War, Politics and Finance under Edward I*, 1972.

——, *The Three Edwards: War and State in England, 1272 – 1377*, 1980.

Priestley, E. J., *The Battle of Shrewsbury 1403*, Shrewsbury, 1979.

Prince, A. E., 'The Strength of English Armies in the Reign of Edward III', *EHR*, xlvi, 1931, pp. 353 – 71.

——, 'The Army and Navy', in J. F. Willard & W. A. Morris (eds), *The English Goverment at Work, 1327 – 1336*, Cambridge, 1940, I, pp. 332 – 93.

Putnam, B. H., *The Place in Legal History of Sir William Shareshull*, 1950.

Richardson, R. C., *Puritanism in North-West England*, Manchester, 1972.

Round, J. H., *Peerage and Pedigree*, 2 vols, 1910.

Rouquette, J., *Le Rouergue sous les Anglais*, Millau, 1887.

Russell, J. C., *British Medieval Population*, Albuquerque, 1948.

Russell, F. H., *The Just War in the Middle Ages*, Cambridge, 1975.

Russell, P. E., *The English Intervention in Spain and Portugal in the Time of Edward III and Richard II*, Oxford, 1955.

Ruthven-Otway, J., *A History of Medieval Ireland*, 1968.

Ryan, L. V., *Roger Ascham*, 1964.

Saul, Nigel, *Knights and Esquires: The Gloucestershire Gentry in the Fourteenth Century*, Oxford, 1981.

Seacome, J., *Account of the Ancient and Honourable House of Stanley*, 1848.

Sharp, M., *Contributions to a History of the Earldom of Chester*, University of Manchester PhD, 1925.

——, 'The Administrative Chancery of the Black Prince before 1362', in A. G. Little & F. M. Powicke (eds), *Essays in Medieval History Presented to Thomas Frederick Tout*, Manchester, 1925, pp. 321 – 33.

——, 'A Jodrell Deed and the Seals of the Black Prince', *BJRL*, vii, 1922 – 8, pp. 106 – 17.

Sherborne, J. W., 'Indentured Retinues and the English Expeditions to France', *EHR*, lxxix, 1964, p. 718 – 46.

——, 'Richard II's Return to Wales, July 1399', *Welsh History Review*, 7, 1974.

Skeel, C., 'The Cattle Trade between England and Wales 15th to 19th Centuries', *TRHS*, 4th Series, ix, 1926, pp. 135 – 58.

Snead, G. A., *The Careers of Four Fourteenth Century Military Commanders Serving Edward III and Richard II*, University of Kent MA, 1968.

Somerville, R., *History of the Duchy of Lancaster*, 1953.

Stewart-Brown, R., 'The Disafforestation of Wirral, 1376', *THLC*, lix, 1908, pp. 165 – 80.

——, 'The Avowries of Cheshire', *EHR*, xxix, 1914, pp. 41 – 55.

Tait, J., 'Knight Service in Cheshire', *EHR*, lvii, 1942, pp. 26 – 54.

Tout, T. F., *Chapters in the Administrative History of Medieval Engiand*, 6 vols, Manchester, 1920 – 33.

Tuck, J. A., 'Anglo-Irish Relations 1382–1393', *Proceedings of the Royal Irish Academy*, 69, 1970, pp. 15–31.

——, 'Richard II's System of Patronage', in F. R. H. du Boulay & Caroline M. Barron (eds), *The Reign of Richard II*, 1971, pp. 1–20.

——, *Richard II and the English Nobility*, 1973.

Tupling, G. H., *South Lancashire in the Reign of Edward II*, Chet. Soc., 3rd series, I, 1949.

Usher, G. A., 'The Black Prince's Quo Warranto', *The Welsh History Review*, 10, 1974, pp. 1–12.

Vale, M. G. A., *English Gascony, 1399–1453*, Oxford, 1970.

Vaughan, Richard, *John the Fearless*, 1966.

Verbruggen, J. F., *The Art of Warfare in Western Europe in the Middle Ages*, Amsterdam, 1977.

The Victoria History of the County of Chester, ed. B. E. Harris, ii, Oxford 1979, iii, Oxford, 1980.

Virgoe, Roger, 'The Crown and Local Government: East Anglia under Richard II', in F. R. H. du Boulay & Caroline M. Barron, *The Reign of Richard II*, 1971, pp. 218–41.

Walker, Simon, 'Profit and Loss in the Hundred Years War: the Subcontracts of Sir John Strother, 1374', *BIHR*, lviii, 1985, pp. 100–6.

Waugh, S. L., 'The Profits of Violence: The Minor Gentry in the Rebellion of 1321–22 in Gloucestershire and Herefordshire', *Speculum*, lii, 1977, pp. 843–69.

White, L., *Medieval Technology and Social Change*, 1962.

Willement, T., *Heraldic Notices of Canterbury Cathedral*, 1827.

Wolffe, B. P., *The Royal Demesne in English History*, 1971.

Wylie, J. H., *History of England under Henry IV*, 4 vols. 1884–98.

INDEX

Delves, Sir John, of Doddington, 3–4, 109, 122, 170, 176, 182
Denbigh, 49, 72, 75, 152, 160
    garrison at, 211–12
Denwall, 197
Derbyshire, 32, 40
    archers from, 103
Derval, 136, 148, 159
desertion, 112–13
Deslayheath, 155
Despenser, Bishop Henry, of Norwich, 161–4, 175
Despenser, Hugh sr., 55
Devon, 80
Dieppe, garrison at, 157
Dieulacres abbey, 27, 78
    chronicle, 189, 212, 214, 216
Doddington, 3–4
Dodleston, 36, 211
Domesday Book, 67, 69, 80, 84, 86
Domville, John jr., 119–20
Domville, John, of Lyme, 209
Doncaster, William, 36
Done, Richard, of Utkinton, 87
Donne, John, 199, 205
Donne, William, 147
Dordogne, river, 159
Dounes, Reginald, 209
Drakelow, 70
Dublin, 172, 174
Dunham Massey, barony and manor of, 34–5, 73, 84–5, 216
Dupplin Moor, battle of (1332), 38
Durham, 74, 191
    county palatine of, 19, 29, 63–4
Dutton, Hugh, 209
Dutton, Peter, 209
Dyserth, 36

East Anglia, 187
    erldom of, 28
Eaton, 211
Eccleston, 169, 211
Eddisbury hundred, 79
    archers from, 142, 209
Edmund, Earl of Cornwall, 31–2
Edward I, 1, 6, 27–32, 34–7, 40–1, 44, 48, 62–6, 72, 77, 85, 98, 112, 114, 149, 185, 193, 226
Edward II, 20–1, 29, 31, 34, 36, 38, 41, 44, 50–2, 125
Edward III, 41–2, 44, 46–7, 49, 52, 54–5, 65, 74, 89, 97–8, 102–4, 109, 120, 125–6, 129, 131, 149, 157
Edward, the Black Prince, 3, 6, 10, 15–17, 19, 29, 40, 64–5, 69, 73–5, 77, 89–91, 97–140, 150, 152–3, 155–7, 160, 162–3, 166, 170, 175, 185, 187, 191–2, 201, 226
    household of, 99, 130, 152
    chamber, 154
    clerk of the household, 99
    controller of the household, 99
    exchequer at Westminster, 99, 105
    tailor and baker, 127
    treasurer of war, 110

Eggerton, David, 209
Eggerton, Ralph, 209
Eggerton, William, 203
Ellesmere, 215
Ellis, Philipot, 167
Elton, Richard, 155
Emeric, Henry van, 161
Englefield, archers from, 140
Essex, archers from, 46
Essoin rolls, see Chester, county court
Eton, John, 127, 209
Evesham, battle of (1265), 32
Eyton, David, 191

Fairchild, John, 156
Farndon, 77
Falkirk, battle of (1298), 33
Falkirk Roll of Arms, 34
Fastolf, Sir John, 15
Felton, Sir Thomas, 136, 159, 162, 164
Ferrers, Sir Thomas, 101, 104, 142
Fillongley, Richard, 126
Fitton, Sir John, 108
Fitton, Lawrence, 209
Fitzalan Earls of Arundel, 35, 71, 73, 85
    lands of, 202
Fitzalan, Richard, Earl of Arundel (d. 1302), 72
Fitzalan, Richard, Earl of Arundel (d. 1376), 74, 104, 126
Fitzalan, Richard, Earl of Arundel (d. 1397), 18–19, 74, 155, 162–3, 188–91, 195–6, 198–9, 217
Flanders, commercial treaties with, 171
Flint, 185, 188, 204, 212
    archers from, 140
    castle, see castles
    county of, 30, 99, 108
    lieutenant-sheriff of, 190
Flodden, battle of (1513), 5
Folville family, 117
forests, 88, see also Delamere, Macclesfield, the Wirral
    forest eyre, 100, 126
    puture, 89
fouage, see Aquitaine, Principality of
Foussat, Amanieu de, 134
Fowler, Kenneth, 157
free companies, 122, 134–5, 137, 160
Frere, 151
Frodsham, 69, 71, 82, 84
Frodsham, Geoffrey of, 148
Frodsham, Thomas, 93
Froissart, Jean, 132, 161, 166, 169, 175
Fronsac, garrison at, 160–1, 163, 165, 170
frontier (Spain), 34

Gairgrave, Thomas, 98
Garonne, river, 159
Gascony, 102, 113, 121, 130
    Gascon lords, 110, 133, 157–9, 161
    march, 111, 157
    Gascon rolls, 134
    Gascon troops, 124, 133
Gascune, Gylymot le, 165